BUSINESS,
ETHICS, AND THE
ENVIRONMENT

BUSINESS, ETHICS, AND THE ENVIRONMENT

The Public
Policy Debate

EDITED BY

W. Michael Hoffman,
Robert Frederick, and
Edward S. Petry, Jr.

From the Eighth National Conference on Business Ethics
Sponsored by the Center for Business Ethics at Bentley College

QUORUM BOOKS
NEW YORK • WESTPORT, CONNECTICUT • LONDON

Library of Congress Cataloging-in-Publication Data

National Conference on Business Ethics (8th : 1990 : Bentley College)
  Business, ethics, and the environment : the public policy debate /
edited by W. Michael Hoffman, Robert Frederick,
and Edward S. Petry, Jr.
    p. cm.
  "From the Eighth National Conference on Business Ethics
sponsored by the Center for Business Ethics at Bentley College."
  Includes bibliographical references.
  ISBN 0–89930–550–4 (lib. bdg. : alk. paper)
  1. Environmental policy—United States—Congresses.
2. Environmental policy—Congresses. 3. United States—Industries—
Environmental aspects—Congresses. 4. Industry—Social aspects—
Congresses. 5. Business ethics—Congresses. I. Hoffman, W.
Michael. II. Frederick, Robert. III. Petry, Edward S. IV. Bentley
College. Center for Business Ethics. V. Title.
HC110.E5N32   1990
363.7'08'0973—dc20   90–8390

British Library Cataloguing in Publication Data is available.

Library of Congress Catalog Card Number: 90–8390
ISBN: 0–89930–550–4

First published in 1990

Quorum Books, 88 Post Road West, Westport, CT 06881
An imprint of Greenwood Publishing Group, Inc.

Printed in the United States of America

The paper used in this book complies with the
Permanent Paper Standard issued by the National
Information Standards Organization (Z39.48–1984).

10 9 8 7 6 5 4 3 2 1

Contents

III. Environmental Problems and Solutions   169

Figures and Tables

Foreword

W. MICHAEL HOFFMAN

Since its founding in 1976, the Center for Business Ethics at Bentley College has sponsored and hosted a series of National Conferences on Business Ethics. The proceedings of all of these conferences have been published and used as texts in courses and as resources for scholarly research in the field of business ethics. They have also provided ideas for pragmatic change within our society, particularly in the world of business activities. This will be no less true of this volume, and its companion work, *The Corporation, Ethics, and the Environment,* also published by Greenwood Press. Together they comprise the proceedings of the center's Eighth National Conference on Business Ethics.

A major reason for the success of these conferences and the subsequent publications is the timeliness of their themes. Over this past decade the conferences have focused on work ethics, ethics and the management of computer technology, ethics and multinational business, and the ethics of mergers, takeovers, and corporate restructuring. These are not only fundamental areas of business with sensitive ethical dimensions but also ones that have captured the public's interest during the 1980s. The question of what is morally right in these areas was of particular social concern and given heightened, even dramatic, attention. Certainly no less can be said of the theme of this book. Perhaps this can best be summed up by remembering that *Time* magazine, in a rare departure from its naming a Man of the Year, designated Endangered Earth as Planet of the Year for 1988.

While concern over the environment is not new, there has been renewed interest. Over the past few years Planet Earth spoke to us even more loudly than before, and we began to listen more than before. The message was ominous, somewhat akin to God's warning Noah. It spoke through droughts, heat waves, and forest fires, raising fears of global warming due to the buildup of carbon dioxide and other gases in the atmosphere. It warned us by raw sewage and medical wastes washing up on our beaches and by devastating oil spills—one despoiling Prince William Sound and its wildlife to such an extent that it made us weep. It spoke to us through increased skin cancers and discoveries of holes in the ozone layer related to our commercial use of chlorofluorocarbons. It drove its message home through the rapid and dangerous cutting and burning of our primitive forests at the rate of one football field a second, leaving us even more vulnerable to greenhouse gases like carbon dioxide and eliminating hundreds of irreplaceable species daily. Its message rained down on us in the form of acid, defoliating our forests and poisoning our lakes and streams. And its message exploded in our faces at Chernobyl and Bhopal, reminding us of past warnings at Three Mile Island and Love Canal.

How will we face up to these problems? This will be the focal point for a public policy debate on our ethical responsibilities toward the environment—a debate that must be a priority for the 1990s.

This effort will not be meaningful without the full participation of its two major players: business and government. The debate must clarify these fundamental interrelated questions: What can business do to help with the environmental crisis? What is the proper relationship between business and government, especially when faced with a social problem of the magnitude of the environmental crisis? Corporations, and society in general for that matter, have yet to answer these questions satisfactorily.

In holding its Eighth National Conference on Business, Ethics, and the Environment, the Center for Business Ethics wanted to lay some groundwork for this public policy debate on the environment for the 1990s. Business must decide what it can and ought to do with regard to our ecological crisis and what its relationship to government can and ought to be. Without responsible dialogue and cooperation between business and government on this issue, I fear our future looks bleak. I hope this volume, and its companion volume, will help bring the movements of business ethics and environmental ethics together for a brighter close to our twentieth century.

Acknowledgments

The Eighth National Conference on Business Ethics and other activities of the Center for Business Ethics were made possible in part by grants from the following: Arvin Industries; Robert W. Brown, M.D.; Champion International Corporation; the Council for Philosophical Studies (sponsored by the National Endowment for the Humanities); the General Mills Foundation; General Motors Corporation; the Goodyear Tire and Rubber Company; Midland-Ross, Inc.; the Motorola Foundation; Norton Company; Primerica Corporation; Raytheon Company; the Raytheon Charitable Foundation; Rexnord, Inc.; Richardson-Merrill, Inc.; the Rockefeller Foundation; Semline, Inc.; Stop and Shop Manufacturing Companies; F. W. Woolworth Company; and Exxon Education Foundation. On behalf of the center, we wish to thank these contributors and all of the participants of the Eighth National Conference for sharing with us their support and ideas. We also wish to thank Anne Glynn, Sally Lydon, and Peter Rubicam for all their help with the conference and this book.

Introduction

ROBERT E. FREDERICK

On October 26 and 27, 1989, the Center for Business Ethics at Bentley College held its Eighth National Conference on Business Ethics. The topic of the conference was Business, Ethics, and the Environment. Prominent members of business, government, academic, and public interest groups made presentations. Many of those presentations are collected in this volume, and others are in a companion volume, *The Corporation, Ethics, and the Environment.*

The conference marked a departure from a number of other discussions on business and the environment since the major focus of the conference was not the monetary cost-benefit of environmental protection. Instead most of the papers were intended specifically to address, in ethical terms, the ethical obligations businesses may have for protecting the environment. If there are such obligations, then businesses are morally required to consider them when business activity has an adverse effect on the environment. But are businesses obligated to protect the environment? Should private enterprises take an active and leading role in solving this national problem? Or should the solution be entirely a matter of public policy, not involving businesses except to the extent that they are required to act by law and regulation?

Environmental problems and concern for the environment are not new. Warnings came out in the 1960s that lakes were dying of industrial wastes. Our foodstuffs were tainted with methyl mercury and radioactivity. The World Health Organization even warned us of the contamination of mother's milk by DDT. It was reported in 1969 by the Atmospheric Sciences Research Center that there was not a breath of uncontaminated air anywhere in the North American hemisphere. In 1970 Thor Heyerdahl found no oil-free stretch of ocean during his *RA II* crossing, and Jacques Piccard in 1971 reported to the United Nations that oil dumping, lead exhaust, and mercury pollution would soon render the oceans incapable of sustaining aquatic life. Paul Erlich shouted from *Ramparts* in 1969 that we were headed for an "eco-catastrophe." Public concern over these and other environmental problems led to the establishment of the Environmental Protection Agency, which over the last two decades has had at best a spotty record of success.

Although public concern for the environment waned in the late 1970s and early 1980s, there has been renewed interest from all segments of the population. As several contributors to this book point out, social groups that have little else in common agree that something must be done about damage to the environment. In part this may be the result of the continued accumulation of scientific evidence about acid rain, the destruction of the ozone layer, and the greenhouse effect, but it is also because the consequences of environmental damage have become much more personal and immediate. We see, either in person or on the news, devastating oil spills, medical wastes on beaches, the destruction of tropical forests, the *Pelicano* roaming the seas looking for a place to dump tons of toxic incinerator ash, and disasters at Chernobyl and Bhopal. Repeated warnings and repeated environmental catastrophes have made it plain to us all, as Senator Albert Gore said in 1988, that "the fact that we face an ecological crisis without any precedent in historic times is no longer a matter of any dispute worthy of recognition." The question, he went on to point out, is not whether there is a problem but how we will face up to it. This will be the focal point for a public policy debate on responsibilities toward the environment, a debate that must be a priority in the 1990s.

Yet granted that there are environmental problems and even granted that business activities have contributed to those problems in large measure, the role businesses should take in solving the problems is not obvious. Public problems, like the environment, would seem to be best addressed by public policies. The role of business in the debate and in the implementation of those policies might seem to be that of a bit player rather than the lead. To some extent, this is correct. The main reason businesses exist is to serve the economic needs of society. By themselves businesses cannot solve, and should not be expected to solve, social problems like damage to the environment. But this does not imply that they have no responsibility to take action in the absence of law and regulation. As I will try to show, when business activities cause damage to the environment, which in turn causes a certain type of harm to persons, then businesses are morally required to alleviate that harm.

An ancient and compelling ethical principle, one that almost everyone accepts, is the brief rule, "do no harm." One reason this rule, usually called the "harm principle," is so compelling is the conviction we share that causing harm violates a moral right not to be harmed. As it stands, however, the injunction to do no harm is much too brief to be of any real help. It needs to be expanded and clarified if we are to use it as a moral guide in complex situations. One way to do it is:

(1) If a certain type of human activity or endeavor causes unwarranted harm to a person or some other entity, then that activity violates the moral right of that person or entity not to be harmed.

Note that this version of the harm principle does not state that all the harm a person may suffer violates the right not to be harmed but only that all unwarranted harm does. In order to apply the principle, then, more needs to be said about the notion of unwarranted harm.

Unwarranted harm is a difficult concept to analyze since there are different kinds of harm and many different circumstances under which someone might allege that harm is unwarranted and hence violates rights. As a rough cut, however, I suggest that the harm an activity causes is unwarranted if the following two conditions are met: the harm is not offset or ameliorated to any significant extent by some corresponding benefit the activity generates, and the harm can be prevented without causing other significant harm that outweighs the benefit of prevention.

This characterization of unwarranted harm suffers from the defect that there is no generally accepted formula that determines when a harm is "significantly" offset or ameliorated by a benefit. Moreover, in my view, harms and benefits may be incommensurable in many cases. There may be no objective standard of measurement, monetary or otherwise, that we can use to quantify harms and benefits and see if the former is to any degree offset or ameliorated by the latter. Nevertheless, judgments about the relative weight of harms and benefits are unavoidable. Surgery is harmful, but in most (not all) cases we judge that the benefit of improved health offsets the harm of the pain caused by surgery, though there is no standard against which pain and improved health can be measured. Economic activity is another example. Industrial accidents happen, factories shut down, the stock market takes a plunge, pollutants are released into the atmosphere, and in all these cases people suffer harm. But here also we judge that in the main the benefits of economic activity offset the harm it causes, although there may be no objective way to measure one against the other.

Sometimes we judge that harms are not offset by benefits. Sometimes surgery causes more harm than good, and the same is true of economic activity. The economic benefits of slavery and child labor did not offset the harm they caused. Much of the debate about business and the environment is about harms versus benefits. It is a serious mistake to think that harms and benefits can be quantified and compared, but it is equally a mistake to think that we can make no judgments at all about their relative weight.

Preventing a harmful activity, even when the harm is not offset by the benefits it produces, may cause other serious harm that outweighs the advantage gained by stopping the activity. For example, the illegal trade in addictive drugs causes harm that is not significantly offset by any benefit, but some argue that preventing this trade would cause other harm too costly to bear. Consequently the trade should not be prevented, but legalized. A more controversial example is clear-cutting tropical rain forests. The long-term ecological harm this causes may outweigh any immediate economic benefit, but stopping the activity would deprive many people of their only means of livelihood and further impoverish certain Third World countries.

If this account of unwarranted harm is provisionally acceptable, then the next step in the expansion and clarification of the harm principle is:

(2) If a human activity or endeavor violates the moral right of a person or other entity not to be harmed, then that harm ought to be prevented by either stopping the activity, or, if it cannot be entirely stopped without causing other significant harm, it ought to be modified so as to minimize the harm it causes.

This is based on the thesis that moral rights imply moral duties. For instance, if Jones has the right not to be harmed, then I have a duty not to harm Jones. Thus, if some activity of mine violates Jones's right not to be harmed, I have a duty to stop or at least modify the activity. Furthermore, if I am unwilling to stop or modify the activity, then the second principle implies that other persons are morally required to see to it that I do not continue harming Jones.

Both principles apply to any human activity that causes unwarranted harm. In a business context they apply as follows. Suppose business activity X has adverse effects on the environment that cause harm to certain persons or entities. Further suppose such harm is unwarranted since it is not significantly offset or ameliorated by the benefits that economic activity brings to those persons or entities, and it can be prevented without causing other significant harm that outweighs the benefit of prevention. Then there are moral grounds for either preventing activity X or modifying it to ensure that the environmental damage it causes is minimized, since to allow it to continue violates the right of certain persons or entities not to be harmed.

To take a specific example, suppose business activity X is disposing of toxic industrial wastes in a way that eventually pollutes area groundwater. If it could be shown that the pollution causes unwarranted harm to the local residents, it would follow that there are moral grounds for altering the present method of disposal.

If someone were to reject the conclusion of this argument, he or she would have to show that the proposed ethical principle is for some reason inapplicable, that no harm is caused, or that it cannot be claimed that the harm caused is unwarranted since it does not satisfy the suggested characterization of unwarranted harm. On the other hand, even if the conclusion is accepted, the controversy is not ended. The argument can continue over how and to what extent the damage should be prevented or minimized and who should ensure that it is prevented or minimized.

It seems unlikely to me that any of the contributors to this book would reject the ethical principle as long as those harmed are existing human beings. But the same is not true if the harm is done to future generations of human beings, animals, or the environment itself. For instance, suppose there will be no significant greenhouse effects from burning fossil fuels for another hundred years. Then someone might argue that although no existing human beings will suffer harm from greenhouse effects, future generations will be harmed. Thus, assuming such harm is unwarranted, burning fossil fuel should be severely curtailed.

Similar arguments can be given on behalf of animals. If animals have the right not to be harmed, then if they are caused unwarranted harm, their rights are violated. On the other hand, if it is, as one contributor to the companion volume claims, "hopelessly sentimental" to believe that they do, then although we may want to avoid harming animals, there are no moral reasons not to do so since the harm principle does not apply to them.

The same might be said about future generations. How can something that does not exist have a moral right that implies a duty on our part to preserve the environment? And if neither animals nor future generations have rights, why shouldn't we exploit the environment as we see fit as long as we do not cause unwarranted harm to existing persons?

In order to answer this question fully we would have to examine in detail arguments for the rights of animals and future generations, but there may be a way to answer without undertaking this lengthy task. Some of the contributors suggest that the broad-based public support for environmental protection cannot be explained by the methods of rational risk assessment. Instead it is a deeply held public value, an attitude or sense of obligation toward other persons and the natural world. If this is correct, then one reason businesses should protect the environment is prudential: when things the public values are damaged or destroyed by what is generally believed to be a willful disregard for the public interest, legislative and regulatory restrictions are usually not far behind. And when these are ineffective, direct public action against the offender is an option sometimes taken. Thus, protecting the environment, even in circumstances where there is no question of the violation of rights, also protects the self-interest of business.

The difficulty with this approach, however, is that it does not necessarily give any particular business a good reason for eliminating or minimizing an environmental problem it causes. A businessperson could quite consistently agree that protecting the environment is a public value that deserves support and at the same time argue that as long as no person is caused unwarranted harm, there is no overriding reason to spend stockholder money to solve the problem. Protecting the environment may be a good thing to do, but in the absence of decisive moral considerations, it must take its place in line with all the other good things to do, had we but time and money enough to do them.

I will leave the public value approach aside for a moment and return to the main argument. The second way to show that no moral right has been violated by an action that damages the environment is to show that no harm was caused to any person, or to animals and future generations, if they have rights. There can be two areas of disagreement here. The first is about what counts as harm, and the second is whether the harm actually occurred or will occur. There are many different kinds of harm, but an uncontroversial example is immediate and undeniable physical harm directly caused by, for instance, toxins discharged into rivers used as a source of drinking water. If the harm is not immediate but supposedly will occur in the future, perhaps years in the future, and if the causal connection between environmental damage or pollutants and physical harm is less than clear, the case that a certain type of business activity causes physical harm by environmental damage is much more difficult to establish. For example, it is sometimes alleged that in twenty or thirty years, certain pollutants will cause an increase in the rate of various cancers or other disorders. But an examination of the evidence that backs up these claims often reveals questionable assumptions and research that is at best in its initial stages.

Furthermore, the problem is not only the empirical one of gathering enough evidence to establish that harm will occur. It is also conceptual. If we can point to no specific person who is harmed now, no rights are violated now. So why should a business be obligated to change its current procedures to prevent harm that may occur at some unspecified date in the future to some unspecified person or persons?

These are complex issues, and at best I can only sketch an answer. The empirical problem of showing that harm will occur at some future date has two distinct parts. The first is to decide on some standard of evidence that, it is generally agreed, is sufficient to justify present steps to prevent future harm. The second is to show in particular cases that the standard is or is not met.

Disagreement about the standard of evidence seems to lie at the center of many contemporary debates about the environment. Some corporations demand a stringent standard. In legal terms, they want the evidence to show beyond a reasonable doubt that environmental damage will cause harm. Others require a less strict standard—only that the preponderance or weight of evidence shows that harm will occur. For example, Du Pont apparently used the less strict standard when it decided to stop making chlorofluorocarbons (CFCs).

I believe the less strict standard should apply. The reason is that the moral requirement not to cause harm overrides whatever qualms there may be about the strength of the evidence. A preponderance of evidence, though it may not be as strong or unequivocal as we might wish, is reason enough to act to prevent harm that may occur in the future. I concede, however, that much more needs to be said about this.

Assuming the proposed standard of evidence is adopted, there remains the problem of determining whether the standard is met in specific instances. For instance, is there a preponderance of evidence that CFCs cause depletion of the ozone layer or that greenhouse gases will cause the icecaps to melt? Individual businesspersons might reasonably object that evaluating the evidence is beyond their competence and that without any determination about the quality of the evidence it would be foolhardy for them to act.

I agree that the objection is well taken but deny that businesspersons are thereby absolved of all responsibility. Businesses have the responsibility to find out whether the evidence justifies action, if not through their own efforts, then by banding together in some way to support independent and objective evaluations of the evidence. For example, suppose the chemical industry agreed to submit the CFC problem to an independent scientific organization for evaluation, to support additional research if needed, and to abide by that organization's decision about the evidence. In my view this would be an ethically responsible course of action. It would also be an action that would require immense changes in business attitudes and government policy. It may seem idealistic to advocate such a course of action, but the alternative is more lengthy debate about the evidence, and continued delay may prove disastrous. Some way to decide about the quality of the evidence must be adopted—if not the one proposed, then some other one. We cannot wait until the issue is moot.

There remains the conceptual problem. In brief, if no one is harmed now, then no rights are violated now, so why should businesses change their procedures? In order to answer this question, consider one of those fanciful examples so dear to the heart of philosophers. Suppose an evil scientist constructs a superintelligent robot. He enters the name and address of every living American into the robot's memory and then instructs the robot to select one of those persons at random and in about twenty years or so to go to that person's home and cause him or her serious physical harm. If we learned about the scientist's nefarious plan, would we be morally justified in preventing him from carrying it out, by force if necessary? Surely we would. And we would dismiss as frivolous any claim on his part that since no one has been harmed, no rights have been violated. It is justification enough for us to act that if we were to allow the scientist to continue, rights would be violated. If this is correct, then it implies that if an action in the present were to cause harm in the future, and thus would violate a right in the future, we are morally justified in requiring action to prevent or minimize that harm. This is an important extension of the ethical principle, which does not obviously have this implication. It allows us to say to an individual manager that he or she is morally obligated now to prevent harm that may occur long after the manager has gone to another job. It may even justify present action to protect the "rights" of future generations.

The final stage of the argument is to show that the harm caused is unwarranted. If both conditions in the characterization of unwarranted harm are not met, then the conclusion does not follow. For example, suppose businesses are convinced that greenhouse gases will cause some warming of the earth's atmosphere and that as a consequence ocean levels will rise several feet and harm some coastal residents. They still could argue that the benefits of the economic activities that generate greenhouse gases offset the harm done to coastal residents. Alternatively, they could argue that stopping those activities would cause other significant harm, such as loss of jobs, that outweighs any benefit gained. If either point could be shown, the harm caused does not qualify as unwarranted in the sense I have characterized it.

The greenhouse case is complex since it asks us to make judgments about the relative weight of present benefits (economic activity) against future harms (rising sea levels) and existing harms (loss of jobs) against future benefits (maintaining sea levels). It is not clear to me how rationally to make such judgments, but it is clear that a procedure for making them is needed. Many kinds of business activity cause some degree of harm and can be stopped only at the cost of causing other harm. If we consider causing any harm at all morally unacceptable, then we will find ourselves in a moral dilemma from which there is no escape. Thus, we need to have some way of determining whether harm is unwarranted and hence morally prohibited.

Finally, if it is shown that a certain economic activity causes environmental damage, which in turn causes unwarranted harm, who should take the lead in stopping the activity or minimizing the harm it causes: business, government, or some other organization? If the preponderance of evidence shows that a certain business activity causes unwarranted harm, then the business in question is morally required to prevent or minimize that harm. But it must be done in a way that takes account of two further problems. The first is that the solution does not place the business at an insurmountable competitive disadvantage. It is pointless for a business to go bankrupt trying to solve a problem that can only be addressed by concerted industry-wide action. George Cabot Lodge, a professor at Harvard Business School, once told a story that illustrates this sort of futility. On Earth Day in 1969 a friend of his, who owned a paper company on the banks of a New England stream, was converted to the cause of environmental protection. He became determined to stop his company's pollution of the stream and marched off to put his new-found religion into action. Later, the story goes, Lodge learned that his friend went broke, and he drove up to see what happened. Radiating a kind of ethical purity, the friend told Lodge that he spent millions to stop the pollution and thus could no longer compete with other firms that did not follow his example. The company went under, five hundred people lost their jobs at the paper company, and the stream remained polluted. When Lodge asked his friend why he had not sought help from the state or federal government to set stricter standards for everyone, his friend muttered something about this not being the American way—that government should not interfere with business activity and that private enterprise could do the job alone.

This brings us to the second problem. Sometimes individual businesses can alleviate damage they cause without going bankrupt. When they can and when such damage causes unwarranted harm, they are morally required to do so. But even in cases where they cannot prevent the harm by themselves, they are not thereby excused from all moral responsibility. If necessary, businesses may have to lobby the government to impose regulation that prevents or minimizes unwarranted harm caused by their activities. This is directly contrary to prevailing business attitudes, but as several contributors argue, the antagonistic attitude between business and government over environmental regulation is an outmoded and self-defeating relic of the mistaken attitude that any government interference with business activity is unjustified. Moreover, it is morally unacceptable for businesses to lobby against regulations aimed at preventing or minimizing unwarranted harm caused by business activity. When individual businesses are prevented by market considerations from acting alone, then collective action may be the only remaining method of discharging their moral obligations.

In conclusion I would like to return briefly to the point that environmental protection is a public value. I centered my discussion around the rights of individuals and argued that the public value of environmental protection does not always provide individual businesspersons with reasons to change their business policies. It would be a mistake to dismiss this value too lightly. The decisions we make now about the environment are decisions about the kind of world we want to live in and the kind of world we want to leave to our heirs. Each decision shapes that world, sometimes in ways that can be changed and sometimes irrevocably. Many decisions about the environment are of the latter kind. No doubt some of them do violate rights not to be harmed. These should be dealt with by appropriate means. But others of equal or greater magnitude do not clearly violate any rights. Perhaps they cannot even be evaluated within the conceptual framework of rights. This seems to me a genuine possibility. It does not mean, I believe, that we cannot evaluate them at all from a moral viewpoint, but it may mean that we need to consider whether we have moral obligations to ourselves, to future generations, to animals, and to the environment that go beyond the rights these things may or may not have. The place to begin this investigation is with the values we hold—the things we hope our actions will preserve, promote, or protect. It is here, if anywhere, that we can truly begin to deal with the environmental dilemmas we face.

I

BUSINESS AND GOVERNMENT: COOPERATION AND REGULATION

Government-Business Relationships for Environmental Protection

DUANE WINDSOR

The passing of 1989 marked two decades of U.S. experience with environmental protection, as measured from passage of the 1969 National Environmental Policy Act. The Reagan and Bush administrations have explicitly endorsed market approaches as a substitute for conventional regulation. We need a systematic reexamination of business-government relationships affecting environmental protection at both the domestic and international levels in order to have a realistic appreciation of the process dimension of environmental policy making. Complexity, fragmentation, and conflict over values and interests among many uncoordinated stakeholders is the situation that characterizes both U.S. policy making and international cooperation on environmental protection. Such conditions compel attention to process as a necessary means for getting at substance. A process-oriented viewpoint should not be a surprising one in the environmental arena. On the contrary, Tribe (1976) emphasized that process would be crucial in environmental policy making, and Frankel (1976) emphasized that plurality of values could be handled only by some form of interest accommodation. I shall stipulate that domestic and multinational enterprises, governments, and individuals all have broad responsibilities or duties for environmental protection (Frederick 1986), which is a long-run community value of high priority but abstract content.

I shall argue three conclusions. First, the most appropriate and now also the most likely approach to environmental protection will be a mixed system of multiple strategies. Four basic strategies are to be combined:

1. Conventional regulation by standards-setting public agencies together with the related strategy of public or trustee ownership of critical environmental resources (like wetlands and forests) that developed in the earlier conservationist movement (see Farney 1989).

2. Stakeholder litigation for enforcement of such regulations.

3. Stakeholder negotiations (including both contracting and bargaining) in lieu of litigation.

4. Improved market incentives for environmental protection.

We need continuing research into the relative strengths and weaknesses of each strategy. Second, there appears to be an increasing need to decide, at least in principle, the desirable balance between the adversarial (regulation cum litigation) and cooperative (negotiation cum incentives) approaches to environmental protection. Cooperative approaches will be especially necessary to international action. The cooperative approach at the international level is akin to a Rawlsian philosophy concerning distribution of benefits and costs (Rawls 1971). Third, arguments in favor of specifying constitutional rights to environmental quality for future generations and nature are simply artificial devices for attempting to sidestep the political processes necessary to resolve environmental issues. Environmental policy is inevitably the product of a particular and highly institutionalized political process in the United States (see Hays 1987) and of a particular situation affecting international cooperation.

The chapter proceeds from four related premises. First, political action is required for environmental protection and is largely an arena of formal authorities and formal organizations operating within limits set by public opinion (Banfield 1961). Second, both market and governmental failure should be anticipated. It is this dual failure that we see at work in the Bhopal and *Exxon Valdez* incidents. Third, short-run benefits and costs to individuals and organizations of environmental protection are very unevenly distributed. Many individuals and organizations thus have strong incentives to disregard long-run or externalized environmental impacts. Fourth, while environmental protection involves long-run global interdependence compelling international cooperation for success, national sovereignties also face strong incentives against cooperation. As in the case of individuals and organizations, short-run impacts are very unevenly distributed. Many developing countries may, like many business organizations, value growth far more highly than environmental protection.

A serious problem in designing and implementing environmental protection strategies is that we must take account of the distinct probability that both markets and political institutions will fail. The underlying "theory" of the environmental protection movement since 1969 has been that because "markets" are bad, their environmental protection dimensions should be handled by government. Public choice theory argues that both market failure and political failure must be expected (Buchanan 1988). The same body of work has been highly critical of conventional regulation (Aranson and Ordeshook 1985). This view is reinforced by studies of bureaucratic politics and governmental processes that find many sources for decision-making failures in political institutions (Allison 1971). Forests may be protected by public ownership (although there are increasing complaints that government agencies may do no better than private firms), but public ownership of nuclear facilities does not seem to be a safeguard based on recent U.S. experience with atomic weapons plants. While markets are certainly defective in the environmental dimension, government is unlikely to be a panacea. The process design problem is much more difficult.

The policy debate may be subject to periodic politicization-depoliticization cycles that affect degree of popular concern and governmental interest (Vogel 1986). The 1960s was a decade of prosperity in which the social costs of environmental protection and governmental intervention in markets were regarded as low. The 1970s and 1980s by contrast saw high inflation focused on energy costs and increasing international competition, accompanied by an emphasis on the benefits of governmental reduction, as reflected in the deregulation, taxpayer resistance, and privatization movements (Reese 1983). This observed evolution may also reflect a widening disenchantment with the adversarial model inherent in the regulatory and litigation strategies conventionally used for environmental protection. It is conceivable that the 1990s will see a resurgence of environmental concerns (Garelik 1989).

The environmental policy debate is highly fragmented, despite a greatly increased appreciation of environmental issues in the United States and elsewhere. It is a technically complex debate among many highly specialized policy elites and organized interest groups (Bosso 1987), who are concerned with a multitude of very different issues only loosely grouped under the abstract rubric of the environment. There is a whole universe of environments affected by human activities. Environmental protection is in no sense a single policy issue arena. On the contrary, a critical problem in environmental policy is that we face an only partially overlapping series of environmental impacts involving different concerns, stakeholders, and institutions. What makes grappling with environmental protection so vital is the cumulative consequences of these many environmental impacts.

The environment is a series of collective-consumption goods. While everyone may ultimately benefit from environmental protection, such benefits are in the future and thus intangible now. The costs of environmental protection are now and tangible. Enterprises, agencies, and consumers have strong incentives to ignore future intangible benefits while responding to existing tangible costs. Tackling this collective-consumption arena involves building a widespread public opinion strongly favoring environmental protection measures. Such public opinion probably exists in the United States today (Weidenbaum 1989).

There are as yet relatively poor prospects for improved international cooperation to deal with environmental impacts of both business and governmental activity. Countries are at different stages of economic and political development and thus take very different views of the appropriate trade-offs between growth and environment. These are significant East-West political and North-South economic cleavages that affect international cooperation (Heath 1984). Environmental destruction is a major problem in many countries outside the Organization for Economic Cooperation and Development (OECD), including the Soviet Union.

The widespread existence of environmental effects, regardless of economic and political systems, indicates that business enterprise in market capitalism is not per se the source of environmental damage. Citizens and governments often do little better; witness the Soviet Union's record on environmental damage, including the Chernobyl disaster, as well as human rights violations, the U.S. government's unsafe nuclear weapons plants, and municipal water pollution. Either business enterprises or governmental agencies may serve as the engines of economic growth.

FOUR STRATEGIES

The appropriate approach to environmental protection is not fully resolved. On the contrary, both the Bhopal and *Exxon Valdez* incidents clearly illustrate how corporate action within a framework of government regulation can fail disastrously. In the *Exxon Valdez* accident, the largest oil spill in U.S. history occurred in an environmentally sensitive area and appears to have resulted from a series of failures in procedures. What should have been contingency cleanup plans were ineffectual. All these errors were contrary to corporate guidelines and government regulation. In the Bhopal accident, thousands of people were killed or injured by a deadly gas leak. It appears that the technology was inappropriate to the situation and that both corporate and government inspection programs failed. (An Indian state was minority owner and the local population was allowed to expand around Bhopal without consideration for the safety hazards.)

There are four basic strategies for coping with environmental concerns:

1. The classic approach has been a conventional *regulatory strategy,* modeled on antitrust and public utility tradition. Conventional regulation emphasizes control of environmental impacts by specialized public agencies like the Environmental Protection Agency (EPA) defining appropriate standards for performance pursuant to statutory authorizations. Public or nonprofit ownership of critical environmental resources is an important instrument in this conventional strategy.

2. Regulation in the antitrust tradition is usually enforced through criminal and civil litigation. *Litigation strategy* emphasizes legal dispute among stakeholders, pursuant to statutory authorizations and common law precedents. The term *stakeholder* is borrowed from the corporate governance literature, where it connotes all the clienteles or constituencies affected by or interested in the activities of a given firm (Freeman 1984).

3. William Reilly, formerly president of the World Wildlife Fund, and appointed by President Bush to head EPA, is said to be an exponent of *negotiation strategy* (Kwong 1988). This approach emphasizes direct accommodation among stakeholders affected by a given environmental issue. Environmental negotiations typically involve mediation by public agencies, along the lines of management-labor dispute mediation. Probably the most critical objection to environmental negotiation is the likely maldistribution of negotiating resources and skills among stakeholders, weighted in the direction of corporations (Amy 1987).

4. Reilly is also said to favor increased use of market solutions (Kwong 1988). *Market strategy* emphasizes the role of property rights and economic incentives (Anderson et al. 1978; Coleman 1989; Weidenbaum 1989) in balancing economic growth against environmental protection. An intellectual understanding of environmental issues, and political pressures for compliance, are important elements of environmental protection. But business enterprise is motivated primarily by materialistic, or tangible, incentives. The most direct method for affecting business activity is to alter its perceived economic environment. While business firms can embrace social, that is nonmaterial, responsibilities (Frederick 1986), in practice they lack strong incentives to consider the unpriced externalities of their economic activities unless forced to by other stakeholders acting directly through litigation or by governmental institutions using penalties and taxes. How to reshape the economic incentives of public enterprises and agencies is very unclear (Weidenbaum 1989), particularly in the case of centralized socialist states.

GOVERNMENT-BUSINESS RELATIONSHIPS

Figure 1.1 translates the four environmental protection strategies into four alternative models of government-business relationships (there is not a precise one-to-one correspondence of models to strategies). Each relationship model is defined in terms of an environmental protection approach and its basic enforcement mechanism. The figure is constructed by distinguishing between environmentally effective and ineffective markets, as well as between ethical and unethical actors. By an effective market, I mean one that actively promotes environmental protection and renewable resources. An ineffective market fails to protect the environment, due either to the ignorance or avarice of economic actors. Unethical actors deliberately ignore the environmental effects of their

Figure 1.1
A Mixed System of Multiple Strategies

	Environmentally			
	Ineffective Markets		Effective Markets	
	Unethical Actors	Ethical Actors	Ethical Actors	
	Evasion	Ignorance	Standards	Responsibility
Environmental protection approach	Government regulation/ ownership	Public information	Industry self-regulation	Corporate codes of conduct
Enforcement Mechanism	Stakeholder litigation	Stakeholder negotiation	Business liability	Property rights
	Model 1	Model 2	Model 3	Model 4

economic activities. Effective markets probably depend on ethical actors as well as property rights, but even ethical actors can create environmental damage through ignorance.

Models 1 and 2 assume that markets are ineffective in promoting environmental protection for different reasons. Model 1 marries regulation and litigation strategies. The conventional regulatory strategy assumes implicitly that markets are ineffective and economic actors are unethical. Since unethical actors will seek to evade regulation, stakeholder litigation is necessary as an enforcement mechanism. Model 2 explicates negotiation strategy. It assumes that economic actors are ethical, so that environmental damage arises through ignorance. In this case, the approach is to disseminate public information, leading to desired changes in behavior. Stakeholder negotiation would be more likely under these conditions. The Bhopal and *Exxon Valdez* accidents indicate that government must be prepared to act rapidly when private systems fail.

Models 3 and 4 explore market strategy. They assume that markets can be made environmentally effective and that economic actors are ethical. Under such conditions, in model 3, environmental standards guided by public information from governmental and nonprofit entities could be created by industry self-regulation. (The industry may act through the legislative process to ensure compliance by unethical companies.) The industry should pay for accidental environmental damages as a form of insurable business liability. By extension, model 4 characterizes environmental protection standards as being included in corporate codes of conduct through a sense of environmental responsibility. Corporate interest in defining and adhering to such responsibilities is best maintained by establishing property rights in environmental resources.

Figure 1.1 is not intended to demonstrate that model 4 is superior to model 1. Rather, two other conclusions are intended. First, environmental protection is easier to achieve and enforce if markets are effective, economic actors are ethical, and property rights provide appropriate incentives for environmental protection. Efforts to establish such a framework are critically important. Second, all four models are needed simultaneously. Regulation cum litigation and public information together with industry standards should help to enhance incentives for corporate responsibility. There will be unethical actors evading environmental standards; even ethical actors may proceed in ignorance. The appropriate mix of strategies is likely to vary by issue and industry characteristics (Sonnenfeld and Lawrence 1978). Effective enforcement mechanisms are an additional topic to be investigated. A great many statutes forbidding undesirable behavior are often violated.

CONSTITUTIONAL RIGHTS AND POLITICAL PROCESSES

The question of constitutional rights to environmental protection is an additional layer to this political analysis. A constitutional system of rules and procedures regarding definition of such rights is in existence in the United States. Three issues affect its use. First, this system has only general form, since environmental protection, like education or housing, is not directly addressed. Such concerns must be handled indirectly through other constitutional rights or legislatively. Indirect treatment is always difficult because conflict among different constitutional principles is highly likely. Historically conflict among principles has been handled by not pushing any single principle too far in determining priorities. Second, do future generations have whatever rights are definable? Third, does nature have whatever rights are definable (Frankel 1976; Nash 1989; Stone 1972; Tribe 1976)?

I shall group the second and third issues together since they turn on the same problem: neither future generations nor nature can in any sense define and protect their constitutional rights. That protection must be placed in the hands of the government or interested private parties acting as trustees. This approach is tantamount to arguing that environmental protections are inadequate (a point with which I fully concur) and that such protections can be best defined by creating them artificially—that is, by assigning them to fictional persons, who will be represented by real persons acting in effect as trustees. (It is in this manner that business corporations are accorded constitutional rights under judicial interpretation. Another analogy is the treatment accorded to juveniles, for whom parents, or under certain circumstances the state acting in the public interest, serve as trustees.)

We may accept here as a given that environmental protection is crucial and that business enterprises have environmental responsibilities and should be accountable for their environmental impacts. This environmental protection axiom inevitably sidesteps two very important problems of constitutional democracy, however.

The first problem is that very few values can be said to be absolute in a democracy. It is easy to say that growth should be reduced or restructured to relieve environmental impacts, but there are areas of the globe in which the immediate practical choice is between the environment and starvation. Which value is more important? Where does the trade-off point fall? How is the growth issue to be handled?

The second problem is that the short-run costs of environmental protection fall on someone in a democracy. Who should bear what costs, and how? While the net economic welfare of a society must properly be measured in terms of economic performance adjusted for environmental effects (Samuelson 1980, pp. 183–85), judging the relationship between growth and environment is inherently a political—that is, a collective decision-making—process. Environmental policy-making processes are complicated by the realities of complex institutions, the fragmentation of environmental issues, and global interdependence in a highly diverse and conflict-ridden world. The function of the democratic political process is to weigh these competing values and determine who gets what in a situation of open access to all stakeholders.

I shall use the term *politics* in the sense advocated by Bernard Crick, who regards it as an admittedly imperfect "process of deliberate conciliation . . . radically different from tyranny, oligarchy, kingship, dictatorship, despotism and . . . totalitarianism" (Crick 1972, p. 19). Politics is compromise and accommodation rather than a struggle for power. I must depart somewhat from Crick in that governments and political systems are inevitably mixes of influence, struggle, and market exchanges (Banfield 1985) rather than the pure forms he tends to suggest.

But the process of interest accommodation, within legal forms, is a hallmark of constitutional democracy, and it may be especially necessary in international cooperation among different forms of government ranging from democracy to totalitarianism. Rawls's (1971) theory of social justice may be a particularly appropriate framework for tackling international cooperation. Invoking a species of social contract theory, he argues that mutual consent among "stakeholders" (whether citizens or countries) is the appropriate standard for social justice. There is a very strong tradition in international law that all states have equal sovereignty; they are akin to electors within a political community. This tradition is in general accord with the Rawlsian approach to social justice.

A political view of environmental policy making should not be confused with a value-neutral view that public policy must be simply whatever results from political interaction. There are two reasons for making a distinction. First, choice problems often have a logical structure that drives interaction in a particular direction. Environmental impacts are real phenomena with real consequences. Bhopal, Love Canal, Chernobyl, ozone loss, deforestation, oil spills, the Yellowstone Park fire, and so on demand concrete action. The survival of civilization may now hinge on how we collectively cope with the environmental question. Second, social interaction can be guided by leadership and persuasion. It matters greatly what attitude the president and other key opinion leaders take toward environmental issues (Garelik 1989). Stakeholders' views and interests can be reshaped by the persuasive efforts of opinion leaders and activists, as well as by events and trends. Environmental interest groups like the Sierra Club and the Wildlife Fund play a vital role in this process. The essence of their role is the creation of formal organizations to promote environmental issues.

International cooperation for environmental protection must also be shaped within a political environment. There are strong incentives opposing international consensus. For example, while the European Community countries have now acted to reduce fluorocarbons affecting the ozone, India and the People's Republic of China in a recent international conference did not agree to limits and blamed the situation on the advanced industrial states. Individual countries, like citizens, may pursue short-run benefits and ignore long-run costs imposed on others as externalities. The OECD may be in a position to exercise leadership and influence in the international cooperation arena.

CONCLUSION

I have proposed a framework for understanding the problems inherent in building a more effective process for government-business interaction toward strengthening environmental protection in both domestic and international contexts. I conclude that a mixed system of multiple strategies is the most desirable—because both market and governmental failures must be anticipated—and the most likely—because the environmental policy arena is necessarily highly fragmented and conflict ridden. Under such conditions, constitutional rights to environmental protection by future generations and nature are simply artificial attempts to circumvent unavoidable politics of interest accommodation. The evolution of a mixed system of multiple strategies will be driven by complex forces of public opinion, environmental leadership, and environmental disasters.

REFERENCES

Allison, Graham T. 1971. *Essence of Decision: Explaining the Cuban Missile Crisis.* Boston: Little, Brown.

Amy, Douglas J. 1987. *The Politics of Environmental Mediation.* New York: Columbia University Press.

Anderson, Frederick R., et al. 1978. *Environmental Improvement through Economic Incentives.* Baltimore: Johns Hopkins University Press.

Aranson, Peter H., and Ordeshook, Peter C. 1985. "Public Interest, Private Interest, and the Democratic Polity." In Roger Benjamin and Stephen L. Elkin, eds., *The Democratic State,* pp. 87–178. Lawrence: University Press of Kansas.

Banfield, Edward C. 1961. *Political Influence.* New York: Free Press.

———. 1985. "Economic Analysis of Political Problems." In *Here the People Rule: Selected Essays,* pp. 317–27. New York: Plenum Press.

Bosso, Christopher J. 1987. *Pesticides and Politics: The Life Cycle of a Public Issue.* Pittsburgh: University of Pittsburgh Press.

Buchanan, James M. 1988. "Market Failure and Political Failure." *Cato Journal* 8:1–14.

Coleman, Jules L. 1989. "A Market Approach to Products Liability Reform." St. Louis: Center for the Study of American Business, Washington University.

Crick, Bernard. 1972. *In Defence of Politics.* 2d ed. Chicago: University of Chicago Press.

Farney, Dennis. 1989. "Nature Conservancy–Led Land-Preservation Plan Outperforms and Out-Innovates Federal Program." *Wall Street Journal,* May 24.

Frankel, Charles. 1976. "The Rights of Nature." In Lawrence H. Tribe, Corinne S. Schelling, and John Voss, eds., *When Values Conflict: Essays on Environmental Analysis, Discourse, and Decision,* pp. 93–114. Cambridge, Mass.: Ballinger.

Frederick, William C. 1986. "Toward CSR3: Why Ethical Analysis Is Indispensable and Unavoidable in Corporate Affairs." *California Management Review* 28:126–41.

Freeman, R. Edward. 1984. *Strategic Management: A Stakeholder Approach.* Boston: Pitman.

Garelik, Glenn. 1989. "A New Item on the Agenda: The Plight of the Planet Is Finally Serious International Business." *Time,* October 23, pp. 60–62.

Hays, Samuel P. 1987. *Beauty, Health, and Permanence: Environmental Politics in the United States, 1955–1985.* New York: Cambridge University Press.

Heath, Edward. 1984. "East-West and North-South Relations." St. Louis: Center for the Study of American Business, Washington University.

Kwong, Jo Ann. 1988. "Environmentalism Gone Part-Way to Market." *Wall Street Journal*, December 30.

Nash, Roderick F. 1989. *The Rights of Nature: A History of Environmental Ethics*. Madison: University of Wisconsin Press.

Rawls, John. 1971. *A Theory of Justice*. Cambridge: Harvard University Press.

Reese, Craig R. 1983. *Deregulation and Environmental Quality*. Westport, Conn.: Quorum Books.

Samuelson, Paul A. 1980. "Beyond GNP to Net Economic Welfare." In *Economics*, pp. 183–85. 11th ed. New York: McGraw-Hill.

Sonnenfeld, Jeffrey, and Lawrence, Paul R. 1978. "Why Do Companies Succumb to Price Fixing?" *Harvard Business Review* 78:145–57.

Stone, Christopher D. 1972. "Should Trees Have Standing?—Toward Legal Rights for Natural Objects." *Southern California Law Review* 45:490ff.

Tribe, Lawrence H. 1976. "Ways Not to Think about Plastic Trees." In Lawrence H. Tribe, Corinne S. Schelling, and John Voss, eds., *When Values Conflict: Essays on Environmental Analysis, Discourse, and Decision*, pp. 61–92. Cambridge, Mass.: Ballinger.

Vogel, David. 1986. "The Study of Social Issues in Management: A Critical Appraisal." *California Management Review* 28:142–51.

Weidenbaum, Murray. 1989. "Protecting the Environment: Harnessing the Power of the Marketplace." St. Louis: Center for the Study of American Business, Washington University.

Making Polluters Pay

ANDREW W. SAVITZ

I am the general counsel of environmental affairs for the Executive Office of Environmental Affairs for the commonwealth of Massachusetts. I am also the assistant secretary of environmental law enforcement. Our office has been in the news lately, as we have started to make good on our promise to make polluters pay. I want to talk about that slogan—making polluters pay—as one of the ethical underpinnings of the current environmental movement.

But first, there is a joke I feel neatly sums up the relationship of business, ethics, and the environment. It goes like this: a young man from Boston goes on a vacation to the Midwest. He spends the night in a farmhouse and, come morning, is having a cup of coffee with the farmer when he notices a pig walk by with a wooden leg. The joke goes on until farmer explains that though the pig is a genius and has saved his life, "a pig like that you don't eat all at once." What makes this joke funny is the ironic situation of the farmer who realizes that he has something unique and valuable in the pig but cannot stop himself from devouring it, so he eats the pig leg by leg, somehow trying to slow the damage he knows he is doing.

The difference between the joke and reality is that even if the farmer eats the whole pig, it is his pig to eat, and he is only hurting himself. But when businesses or individuals decide to swallow up the environment, it is not just their environment, and they are hurting others as well as themselves. That is where ethics, government, and environmental law enforcement enter the picture.

Before we enter that picture, I want to take a step back and look at the bigger picture. One of the central questions of moral philosophy is whether altruism is possible. Isn't all action, even action that purports to be altruistic, really based on crude self-interest? To put it another way: are we really just selfish pigs ourselves?

As far as corporations go, we have to assume that they are quintessentially self-interested actors as well. This is not meant as criticism. Corporations are created specifically to promote their own self-interest, and it would be foolish to assume they do anything but that. You and I can get together and do good deeds, even those that appear to be altruistic deeds. But let us form a corporation, and immediately that artificial entity takes on a life of its own. Duties of care are imposed by law; I suddenly have fiduciary responsibility. If the business is a for-profit corporation, the need for profit becomes paramount. That need becomes a very powerful engine that drives our corporate behavior.

Environmentalists must appeal to corporate self-interest in order to obtain positive results for the environment. Corporate altruism on the environment may be possible, but I fear it is several years away. Companies that do make a good-faith effort to obey the environmental laws—and they are, thankfully, in the majority in Massachusetts—have a basic economic self-interest in seeing those laws vigorously enforced against companies that willfully violate them. Good corporate citizens find themselves facing unfair economic disadvantages because it is more expensive to comply than to violate, especially if you stand a good chance of getting away with the violation. Law-abiding companies must either swallow the cost of compliance or, more likely, pass the costs of compliance on to their customers. Either way, they face an unfair competitive disadvantage against those few companies that intentionally violate the environmental laws.

To go one step further, given the limited resources the state has to catch violators and the relatively low levels of fines and penalties that have been imposed in the past, companies may actually experience a perverse desire to try and beat the system. I call this the reverse Megabucks phenomenon: the chances of being caught are low, and those who were caught in the past often paid little more than the cost of doing it right the first time.

That will not happen again. Massachusetts is sending a message to those who intentionally violate the environmental laws: the 1990s will be your unlucky decade. It may have been a winning bet before, but we are changing the odds. We are bound and determined to change the equation, level the playing field, stack the deck, fight the good fight, and generally put the wood to polluters.

Not only are we working harder to catch violators, but we are raising the stakes for those who do get caught. We are, in a sense, acknowledging our limited resources and working to make the gamble of noncompliance a very costly one for those who gamble and lose. We are trying to protect those law-abiding companies that are spending their money on compliance. We are protecting their investment in playing by the rules. We are committed to this both as a matter of law and as a matter of basic fairness to honest companies.

But is our approach fair to dishonest companies? Are we being fair to the developer who, having ignored two cease-and-desist orders for bulldozing wetlands, suddenly finds an environmental police officer on his doorstep at 8:00 A.M. with a penalty assessment notice for $200,000 and an enforcement order for another $250,000 in remediation? Are we making an unfair example of this man?

Is this ethical? Is this fair? His lawyer said this was like a life sentence for running a traffic light. We think it was more serious than that, and also he was fleeing from the police at the time of his most recent violation.

One thing is absolutely clear: when the story of this enforcement action made the front page of the business sections of the *Boston Globe,* the *Boston Herald,* and the local papers where the developer lived, the world changed; developers took notice.

Here is another central, ethical question raised by pollution that is especially poignant in these tough fiscal times: who should pay to clean up pollution in the first place? Should the taxpayers pay, or should we make polluters pay? Making polluters pay makes sense both fiscally and from a public policy point of view. Moreover, why should the taxpayers have to reach into their pockets to pay the price of these multimillion dollar cleanups when they are not at fault and cannot afford it.

The federal and state Superfund laws appear to resolve this fundamental question of who pays in favor of the taxpayers—even in the case of nonwillful pollution. Under the Superfund laws, the government is authorized to recover the costs of cleanup from private parties, whether they actually caused the pollution or not. The law designates potentially responsible parties (PRPs) as those who caused the pollution, those who currently own the land, or those who at any point owned the land. Each PRP is liable for the entire amount of the cleanup but can split that amount with the other parties. We are talking about strict, joint, and several liability. According to strict liability a manufacturer or seller is liable for any and all defective or hazardous products which unduly threaten a consumer's personal safety. According to joint and several liability parties can be held responsible together and individually.

This tough liability has been the subject of tremendous debate. Is it fair to hold someone liable for pollution who may not have known about the buried drums or oil leak that has appeared under his or her land? I believe the public policy behind these laws is sound and clear: get the sites cleaned up before the toxics do more damage to people and the environment. In order to accomplish this overriding public purpose, the government is authorized to get right to the cleanup without first having to determine who is at fault. The government recovers its costs from the polluter or from the landowner in strict liability and moves on to clean up another site. The private parties are then left to determine who ultimately bears the costs.

Massachusetts has recently proposed legislation to exempt innocent home owners from strict liability under the state Superfund law. At the same time, we have implemented regulations that specify that the state may recover not only the costs of cleaning up sites but also a percentage of the oversight costs for cleanups that are conducted by PRPs and overseen by the state. In other words, a percentage of administrative costs, including salaries, will be charged back to private parties, most of whom are cleaning up the sites themselves.

This raises some interesting ethical and legal questions. For example, which industry association holds the modern land-speed record for filing a lawsuit against the state? A lawsuit was filed within nanoseconds of our promulgating those cost recovery regulations on the grounds the charges are an unauthorized tax on PRPs. We argue that we are authorized, indeed required, to recover all of our costs and that we need to do so to keep the cleanup program moving forward.

Leaving aside the fact that the plaintiffs in this case are also generally opposed to higher taxes to pay for the oversight costs, I find it disturbing that the only issue at stake in this lawsuit is who pays. In these tight fiscal times, even the state is reduced to arguing how to protect the budget rather than how to protect the environment. In a case involving an admitted threat to public health and safety, all sides are arguing solely from the point of view of economic self-interest.

Unless we get the argument onto higher ground, we are going to squabble the environment away. The central question is how we can elevate concern for the environment above economic self-interest. (At the moment I wrote that sentence, the telephone in my office rang, and it was a John O'Leary, a private investigator who had just started a company specializing in hunting down potentially responsible parties, for a large fee. He asked me if anyone in the state had a use for his services. I said to him: "Excuse me, Mr. O'Leary, but is environmental altruism possible?" And he said: "Yes it is, for a large fee.")

I think that it is possible to move away from economic self-interest toward more disinterested action on the environment. It is vital that we do so. Unless we have a fundamental change in attitude, we are going to lose the fight on the environment. Economic self-interest may be the greatest motivating force the world has ever known, but all the Mr. O'Learys in the world will not get the job done, at least not in time. Call it altruism or call it survival, but we need a noneconomic approach to protecting the environment. In many ways, that is what our environmental law enforcement campaign is all about.

In moving to higher ground, we do have some things to work with. Let us start with the public. The public is angry about the environment, and the anger is not based on dollars and cents. Maybe it was the sight of 11 million gallons of oil spilling over Prince William Sound and realizing all the money in the world cannot fix it. Maybe it was the cyanide in Tylenol, or the strychnine on fresh fruit, or simply the constant bombardment of information about the destruction of the ozone layer and the tropical rain forests. But, for whatever reason, the public wants a cleaner world, now.

I see a subtle but fundamental change in attitude about illegal pollution. Environmental protection is becoming both a neighborhood issue and a law enforcement issue. People are starting to see that environmental crime is violent crime. This is another positive step toward a noneconomic position on the environment. And this is violent crime on a large scale, crime that threatens not one or two or ten people at a time but entire communities—with contaminated air and contaminated water. People are now being poisoned by pollution. With this widespread realization has come neighborhood activism. Unlike the essentially suburban environmental activism of the 1960s, today's activism comes out of

places like Lawrence and Woburn, Lowell and Boston. And there is an interesting circular effect as people in cities are more prone to see this issue in terms of
law and order to begin with.

The victims of pollution are coming forward to tell their stories: families who
have had to move from their homes, families who have had loved ones die from
contaminated water or from breathing in asbestos. They want justice and their
message is being heard: pollution is not a victimless crime.

Environmentalism is becoming a law and order issue, and I see this as a
positive development. As with other law and order issues, questions of right and
wrong have begun to replace the economic calculus of self-interest.

In terms of public attitudes, environmental crime can be compared to attitudes
toward drunk driving ten years ago. It used to be that drunk driving was not
considered a very serious crime. Now, because the consequences are more widely known, because victims have come forward and have gotten organized, and
because the government has taken a leadership role in forming public opinion,
we all know that drunk driving is an extremely antisocial, criminal activity.
Public attitudes about pollution are on the edge of change. We are moving from
an "everybody does it" attitude to a "this is the wrong thing to do" attitude. The
social stigma that now attaches to drunk driving will, I believe, become associated with those who pollute. In some small part, environmental law enforcement
can drive us to a more socially conscious, if not ethical, place on the spectrum.

Once people see protecting the environment as a law and order issue, they
begin to consider aspects like deterrence and punishment. When the police begin
working side by side with the scientists on a systematic basis, as they have with
our new Environmental Crime Strike Force, attitudes inside and outside of government change. Deterrence is essential to effective law enforcement, especially
in times of diminishing resources. Like more traditional forms of law enforcement, environmental law enforcement does not have the resources to investigate
and prosecute every case. We must therefore try to stop illegal pollution before it
occurs. It is much cheaper that way. Consider the cost of cleaning a gallon of
waste oil while it is still in the bucket compared to dealing with the million
gallons of water it can pollute when it is tossed into a lake. And unlike certain
other violent crimes, most illegal pollution is premeditated. It often boils down to
a cold business decision.

We have been cracking down. In Massachusetts we set up the Environmental
Crime Strike Force to go after intentional polluters using old-fashioned law
enforcement tools like surveillance, stakeouts, and high-powered investigative
teams. For the first time in the history of our state, we have environmental
scientists, attorneys, and police officers working as a team to investigate and
prosecute environmental crime. We have also created a new enforcement unit
within the Department of Environmental Protection to strengthen ongoing enforcement efforts within the agency. This office is responsible for most of the
administrative penalties we levy. And we have been ratcheting up the fines:
$300,000 on Mobil Oil and an $11 million remediation order for failure to

disclose a leaking underground storage tank; $600,000 to an Everett plating company for the illegal discharge of heavy metals into the Boston sewer system; and $200,000 to the developer who continued to bulldoze his wetlands in the face of two cease-and-desist orders.

We are removing the economic incentives to cheat, but we are also, we hope, changing attitudes about trying to cheat in the first place. We hope to change attitudes about the environmental laws much the way that rigorous enforcement of the drunk driving laws helped to change attitudes about that crime.

By cracking down and by publicizing our efforts, we are trying to raise concern for the environment to a higher ground than economic self-interest, even among those businesses and individuals who might not see it that way. It is a two-step process. First, we have to make businesses and individuals aware that if they swallow the pig, they are going to pay the price. Then at some point we have to convince them that it is simply wrong to swallow the pig, regardless of the price they might have to pay.

I hope we are on the verge of an ethical breakthrough on the environment. But until we reach that point, expect tougher, more aggressive, environmental law enforcement in Massachusetts. We are determined to save the pig.

The Civic Society and Hazardous Waste Management

ROBERT L. SWINTH

The generation and accumulation of hazardous waste in the United States has reached alarming levels under existing management systems. This problem is in part the consequence of the individualistic ethical stance in business and other institutions toward the environment. Here, as in several other aspects of the environment, such as ozone depletion, the greenhouse effect, and acid rain damage, the limits to this value framework are revealed.

THE ISSUE

Industry generates 265.6 million tons of hazardous waste per year in the United States (Congressional Budget Office 1985). More than half of it, 144.6 million metric tons, is emitted into the environment through wastewater treatment plants, illegal dumping, and shallow wells. One hundred one million metric tons is stored in hazardous waste landfills and deep injection wells where it must be managed for hundreds of years and where there are leaks and spills. Only 20 million metric tons is treated, and even here the main method, incineration, raises community concerns about accidents similar to those that arise with nuclear power plants.

The troubled feelings of society are well founded. The social and environmental consequences of the hazardous waste among us has been demonstrated in numerous studies. Bailar (1987) points out that the age-adjusted cancer rate in the United States is rising rather than falling, as we have been led to believe, in part due to hazardous waste exposure. The Council on Environmental Quality (1988) has found long-term declines in waterfowl breeding populations, a general environmental indicator—in part due to hazardous waste exposure. In support of these trends are numerous studies of cancer and other diseases associated with specific hazardous waste exposures and wildlife degradation stemming from such exposure.

It would appear that continuing to travel the present path takes society through many future crises and possibly major catastrophes. This backwash of hazardous waste into our lives forces us to confront a dark picture. Not only is it showing that a policy of out of sight, out of mind is unworkable, it calls into question our sense of ourselves as civilized, right-living people. Fundamentally we need to feel good about our actions but are finding that we cannot be comfortable with the consequences of current hazardous waste policies.

INDIVIDUALISM

Although the legitimation of individualism has served society well in many domains, it has led to troublesome results with the environment because of the commons nature of the relationship between environmental quality and economic production (Aram 1989). Production that generates hazardous waste has little impact on the environment below some threshold amount because of the capacity of the environment to assimilate it. When a critical level is reached, though, the environmental response may be catastrophic. Thus in threshold regions, small changes in production may lead to large consequences in environmental degradation. Individualism, on the other hand, is predicated on the assumption of equilibrium conditions where there are many actors, each with relatively equal capacity to influence events. Here, the self-interested action of any one player has only small consequences, and the tendency of the system is always toward the mean.

Scholars are beginning to recognize this difference, and the use of economic justification for private decision making on issues that affect ecological performance is being criticized by ethicists (Sagoff 1988). There are practical problems with the emphasis on the priority of the self, separate persons choosing and the rights of the individual (Sandel 1984) when settings are highly interdependent. The unique ethical feature of individualism is not self-interest but the reserving to oneself the right to choose unilaterally when there is a conflict between goals. Although such a manager may be environmentally conscious, the individualistically oriented executive still feels legitimate in personally deciding to put company needs ahead of environmental protection "when necessary."

As Sagoff notes, corporations must put aside their power in this area (p. 47). These organizations must reflect on their interests for the long term (Aram 1989). They and the society with which they are interdependent may well be better served by their agreeing to accept the equal importance of standards, such as the elimination of certain hazardous waste.

AUTHORITY APPROACHES

There are legal authority alternatives to individualism for dealing with issues where the interdependence between environment and production is high. In this section two possibilities are discussed.

Institutionalism

Organizational theorists are beginning to recognize the potential for institutional pressures in improving organizational performance (Zucker 1987; Scott 1987). These researchers are showing that effective organizational functioning is dependent on strong environmental forces—meaning in this context, social, political, and economic. They are saying more than that coercion affects behavior; rather it is a notion of pressure bringing out change. Thus we should be able to obtain better protection of the natural environment by imposing stronger institutional forces on organizations. As Barry Commoner (1987) points out, our successes in managing hazardous waste have come where society mandated elimination. When industry was told that it had to get the lead out of gasoline, it found ways to do it. These organizations rose to the demands of the strong institutional pressures.

Socially Managed Production

Some commentators on business and the environment call into question the whole notion of economic efficiency as the guide to decision making where the environment is involved (Chandler 1987, p. 194). Barry Commoner expresses this view quite clearly:

Perhaps the most profound question raised by environmental issues is to what extent the choice of production technologies should be determined by private economic considerations and to what extent by social concerns like environmental quality. These values are in sharp conflict. . . .

Recognition that significant environmental improvement depends on social rather than private governance of production decisions helps us understand why the considerable effort to improve the environment has had so little effect. (pp. 62, 64)

Those who urge socially managed production are not specific on the organizational mechanisms by which this approach would be implemented, but they do bring out the intimate connection between performance and production and show that a decision-making framework incorporating both is needed. One way to bring social values to bear on environmental decisions is to require that organizations legitimate environmental values by designating a department or office within their organization as carriers of these values. This spokesperson for the values would prepare a publicly released environmental impact statement (EIS) on all business proposals. This approach is modeled after the government's EIS law. Taylor's (1984) extensive analysis of the role played by these legitimated environmental value carriers in the division offices of the U.S. Forest Service showed that it can improve environmental protection.

THE CIVIC SOCIETY

The management of hazardous waste confronts society with a dilemma in social organization. Is it better for society, acting through government, to regu-

late the generation of hazardous waste by organizations, leaving them to maximize production within these boundaries, or should it take a civic approach
(Stanley 1983)? In the civic view society is seen as having a sense of the whole, a
set of values, myths, and morals that guide policy making. Here conflicts are
dealt with in the context of larger purposes. The hazardous waste issue is seen as
a difficult problem for a set of people who subscribe to both maintaining a viable
socioeconomic system and who strongly want to protect the natural environment
that is the basis of their existence. Their shared values and sense of community
will enable them to find a solution. The hazardous waste issue is seen as intracta-
ble to social organization based on individual interests and therefore an overt
commitment by the principal actors to a civic society approach is essential.

I call this the "civilization of the commons," the protection of the commons as
a moral value. Sandel (1984) speaks of the politics of the common good and
citizenship and of political arrangements with reference to common purposes and
ends. Here the self is conceived of in terms of roles as a participant in the
community. Managers commit themselves to search for solutions that satisfy
both environmental and economic goals. Prioritizing efficiency over the environment is not acceptable, and one does not take it upon himself or herself to make
such judgments. Difficult dilemmas are worked out jointly with the community,
without resorting to one's power. One's civic sense of the whole is his or her
guide. One trusts that in search, integrative solutions to dilemmas in the commons can be discovered.

The workability of this perspective is illustrated by two examples. First, some
industries that generate hazardous waste are structured into two tiers: a few large
organizations and many small supporting businesses that supply the larger ones
with components and materials. Some high technology manufacturing sectors
take this form. Often it is the smaller firms that are the worst generators because
they lack the expertise and capital base to install waste reduction technologies. If
managers of the major corporations were to take a civic society perspective
toward this situation, they would see the industry as a whole and search for ways
to assist the smaller companies in reducing their waste production. Possibly
through a franchising form of organization, the major firms could incorporate the
costs of this service into the price of the components and materials they obtain
from these suppliers.

Second, a major gain with the civic society framework is the opening up of
additional alternative solutions. Because the participants are in a more trusting
relationship with improved interaction, they can discover and are more willing to
be dependent on integrative solutions. In Santa Clara County, California, the
hazardous waste generators, local government officials, and representatives from
environmental organizations jointly formulated a management plan for the storage and handling of hazardous materials. They were able to develop procedures
acceptable to all. Although most generators, such as gasoline stations, had to
raise their storage standards dramatically, they gained a much more workable
formulation of the regulations.

CONCLUSION

The temptation for hazardous waste generators to take an individualistic approach is great. It is appealing to think that with regulation and assistance, such as the Superfund, the worst contaminations can be cleaned up. In many sectors this approach may be sufficient, but in hazardous waste, with its high interdependence between production and the environment, society risks catastrophe under business as usual. In a crisis there will be pressure to bring hazardous waste under control by abandoning our democratic values. Authoritarian regimes are very efficient in mobilizing action to eliminate the threat of environmental catastrophe or in suppressing the complaint of those affected by hazardous waste. There is a profound need for the key players to think in terms of the civic society. Protection of the commons protects democracy.

NOTES

This research was conducted in part while the author was a visiting scholar at the Stanford Center for Organizations Research, Stanford University.

REFERENCES

Aram, John D. 1989. "The Paradox of Interdependent Relations in the Field of Social Issues Management." *Academy of Management Review* 14:266–83.

Bailar, John C., III. 1987. "Rethinking the War on Cancer." *Issues in Science and Technology* 4:16–21.

Chandler, William U. 1987. "Designing Stable Economies." In *State of the World, 1987*, pp. 177–95. Edited by Lester R. Brown. New York: W. W. Norton & Co.

Commoner, Barry. 1987. "The Environment." *New Yorker*, June 15, pp. 48–71.

Office of the President. U.S. Council on Environmental Quality. 1988. *Environmental Quality 1986: Seventeenth Annual Report.* Washington, D.C.: White House.

Sagoff, Mark. 1988. *The Economy of the Earth: Philosophy, Law, and the Environment.* Cambridge: Cambridge University Press.

Sandel, Michael J. 1984. "Morality and the Liberal Ideal." *New Republic* 3:616 (May 7, 1984):15–17.

Scott, W. Richard. 1987. *Organizations: Natural, Rational, and Open Systems. 2d ed.* Englewood Cliffs, N.J.: Prentice-Hall.

Stanley, Manfred. 1983. "The Mystery of the Commons: On the Indispensability of Civic Rhetoric." *Social Research* 50:851–83.

Taylor, Serge. 1984. *Making Bureaucracies Think: The Environmental Impact Statement Strategy of Administrative Reform.* Stanford: Stanford University Press.

U.S. Congress. Congressional Budget Office. 1985. *Hazardous Waste Management: Recent Changes and Policy Alternatives.* Washington, D.C.: U.S. Government Printing Office.

Zucker, Lynne G. 1987. "Institutional Theories of Organization." In *Annual Review of Sociology, 1987*, 13:443–64. Edited by W. R. Scott and J. F. Short, Jr. Palo Alto, Calif.: Annual Reviews.

Community Involvement as an Integral Component of Siting: A Case Study of Siting Low-level Radioactive Waste Facilities

LINDA S. WENNERBERG

Public resistance to the siting of waste disposal facilities has become viewed as a cliché, the so-called NIMBY ("not in my backyard") syndrome. However, such resistance often rests on reasonable concerns, perceptions, and lack of understandable information. Such resistance may stall or stop an ongoing siting process, and no siting can be successful without some form of community acceptance. Community acceptance of a waste facility is not likely without consistent agency outreach and application of staff resources to address individual concerns of the impacted community.

This chapter summarizes the general equity issues that generate public resistance to a controversial siting effort such as the development of a waste disposal facility. Many environmental management technologies require the siting and operation of facilities to treat, store, or dispose of waste products. These waste products result from various processes or services that help society and provide economic benefits. Benefits to society are often diffuse and difficult to quantify by the individual citizen. The costs to treat, store, or dispose of the waste, however, are borne generally by society and, more acutely, by the communities proximate to the site.

Basic questions of equity fuel much of the community resistance to accepting a controversial site. Disposal of radioactive waste serves to highlight the general equity issues faced by any siting effort and the specific issues inherent in the disposal of a toxic substance. Public involvement in the siting of a radioactive waste disposal facility is a crucial component of any successful siting process.

Experiences in three states address general concerns and their specific relationship to the siting of a low-level radioactive waste disposal facility. California, Illinois, and Nebraska officials were interviewed to define general concerns and the process applied to develop viable community outreach in different communities. Their programs are presented as examples of problem solving—both successful and unsuccessful—in the siting of a controversial facility.

CONTRASTS WITH PAST PRACTICES

The three states were examined to illustrate key general considerations for a successful siting effort and the specific methods employed to maintain community involvement. Overall the efforts to site a controversial activity such as a radioactive waste disposal site stress community acceptance and involvement from the beginning. These principles are in direct contrast with past practices of siting, which often fueled public resistance. Some of the past, unsuccessful practices, listed below, underscore the need for an individualized, open process that educates and allows community access:

1. Structuring the siting process to bar communities from participation until the final site is selected.
2. Restricting input to highly complex, technical issues or minor details of the siting.
3. Siting a facility but allowing no local community role in decision making.
4. Offering a standardized economic compensation package, not community education or access. Generally this action fuels fear and uncertainty in the community.
5. Promoting an adversarial relationship among the siting entity and the communities. Technical complexities create a gap between the siting experts and the local community.

Past practices generally drew public resistance because meaningful, localized involvement was precluded or misdirected. Trivialization of the community's involvement in a process limited public interaction and encouraged resentment and resistance. A complex technological process may have overridden the individual community's basic concerns related to equitable treatment.

IMPORTANCE OF NONTECHNOLOGICAL FACTORS

Any siting of a controversial activity requires a technically sound site with a relevant, well-engineered design and a community willing to accept (or at least tolerate) the activity. A waste disposal site, for example, should be chosen and developed to protect health and safety while maintaining its integrity for waste containment and environmental protection. Design requirements are often technologically feasible and increasingly cost-effective. A sound design and robust technology will not automatically result in a successful siting. Siting is generally stalled or stopped by the nontechnological factors of community resistance. Public outcry over such diverse examples of environmental management as incinerators, landfills, transfer stations, sludge disposal sites, hazardous waste facilities, composting, and recycling centers indicate this resistance often is more than a simple knee-jerk reaction.

Historically, controversial facilities had a checkered record of performance and often placed the local public and/or the environment at increased risk. Current resistance is an outgrowth of local experience with a limited public involvement in the siting process and distrust resulting from previous governmental attempts to manage wastes.

QUESTIONS OF EQUITY
AND RISK ASSESSMENT IN SITING

Community reactions can be manifested between the two extremes of violent confrontation and volunteerism. Resistance to the siting process may be an individual response or an organized group activity. Acceptance of the siting can also vary from open volunteerism to resignation by individuals or groups. Reaction to events and perceptions produces localized responses in the community as the siting process progresses.

Resistance to siting rests on the following general public perceptions:

1. Inequitable distribution of benefits and burdens.
2. Gaps in technical understanding.
3. Fear of the unknown.
4. Perception of risk and uncertainty.
5. Distrust of authority.

The perception of inequality in the distribution of benefits and burdens causes the communities to resist assuming a larger share of the cost and risk associated with a controversial activity such as a waste disposal facility. These burdens may be derived from economic dislocations such as a feared loss of property values, a perceived stigma associated with the controversial stigma, or actual increased costs to maintain community infrastructure, such as roads or public safety measures.

A more basic inequality stems from another major concern: the perception of risk to human health and safety. Economic compensation may allay concerns about the economic dislocations; however, fear for one's family and their health creates the perception of an unequal burden for the citizens of an affected community with the benefits allocated to the society as a whole. This perceived inequality cannot be addressed in economic terms alone, or the public perception of the inequality will resist strictly economic compensation as a bribe. Economic compensation is not intended to address the increased health risk perceived by the community. A compensation package may equalize financial inequalities, but public involvement is the only means to address human fears related to health risks.

Siting a low-level radioactive waste disposal facility should be a process employing sound scientific, engineering, and environmental principles. This is common sense but often emerges as a highly complex, technological process. The tension of seeking a technology "robust under uncertainty" may result in layers of models, data, and projections. A gap in technical understanding cannot be answered by the assurances of experts when a community is struggling to understand the process, the waste form, and potential risks to health and property. Education in an understandable framework is critical due to the complex technology required to site a facility.

Low-level radioactive waste carries the singular personification with nuclear weapons and the ability to poison or kill. Radionuclides are colorless, odorless, and not generally perceived by the human senses, which adds to the fear in the local community. The ability to cause cancer in individuals and destroy populations at war has fueled a growing fear of any use or disposal of radioactive isotopes in the United States. Regardless of one's individual position on the use of nuclear materials, any siting effort must address this fear of the unknown directly and sensitively.

The public's fear is also fueled by the inability to define short- or long-term risk. Uncertainty compounds the fear toward anything radioactive, especially due to the potential in some radioisotopes to be harmful for thousands of years. Human institutional mechanisms to manage and isolate long-term risks are viewed with skepticism and distrust. Impacts on future generations are poorly quantified by the short-term political system seen in state or local government.

Distrust of authority is not based on a general disregard for any institution or ideology. Experience with governmental inabilities to manage waste disposal technologies safely has bred fears that any local, state, regional, or federal agency will not adequately protect public health and the environment. This may stem from a perception of the dangerous nature of the waste itself or the poor record of previous governmently approved facilities. Distrust and lack of knowledge cannot be abridged by the reassurances of experts. The siting agency must act consistently and openly, to educate and involve the public.

The NIMBY syndrome is of concern because the proposed site is not always the focus of individual resistance to the siting process. Arguments against the low-level radioactive waste disposal facility, for example, may be based on a stance against nuclear power generation. This reaction assumes nuclear power is the wrong path to take, and stopping disposal of radioactive waste will stop the use of nuclear fuel. I mention this issue because it may be a specific issue in the siting of a low-level facility, but similar philosophical stances against any generating industry may promote community resistance against the siting of treatment or disposal treatment facilities.

The issue of siting a low-level radioactive waste facility emerged as a state and local issue within the past decade. Successful siting of low-level radioactive waste facility requires states or groups of states to address a range of issues, which have technical and equity components.

CHANGES IN FEDERAL AUTHORITY

Radioactive materials and waste have traditionally been the responsibility of the federal government from the early days of the Manhattan Project in the 1940s until 1980, when the three federally sited facilities in Washington, Nevada, and South Carolina pressed for a more equitable sharing of waste management responsibilities among all the generating states. Congress delegated the siting and management responsibilities of future low-level radioactive waste facilities to all the generating states to promote greater equity (P.L. 96-573, as amended). Subsequent amendments in 1985 strengthened the requirement that generating states or compacts of states actively site low-level radioactive waste facilities. Existing licensed facilities exacted increasingly burdensome surcharges on the volume of waste disposed and held the power to refuse access to states developing siting. Federal milestones served as deadlines by which state compliance could be judged. The Department of Energy could withhold the return of surcharge dollars, and existing facilities could block the access of any generating state for nonattainment of the milestones.

Individual states and compacts responded with a range of actions, creativity, and effectiveness. The practical and ethical considerations of siting were focused for the first time on the generating state and locally affected communities. Nuclear waste management emerged at the local level as another issue of inequitable distribution of risks, gaps in technical understanding, fears, uncertainty, and distrust of authority. The interviews in the three states described the factors that fueled local resistance to the siting of a low-level radioactive waste facility and institutional attempts to promote community involvement.

CALIFORNIA'S APPROACH

The firm U.S. Ecology, Inc. conducted the site selection process for the state of California. An interview with Steve Romano of U.S. Ecology outlined the local approach developed to encourage community involvement and acceptance.

Local officials were contacted as soon as a general screening of the state excluded obviously unsuitable areas. Early volunteerism by communities, prior to the initial screening, was not encouraged because siting was assumed to require both a sound site and an accepting community. Three rounds of meetings with local officials, including individuals and groups of citizens, were established once potential areas suitable for siting were designated. Each meeting solicited input from the local communities prior to the next phase of screening. The subsequent meeting explained how previous community input affected the screening and then structured discussion with the public to provide input for the next stage of site characterization and screening.

California's strategy was to involve citizens in the more discretionary, socioeconomic aspects of siting, such as the impacts on transportation and setbacks. The communities responded to locally important and specific issues, as well as general technical concerns. Citizens, the Citizens Advisory Committee, and local communities were clearly involved at crucial decision points, but the affected communities were not given the legal right to refuse the site.

Once three candidate sites were chosen, local offices with locally hired staff were established by the state in all three sites. Committees of officials and citizens used the local office as the liaison and facilitator with state officials and U.S. Ecology staff. Outreach was extensive. Approximately 100 meetings with all the service organizations found in the three areas were conducted over a six-month period. The popularized term of the NIMBY syndrome trivializes the affected communities' response as close-minded and emotional. Individuals may hold extreme NIMBY-like views; however, resistance to siting is realistic when considered in the light of the specific concerns of the community. Successful siting of a waste facility in California required that these concerns be addressed.

Public resistance to the siting of a low-level radioactive waste disposal facility draws from the general perceptions discussed earlier. However, unique perceptions of this waste form reinforce the need to focus on dynamic, specific concerns throughout the siting process. California officials addressed the issue of public involvement at all stages of the process.

Several suggestions were offered highlighting California's approach to facilitate siting of any such controversial facility:

1. Remember the public is the customer, not the generator. Goodwill and partnership are essential to a successful siting.
2. Begin outreach prior to screening in order to educate the public about the waste stream, disposal options, and the site's plan to promote safety.
3. Avoid faulty, conflicting data and the use of external siting experts when addressing the socioeconomic topics that would benefit from local input.
4. Stress economic compensation tailored to the needs of the communities. This is meant to be an incentive package, not compensation that encourages distrust.
5. Accept the high visibility of the project and proceed openly.
6. Work closely with local advisory committees and local groups.
7. Allocate adequate staff and resources to all phases of the site selection through screening, site characterization, and final selection. It is essential to increase community involvement, education, and communication as the process evolves. It is not wise to underfund these activities.

California has several candidate areas currently under consideration. These are in desert areas, remote from population centers and in need of economic development. These characteristics themselves do not preclude the potential for community resistance. Public outreach empowered the affected communities into an openly accepting position. This system has applicability elsewhere in the country and for the siting of other controversial facilities.

ILLINOIS' APPROACH

Illinois, like California, is in the final stages of site selection. Technical considerations for sound siting and the strategies for community involvement varied between the two states. Each state was committed to technical excellence and public acceptability but developed a path to successful siting that was an individualized response to a process.

An interview with Thomas Kerr of the Illinois Department of Nuclear Safety defined an outreach process that focused at the county level. Illinois officials wished to avoid a screening and then rescreening process. Originally all 102 county board chairmen were contacted with information and questioned on their interest in participating in the siting process. The outreach program focused on 23 counties, but local community interest or vocal disinterest caused Illinois officials to target 10 counties.

In an effort to build trust and lessen uncertainty, Illinois did not structure its outreach to focus on specific decision points relating to locally determined socioeconomic concerns as in California. Illinois chose the decision point for the affected community to be the option to veto the site. This was a policy decision, not a statutory requirement. Illinois officials expanded this policy to include the need for consent to enter individual landowners' holdings during site characterization and to require all land sales for the final site to be voluntary. This strategy was risky and nearly resulted in the loss of all sites, but the siting process built credibility. The promise to accept local decisions caused several candidate areas to be abandoned.

Community involvement in a voluntary process can be very sensitive to local resistance. The Illinois siting effort was vulnerable to local resistance due to the local option to veto the site. As the process progressed from its initial total of 102 counties, to the 23 targeted counties, and then to 10 after initial resistance to siting, a sudden dramatic drop in community support cut the number of available counties to one. The siting process remained viable when a municipality not in the original area volunteered to be considered.

As in California, once the two communities volunteered, Illinois opened local offices, hired local staff, and intensified its outreach efforts through local committees. Early interest by local economic development officials was acknowledged and was used to facilitate information transfer to the general public. Approximately 250 meetings have been held in the communities, almost saturating each local event and group with Illinois officials and local office attendance. Citizen advisory committees were used to solicit public input but did not serve as players in the decision process.

This process has been expensive and staff intensive, as in California. The two communities remain in the process and are in the final stages of site selection. This experience offers several suggestions in addition or complementary to California's observations:

1. Focus local outreach on the unit of government most appropriate for the siting effort. Illinois cited a much greater interest from municipalities rather than the county-by-county approach that was originally applied.

2. Voluntary relationships between the state and the affected communities may be fragile. Once an area rejects the process, it is lost from consideration. The communities may say no at any time in the process but have, in effect, only one decision point.

3. Avoid heavy reliance on GIS (geographic information system) data or other technical screening studies that do not allow any flexibility. The quality of the data may not warrant exclusion of an area without further site characterization. An exclusion is an irreversible decision unless a loss of credibility is acceptable to the siting agency. Siting officials must develop a site with technical excellence and community acceptance to be successful.

4. It is possible to site a facility in a humid, well-populated area. The final areas in Illinois are within a few miles of population centers and are in producing, agricultural areas. California, by contrast, has final sites at least 30 miles from towns and with depths of up to 800 feet to groundwater.

Illinois structured and modified its community outreach program to respond to community needs, concerns, and events.

NEBRASKA'S APPROACH

Nebraska is applying the California approach to community outreach in siting. The state is also using U.S. Ecology, Inc., to conduct the process. Jim Neal of U.S. Ecology was interviewed to explain how the California process was applied to Nebraska. Three counties remain in the final state site selection process, but community resistance has emerged to stall the siting. It is essential to understand that historic and political events may merge to stall a siting process regardless of its original commitment to community involvement.

Nebraska is a member of the Central Interstate Compact and does not act as an independent siting state. Prior to the siting process, four events occurred that have affected the siting process to this day. First, a referendum to withdraw Nebraska from the compact was proposed on the ballot. The referendum had extensive provisions to require state and local consent for any siting of a radioactive waste disposal facility. A statewide vote rejected the referendum, but supporting communities are now affected by the siting process. These communities are voicing opposition because they never felt they would have to assume the actual responsibility for the site. The general referendum defeat is now perceived as an ill-defined inequitable burden placed on the unsuspecting communities.

Second, the governor publicly stated the policy that community consent is required to site the facility. No clear definition of community or consent has been determined, so the uncertainty factor is extremely high in the three communities.

A third additional complication in the community outreach program has raised fears, uncertainty, and resistance. As in California, local committees were to be nominated to facilitate discussion with U.S. Ecology, state officials, and local officials. Individuals from outside Nebraska are being appointed to local committees and using the position to resist any siting as a protest against nuclear power. Nebraska did not clearly define the roles, focus, and membership for crucial committees.

Fourth, one of the communities is also resistant because it was not chosen in the initial screening of the three representative areas for site characterization. Review of the three representative areas forced one to be rejected on technical grounds and recommended an alternative community be substituted into consideration. The substituted area responded with intense resistance, feeling hoodwinked by a process that made a decision, reneged on an earlier promise, and forced the burden onto an unprepared community.

The flaws in the process and the lack of clear, consistent procedures have caused the siting process to stall in Nebraska. The following suggestions were given to other states attempting such a siting process:

1. Acknowledge the population and land use patterns of the state or available area. No areas of low population density may exist, and current land uses such as agriculture must be taken out of production to site a facility. Sensitivity to the characteristics of an area allows the public to perceive less distrust of governmental agencies.

2. A poorly defined process or the appearance of inconsistency may allow internal or external opposition to obstruct the process.

3. Reactions against nuclear power often are expressed as resistance in the siting process for a low-level radioactive waste facility.

4. Economic incentives have the appearance of a bribe or payoff when vocal resistance is present. Local officials are pressured to avoid these payments, and the credibility of the siting agency is diminished.

5. A large staff is needed to maintain close contact with local committees and officials. This is not a public relations effort; it is a dynamic process with many players.

6. Siting officials must disseminate information in a manageable and informative manner. A siting process requires a solid framework of information and exchange through the process.

LESSONS FOR FUTURE SITING OF WASTE FACILITIES

Officials and communities need to develop a partnership, not an adversarial relationship. The general concerns based on fear, uncertainty, and distrust of the government must be addressed in an equitable process that empowers the community. Education and focused community outreach are essential first steps.

Experience in the three states highlights the integration of public involvement into all phases of the siting process. A framework of general education in the initial phases supports subsequent attempts to bridge gaps in technical knowledge. This integration of information is most effective when it targets defined decision points or crucial steps in the siting process.

Information alone will not foster community involvement. Clearly defined roles and responsibilities for all involved parties must be established and followed throughout the process. Illinois' voluntary process or the integrative approach developed in California may be equally effective. Both emphasize the need for consistent, open community involvement. Nebraska's current controversy is partially in response to the uncertainty generated by a poorly defined process and the option to veto a site. Uncertainty and inconsistency are costly due to delays, increased public resistance, the need for increased mobilization of staff resources, and the loss of credibility.

Access to the siting process and definition of the community's role may not result in actual involvement if only an illusion of choice is available. The illusion of choice rests on the premise of a clearly defined community outreach effort with little or no actual input allowed. Past practices of siting that restricted input to technical or minor details often generated explosive resistance. Public perception to the illusion of choice could encourage resistance at any point during the siting process. All three states profiled took steps to minimize this perception and the distrust it promotes. An open process with clear decision points remains the best mechanism for diffusing uncertainty, fear, and distrust while addressing the basic equity issues affecting the local community.

Access is crucial at all stages of the siting process and does not function separately from the technical considerations of siting. Experience with low-level radioactive waste disposal siting underscores the need for the allocation and support of staff throughout the process of siting on any controversial activity. Each state stressed the expense and planning necessary for successful community outreach programs. This allocation of resources was essential and served to counter many of the public perceptions stemming from perceived inequities and from past experiences with poorly managed siting efforts. To site a controversial facility successfully, state officials are encouraged to fund and support community outreach efforts as an integral component of the siting process. Equity issues are the basis for the diverse community responses and potential resistance to accepting a controversial siting such as a low-level radioactive waste disposal facility. Anyone ignoring the general and individual equity concerns of the community will intensify public resistance to any siting of a controversial facility.

NOTE

This chapter resulted from interviews with individuals directing siting efforts in California, Nebraska, and Illinois. I thank Steve Romano and Jim Neal of U.S. Ecology, Inc., and Thomas Kerr of the Illinois Department of Nuclear Safety. Mary English of the Energy and Environmental Resources Center at the University of Tennessee and Susan Wiltshire of J. K. Research Associates, Inc., reviewed early drafts and offered insightful guidance. Linda Nappi served as the typist. I thank all involved and assume responsibility for any errors remaining.

Business Responses to Environmental Policy: Lessons from CFC Regulation

DANIEL J. DUDEK
ALICE M. LEBLANC
AND KENNETH SEWALL

This is the third in a series of stratospheric ozone reports by the Environmental Defense Fund. The first two chronicled the need for policy action and outlined policy choices regarding the production of chlorofluorocarbons (CFCs), the widely used chemicals that have been implicated as the main cause of stratospheric ozone depletion. The purpose of this chapter is to derive lessons about environmental management based on business response to CFC regulations.

Unfortunately, much environmental policy is based on an inadequate understanding of the dynamics of business firm behavior. The dominant perspective of government regulators is that the firm is little more than an entity seeking to minimize its own costs while ignoring the social costs of its operations. The desire to minimize costs is an important driving force in the behavior of the firm; however, it can be channeled within the regulatory framework to bring about innovative, cost-effective solutions to environmental problems.

Because property rights for the use of the environment often are not clearly defined, the unconstrained, cost-minimizing firm uses the environment as if it were free. Sometimes the cost of the resulting environmental damages vastly exceeds the value of the benefits that firms and society obtain. For pollution problems such as stratospheric ozone depletion and greenhouse gases, the damages may be catastrophic because global habitability is threatened.

A legitimate role of government is to protect society from excessive levels of pollution. The government typically determines what is acceptable and requires each polluter to cut back by a prescribed amount or to adopt the best available technology for pollution reduction. In extreme cases, bans on production are instituted, such as the ban on CFCs as aerosol propellants in the United States in 1978. To ensure compliance with the regulatory system, firms are monitored and fined if they do not comply.

Government regulators also have responsibility for determining how to implement government-mandated pollution goals. They devise a system to allocate the cleanup among firms and/or specify the technologies that firms must adopt. Often they do not have an insider's knowledge to evaluate all the options available to the firm to reduce pollution. Nor, as regulators, are they capable of fully tapping market forces in achieving the best solution.

There are other factors that hamper government's ability to obtain the most cost-effective means of pollution reduction. Because regulators do not fully understand the effects of regulation, firms are able to disguise potential cost benefits deriving from the regulations or to make a convincing case that the regulations involve excessive costs. The political process sometimes requires consideration of a host of equity issues in the implementation of pollution goals. These include differential impacts of regulations on small and large firms, the implications for regional economies, and the effects of international competitiveness on domestic firms. Addressing these issues in policy formulation tends to lessen the costs to the firm and render the policies less effective.

Perhaps most important, much environmental regulation does not tap the extensive human capital in the work force of polluting firms. Firms often do not have incentives to clean up the environment more than is required, and the creative energy they deploy in solving environmental problems is limited. The consequence for society is larger-than-necessary expenditures on pollution control. Because meeting environmental regulations is costly, industry and its associations have often gone to court. In these cases, an adversarial relationship between firms and government has delayed the implementation of pollution reduction measures.

This chapter supports a more liberal concept of the decision-making capabilities of the firm and the relationship of the firm, the generation of pollution, and the government. The firm is viewed as more than a cost minimizer seeking to ignore the social costs of pollution and escape responsibility for cleaning up the environment. The same cost-minimizing calculus that created environmental problems is seen as a source of creative energy to be harnessed in their elimination. Firms that contribute to environmental problems are in an excellent position to solve them. Government is not expected to determine the technical solutions. The primary role of the government is to establish environmental policies that set pollution limits and create profit motive incentives for firms to solve their own environmental problems. This approach results in a more cooperative relationship between firms and government concerning environmental protection, as well as tremendous cost savings ·in achieving environmental goals.

This report focuses on business reactions to CFC regulations over the past decade. We selected this environmental problem because of its global scope and the variety of policies used in attempting to manage it. As we look forward to the needs of international cooperation in solving the ever more complex policy problems posed by the greenhouse effect, we need to assimilate and digest the lessons of the past.

HOW COMPANIES RESPOND
TO ENVIRONMENTAL REGULATION

Evaluating Firm Response

The conceptual framework used in this chapter is based on the work of Michael Porter of Harvard Business School (1980). It views the business firm as an entity striving to maximize its rate of return on invested capital. Competition within an industry, defined as a group of firms producing products that are close substitutes to one another, drives the rate of return on invested capital toward the cost of capital. In the long run, investors will not tolerate rates of return lower than the cost of capital, and a firm not earning this rate of return will go out of business. Rates of return higher than this level will attract additional capital into the industry and drive down the rate of return. The essence of a firm's competitive strategy is the search for a favorable competitive position within an industry—that is, a favorable rate of return on capital.

A favorable competitive position within an industry is a function of the value a firm is able to create for the buyers of its products or services, as well as its cost of creating that value. Superior value results from offering a lower price for equivalent benefits or from providing unique benefits that more than offset a higher price. An important question in determining the profitability of a firm is whether that firm can capture the value it creates for buyers or whether this value is competed away to others.

Competition within an industry depends on five basic forces: threat of new entrants, threat of substitute products, rivalry among existing firms, bargaining power of suppliers, and bargaining power of buyers. A firm seeks to position itself so as to defend against these competitive forces or to influence them in its favor. These five competitive forces determine a firm's profitability because they influence price, costs, and required investment. For example, rivalry among firms determines whether the value that the industry creates for customers is passed on to buyers in the form of lower prices or dissipated in the form of higher costs. The threat of entry determines the likelihood that new firms will enter an industry and lower profits for existing firms by either reducing prices or raising the costs of competing. The threat of substitutes determines the extent to which some other product can meet the same buyer needs and thus limit the price a buyer is willing to pay for an industry's product. The market power of suppliers determines the extent to which value created for buyers will be appropriated in the form of higher input costs. Finally, the market power of buyers affects product price and service and, therefore, revenues and profits of firms within an industry. A large buyer can obtain price concessions and increased service.

In coping with these five competitive forces, a firm has two ways to outperform other firms in an industry and earn above-average returns on investment: by being the low-cost producer or by differentiating its product or service from competitors. Changes in environmental regulations provide significant opportunities for firms to exploit each of these avenues.

Understanding the Effects of Environmental Policies on Firms and Industries

The framework described is useful in evaluating the effects of environmental policies on firms and industries. A firm or industry may face added costs as a result of environmental quality regulations. Since cost is an important dimension of competition, firms and industries may find themselves in changed competitive positions. Some may find that they cannot remain profitable unless they pass on added costs in the form of higher prices. Others may develop ways to meet the requirements of environmental regulation without raising prices, thus maintaining or even improving their competitive position.

The costs of meeting regulations can be related to the size of the firm. There may be techniques for reducing pollution that are cost effective for large but not small firms. For example, recycling may be less costly for large firms because of scale economies of recycling technologies. Large firms may be able to afford an on-site professional waste manager, while small firms may not have the waste disposal cost savings to justify such an expense. Larger firms are also more likely to have greater in-house technical resources or to have funds to contract with outside consultants. In these cases, environmental regulations are a source of competitive advantage for large firms. In contrast, smaller firms may be less constrained by rigid decision-making hierarchies and more able to experiment and innovate.

The costs of meeting regulations can also affect firms differently depending on the firm's profitability. Profitability varies because of different management skills, technologies, economies of scale, and input costs. Firms that are only marginally profitable may become unprofitable as a result of environmental regulation and leave an industry. In this case, environmental regulations are a source of advantage for the remaining firms if increased profits from their competitors' departures more than compensate for the increased costs of the regulations. For example, suppose there are only two firms in an industry, each earning revenues of $10 million per year. One firm has costs of $9 million per year, while the second has costs of $9.5 million per year. Both of these firms are required to adopt the same technology to reduce atmospheric emissions at a cost to each of $.75 million per year. The first firm will earn profits of $.25 million; the second will lose $.25 million per year. If the second firm leaves the industry, the remaining firm will have a monopoly; it may be able to raise prices and will gain the other firm's business.

Environmental regulations affect polluting firms and industries in ways other than increasing their costs. Some firms may benefit directly from regulations that create new market opportunities, change the relative costs of competing products, or provide barriers to potential competitors. Firms should adopt a strategic view of the choices posed by environmental regulation. For example, aggressive marketing of nonpolluting green products capitalizing on consumer interest is a business response that played a key role in changes in the U.S. aerosol industry.

Firms may also obtain competitive advantage by differentiating their products or by developing unique ways of controlling nonpolluting substitutes. In some cases firms have actually benefited because production costs fell as a result of environmental regulation. Management attention directed toward decreasing waste can lead to increased efficiency of input use and reduced costs. Better worker health and productivity can be a by-product of less pollution at the workplace.

This framework can be used to explain the intense lobbying of individual firms and industries in response to proposed environmental regulation. Potential winners lobby for the regulations, and potential losers lobby against them. This type of strategic behavior can also be seen in the lobbying related to the development of international agreements for protecting the environment, when nations are concerned with protecting or improving the competitive advantage of their industries.

One of the most important strategic decisions faced by firms, the capital investment decision, is particularly sensitive to regulatory uncertainty. This decision involves comparing the present value of expected net investment income (revenues minus variable costs) with investment cost. If the present value of expected net investment income is greater than investment cost, the investment is profitable. Otherwise it is not profitable. Regulatory uncertainty makes this decision difficult because the revenues and variable costs become less predictable. Firms subject to environmental regulation may attempt to protect their investments by postponing regulations as long as possible. On the other hand, firms contemplating new investments might want to speed up the regulatory process so as to make their investment decisions more predictable.

Finally, the competitive drive can be harnessed by the government to manage the environment. To do this, the government must raise the firm's cost of pollution by either penalizing it for polluting beyond the legal limit or allowing it to benefit from pollution levels less than the limit. As firms seek to gain competitive advantage, this incentive will stimulate the market for innovative, less costly solutions to environmental problems and produce substitutes that do not pollute. For example, suppose the government imposes a tax on emissions of a pollutant of $10 per unit. A firm has two choices: pay the $10 per unit or reduce discharges. The firm has a market incentive to find a way to reduce discharges for less than $10 per unit as a means of avoiding the tax and reducing costs. If it can do so, it can also gain a competitive advantage over other firms that are forced to pay the tax. (See Dudek 1987 for a detailed discussion of alternative market incentive approaches to clean up the environment.)

BACKGROUND OF CFC PROBLEM

In 1974 University of California researchers F. Sherwood Rowland and Mario J. Molina presented a theory that explained the destruction of the atmospheric ozone layer by man-made CFCs. Ozone depletion results in an increase in the amount of ultraviolet radiation reaching the earth's surface, which causes skin cancer and affects the earth's climate, weather, and environment. Among the consequences are lower crop yields, shifts in weather patterns, and the spatial location of agriculture, possible collapse of complex aquatic food chains, and destruction of coastal property. (See Dudek 1986 for a thorough analysis of the effects of ozone depletion.)

Reasons for Delay in Policy Action

Several factors have inhibited government actions concerning CFCs. First, conclusive proof of ozone layer destruction was not available until recently. Second, economic losses to the CFC industry and CFC user industries were potentially very large. According to a study of the effects of the U.S. CFC aerosol ban by JACA Corporation, society would incur an economic penalty from lost aerosol and chemical sales of $1.038 billion in 1976 dollars over the period 1975–1990 (Ando and Marshall 1983, p. 10).

CFCs are used widely in modern society in aerosols, refrigeration, air-conditioning, insulation, cushioning foam, solvents, and a range of other products. Table 5.1 shows the economic scope of CFC user industries in the United States. Table 5.2 illustrates how CFC uses contribute to ozone depletion. In the United States, plastic foams and automobile air conditioners pose the greatest threats to the ozone layer. Emissions of both of these products are difficult to capture after the products are in use.

Compounding the issue of the cost of converting away from CFCs was the industry claim that effective substitutes did not exist. In table 5.3, a 1986 industry evaluation of CFC substitutes is depicted. None of the substitute fluorocarbon formulations that were undergoing testing is listed despite widespread knowledge among CFC producers about alternative chemicals.

A third reason for the slow response time of government to the ozone depletion problem is that the reduction of CFC emissions is a global public good. A public good is one that does not permit exclusion from consumption. A nation that reduces its CFC emissions is producing the benefit of reduced ultraviolet radiation, which other nations cannot be excluded from sharing. There is a tendency for nations to underproduce global public goods because any nation receives the benefits of other nations' production without incurring a cost. This characteristic of common property resources lowers the motivation to act unilaterally. In fact, nations have an incentive to wait for others to act.

Government Policies before the Montreal Protocol

Global cooperation in the management of CFCs was not achieved until 1987 at the Montreal Protocol meetings. However, some governments began to act in the mid-1970s despite the scientific uncertainty and lack of global coordination. The U.S. government held hearings on the subject soon after the publication of the research paper by Rowland and Molina in 1974. The U.S. Food and Drug

Table 5.1
Economic Scope of CFC Applications in the United States

USE	VALUE (billions of $)	EMPLOYMENT (thousands)
Refrigeration	6.0	52
Air-conditioning	10.9	125
Mobile air-conditioning	2.0	25
Cooling servicing	5.5	472
Plastic foam	2.0	40
Food freezing	0.4	<1
Sterilants	0.1	<1
Totals	26.9	715

Note: "Value" represents the value of goods and services directly dependent on the availability of CFCs to the 5,000 companies that purchase CFCs from producers. These goods and services have a value to end users of about $135 billion. Solvents are not included in this table because of data availability even though their value is in the billions. "Employment" is direct CFC-related industry employment.

Source: Alliance for Responsible CFC Policy (1986).

Table 5.2
How Uses of CFCs Contribute to Ozone Depletion

Application	Percentage
Aerosol propellants and other miscellaneous uses	5
Solvent cleaning of metal and electronic parts	12
Sterilization of medical equipment and instruments	4
Production of plastic foam insulation products	28
Mobile air conditioners	19
Refrigeration and space air conditioning	9
Unallocated production [a]	22

[a]The difference between total usage and estimated usage in the U.S. categories shown.

Source: The U.S. Environmental Protection Agency (1986).

Table 5.3
Potential CFC Alternatives and Consequences of Using Alternatives

Application	Substitute	Trade-offs
Refrigeration and Air-conditioning	Ammonia Sulfur dioxide	Toxic, explosive Combustible, less efficient
Plastic foams	Pentane Methylene chloride	Flammable, smog precursor Suspected carcinogen
Food freezing	Cryogenic systems	Less energy efficient

Source: Alliance for Responsible CFC Policy (1986).

Administration and Environmental Protection Agency (EPA) began to phase out CFCs used in nonessential aerosols in 1976 and banned them in 1978. Norway, Sweden, and Canada also instituted prohibitions on nonessential CFC aerosol use, and Japan and Australia introduced voluntary programs to reduce CFC propelled aerosols. In 1980 the European Economic Community (EEC) established a production limit for CFC-11 and CFC-12 of 480,000 tons per year, to be modified when Portugal and Spain entered the EEC. The limit was defined as the sum of existing plants' nameplate capacities. The EEC also agreed on a 30 percent reduction by December 31, 1981, of CFC-11/12 aerosol use relative to 1976 levels and encouraged the adoption of best alternate technology for nonaerosol uses. Implementation of EEC policy was left to voluntary action by industry sectors in member states. In addition, Belgium, Denmark, and Portugal implemented regulations directly affecting CFC production and use. The Netherlands and Germany instituted indirect regulatory action: the Netherlands by requiring aerosol cans containing CFCs to bear a warning notice and Germany by placing a limit on the CFC concentration in the ventilation air discharged from foam plastic production plants. (See Bevington 1986, pp. 3–5, for details about EEC member state regulations.) Japan and Brazil also instituted production capacity caps.

The U.S. government postponed until recently the implementation of regulations on the use of CFCs in nonaerosols. In 1980, the EPA issued an Advance Notice of Proposed Rulemaking, "Ozone-Depleting Substances: Proposed Production Restriction," but it was not implemented because of CFC industry opposition. Late in 1984, a suit was filed by the Natural Resources Defense Council, an environmental group, against the EPA for failure to provide additional CFC regulations as required by the Clean Air Act.

Thus, the early history of CFC regulation was characterized by two general policies: a selective ban on one use of CFCs in the United States and a production cap that potentially affected all uses of CFCs in the EEC. Two different management philosophies are embodied in these policies. The U.S. ban restricted the aerosol manufacturers' production choices by prohibiting the use of CFC propellants. This policy reflects a social decision that the use of CFCs as propellants is undesirable but that other uses are acceptable. Unfortunately, this limited action against a single sector of the CFC industry translated into a green light for continued growth in the other sectors. The common public sentiment in the early rounds of negotiations leading to the Montreal Protocol was a belief that the CFC aerosol ban had solved the problem of ozone depletion. While the ban did not prevent the overall growth of CFC production, it did catalyze public opinion and initiate a round of industry research on alternative CFC formulations.

The production capacity limit adopted by the Europeans represents a different approach. Total production of CFCs was restricted to the amount that could be produced by existing plants. While the European action avoided the doomsday scenarios of unlimited future growth in CFC emissions, it did not reduce current emissions. Since total production capacity was significantly greater than production, the limit did not exert an influence on CFC pricing or use decisions. The adoption of a production capacity limit by the EEC was largely conditioned by the policy tools available. The chief guiding principle of European integration, laid down in the Treaty of Rome, is the prohibition of policies that restrain trade. It was therefore much easier for the EEC to adopt a capacity limit than a specific use ban.

Montreal Protocol

These contrary policies were discussed in talks leading to international negotiations at the Montreal Protocol. Significant debate centered around the effects of both the aerosol ban and the production cap. Numerous international conferences on the ozone depletion problem were held; but negotiators failed to agree on worldwide CFC regulations until September 1987. At that time forty-three nations signed the Montreal Protocol, calling for eventual worldwide CFC reductions of 50 percent. The participants agreed to a freeze of production of CFCs -11, -12, -113, -114, and -115 at 1986 levels by mid-1989; a reduction of 20 percent by mid-1993; and an additional 30 percent cut by mid-1998. The volume of a weighted composite of these CFCs, not each CFC, is controlled. The weighted composite is the sum of the relative ozone depletion potential of each CFC times its consumed quantity. Third World countries were given an extension so that their economic growth would not be jeopardized. At the insistence of the U.S. delegation, the protocol also provides for periodic reevaluations of its adequacy, and representatives from signatory countries can be reconvened. Thus, it is an evolutionary agreement that can be modified.

Subsequent to the signing of the Montreal Protocol, scientists obtained evidence that greater-than-expected ozone losses have occurred. In Helsinki in early May, signatory countries expressed their intent to phase out production of CFCs no later than the year 2000. A CFC phaseout is expected to be formally adopted. Developing countries opposed the new timetable, citing the costs of substitutes and scientific uncertainty. Some environmental groups and politicians think the year 2000 is too late (Zurer 1989, pp. 8–9).

In the United States, the first restrictions on the manufacture of fully halogenated CFCs recently went into effect. Since production of these chemicals has increased by 15 percent since 1986, CFC manufacturers were required by EPA regulations that implement the Montreal Protocol to reduce production by 15 percent (Zurer 1989, p. 7). In addition, twenty states have proposed or passed legislation related to CFCs. For example, Vermont has outlawed the registration of automobiles with air-conditioners that use CFCs, beginning with 1993 models. Other state bills require recycling of CFC-12 when auto air-conditioners are serviced, impose bans on the sale of small cans of refrigerants for home use, and mandate labeling of products that contain or are made with CFCs (Zurer 1989, p. 11).

EFFECTS OF CFC REGULATIONS
ON FIRMS AND INDUSTRIES

The long and varied history of CFC regulation makes it possible to observe firm and industry response to different policies and to derive critical lessons about how to manage and solve other environmental problems.

Effects of CFC Regulations before the Montreal Protocol

On the Use of CFCs

The most striking feature of overall global policies prior to the Montreal Protocol is that production of all CFCs has increased. The major policy initiatives, the ban on CFC use in aerosols in the United States and the ceiling on production capacity in the EEC, were ineffective in reducing production. The reduced use in aerosols was countered by increased use in nonaerosol applications. Increased use resulted from the failure of government policies to raise CFC prices significantly and thus to create incentives for users to find alternatives. The failure to achieve any internalization of environmental effects allowed new markets to be developed and maintained CFCs' price-performance dominance over potential substitutes.

Table 5.4 shows how the production of CFC-11 and -12 has varied from 1970 to 1987 in the world, the United States, and the EEC. Table 5.5 compares the composition of 1985 CFC use in the United States and the rest of the world.

From 1978 to 1984, combined CFC production for all uses in the United States increased by approximately 48 percent (U.S. International Trade Commission, as reported by Mooz, Wolf, and Camm 1986, p. 36). The virtual elimination of CFC -11 and -12 in aerosols after 1978 was countered by their increased use in nonaerosols, leaving total use virtually unchanged in 1987. Use of other CFCs increased substantially. CFC-22 production increased from 204 million pounds in 1978 to 255 million pounds in 1984, and CFC-113 increased from 86 million to 150 million pounds in the same time period. CFC-114 production decreased from 21 million pounds in 1978 to 15 million pounds in 1984.

Total CFC production increased in the EEC from 1976 to 1985 in a pattern similar to that of the United States. Nonaerosol uses of CFC-11 and -12 rose at approximately the same rate as in the United States. CFC aerosol use declined about 35 percent—more than the level targeted by the EEC regulations. Overall production of CFC-11 and -12 stayed about constant. Production of CFC-113 and -114, however, increased 127.7 percent, from 23,524 tons to 53,568 tons (EFCTC, as reported in Bevington 1986, p. 20).

CFC Production Capacity

Table 5.6 shows historic plant capacity for all CFCs in the United States. Between 1970 and 1975, capacity steadily increased from 950 million pounds to

Table 5.4
CFC-11 and CFC-12 Production
(millions of kilograms)

Year	World Total	United States Total	Aerosol	Nonaerosol	European Economic Community Total	Aerosol	Nonaerosol
1970	577.8	281.2	162.0	119.2	*	*	*
1971	627.1	293.7	169.3	124.4	*	*	*
1972	712.8	335.1	189.6	145.5	*	*	*
1973	801.7	373.1	218.6	154.5	*	*	*
1974	851.0	375.8	210.6	165.2	*	*	*
1975	741.9	300.6	167.9	132.7	*	*	*
1976	806.3	294.8	144.3	150.2	325.4	176.9	149.5
1977	767.7	258.9	83.9	175.0	319.1	162.6	156.5
1978	756.5	236.3	74.8	161.5	307.0	150.4	156.6
1979	735.3	209.1	9.5	199.6	304.2	136.6	167.6
1980	742.7	205.5	9.5	196.0	295.7	126.4	169.3
1981	759.3	221.4	9.5	211.9	300.1	116.1	184.0
1983	753.9	180.7	9.5	171.2	289.0	117.7	177.3
1983	*	216.9	9.5	207.4	310.0	114.0	196.0
1984	*	238.6	9.5	229.1	322.0	115.0	207.0
1985	*	217.2	*	*	336.0	116.0	220.0
1986	*	238.3	*	*	*	*	*
1987	*	242.1	*	*	*	*	*

Note: * = missing data values.

Source: EPA (1985) and Pearce (1986).

Table 5.5
Aggregate Use of Controlled CFCs in 1985
(percentage by volume)

USE	United States	Rest of the World
Refrigerants	45	20
Blowing agents	30	25
Aerosols	5	35
Cleaning agents and other	20	20

Note: The CFCs included in this table are those named as controlled substances by the Montreal Protocol: CFC-11, -12, -113, -114, and -115.

Source: Alliance for Responsible CFC Policy (1986).

Table 5.6
Historic CFC Plant Capacity in the United States
(millions of pounds)

Producer	1970	1972	1975	1978	1983	1985
Allied	200	310	310	370	300	330
Du Pont	500	500	600	500	650	650
Kaiser	50	50	75	80	80	80
Pennwalt	80	115	115	90	90	120
Racon	20	20	20	45	80	85
Union Carbide	100	150	200			
TOTAL	950	1,145	1,320	1,085	1,200	1,265

Source: Mooz, Wolf, and Camm (1986), p. 34.

1,350 million pounds. The aerosol market required much of this capacity. In anticipation of the aerosol ban in 1978, capacity declined to 1,085 pounds. Union Carbide left the market, and Du Pont and Pennwalt closed plants. Allied, Kaiser, and Racon, however, each increased capacity. Between 1978 and 1983, Allied's capacity declined, perhaps a delayed reaction to the aerosol ban, but Racon's approximately doubled. Du Pont also increased capacity above its pre-aerosol ban level. Racon, Pennwalt, and Allied further augmented capacity between 1983 and 1985. Overall between 1978 and 1985, producers increased capacity by 17 percent (Mooz, Wolf, and Camm 1986, pp. 33–36). What is most striking about these figures is that producers reduced capacity in response to a proposed aerosol ban. However, the same producers, even under the threat of nonaerosol CFC regulation for close to a decade, increased capacity.

One explanation for the increase in production capacity despite a high probability of future regulation of nonaerosol CFC usage is that the share of capital costs in the production of CFCs -11 and -12 is small. According to Farhad and Elkin (1985), capital cost shares range from 15 percent to 30 percent, depending on the size of plant and utilization rate. According to a report by Rand Corporation, CFC prices would have to rise 10 percent or less for companies to recover investments in five years of operations. Therefore, the possibility of future regulation would not deter producers from augmenting production capacity (Mooz, Wolf, and Camm 1986, pp. 48–50). Producers knew that significant price increases would accompany future regulation, especially because substitutes did not exist for many CFC uses and would take several years to develop. Because CFC-11 and -12 production is not capital intensive, producers were able to break even on their investment in a relatively short period, even at existing price levels.

EEC production capacity of CFCs -11 and -12 remained at 480,000 metric tons, the production capacity limit set in 1980. As of 1985 the EEC was producing at 70 percent of this capacity limit and was not expected to produce at the cap until 1996 (Pearce 1986, p. 4). The EEC production cap was never a practical constraint for producers or users of CFCs. It is notable that producers did not reduce surplus capacity.

On Substitute Development

Because the price of CFCs did not rise significantly in response to U.S. policy, development of CFC substitutes was not encouraged. Du Pont, the major worldwide producer of CFCs, initiated a program to develop substitutes shortly after the ozone depletion hypothesis was proposed in 1974. After spending about $15 million, Du Pont gave up, citing projected higher costs, toxicity, lack of commercially viable manufacturing processes, and probable environmental problems of the most promising substitutes (Alliance for Responsible CFC Policy 1986, p. 1). In 1986 Du Pont reinitiated its research efforts because management felt that regulation of CFCs would eventually limit availability of some CFCs to less than market demand (Du Pont 1987, p. 1). In other words, Du Pont felt that the price of CFCs would rise, making substitutes competitive. In 1987 a group called the Chlorofluorocarbon Chemical Substitutes International Committee, led by Richard Lagow of the University of Texas, concluded that the only constraint for availability of substitutes was a worldwide market for such materials. They concluded "that such a market can only be created by government regulations worldwide for stratospheric ozone depleting chemicals to create a demand for materials that are not ozone depleting" (Lagow 1987, p. 2–2).

While substitutes for most CFC uses were not developed, alternatives to aerosol products containing CFCs were created in response to the ban on nonessential aerosols in the United States and the cutback in the EEC member states. During the debate preceding the ban, the aerosol industry expressed concerns about hydrocarbons (HCs) as substitutes for CFCs. These concerns included flammability, quality, and odor. In addition, 18,280 out of approximately 30,000 aerosol products would have had to be reformulated to use HCs. Eventually U.S. industry resigned itself to the ban and managed to find solutions for most of the problems associated with using HCs as aerosol propellants. A study of the effects of the ban by the ICF Corporation determined that society enjoyed an economic benefit from propellant conversion (ICF 1986) apart from benefits to the environment. In addition, some companies developed new propellants with more desirable properties than HCs for applications in fragrances. These include HCFCs and Du Pont's blends of dimethyl ether (Daly 1984, 1988; Dunn 1988).

Research and development has also led to innovative and successful packaging forms. Two examples are Grow Chemical's Enviro-Spray and Container Industries' Exxel propellantless system. Enviro-Spray generates its own propellant (CO_2) through controlled mixing of citric acid and sodium bicarbonate. The propellant is nonflammable and maintains constant pressure. According to David Magid of Grow, "If fluorocarbons were still around, there might not be any Enviro-Spray Division" (Giovanni 1980). Exxel uses an elastic component tensioned by pressure filling. The pressure of the filling process forces the inner bag and sleeve to expand. This sleeve then exerts pressure on the contents of the container but not on the container's outer wall, producing a spray without a gaseous propellant.

The reaction of aerosol fillers in the EEC nations was to increase research into alternative propellants, propelling methods, and product formulations. Research was also undertaken by suppliers of aerosol valves and containers. Dissatisfaction with the quality and safety of products using HCs prevented fillers from marketing them. Other obstacles to more widespread use of HCs included an EEC requirement that an aerosol product containing more than 45 percent by weight of a flammable ingredient be labeled as flammable. Fillers developed formulations based on mixed CFC-hydrocarbon propellants to achieve the desired reduction of 30 percent in CFC propellant use (IAL Consultants 1986, sec. 3).

On Industry Structure

The ban on the use of CFCs in nonessential aerosol products in the United States resulted in some reallocations in the U.S. aerosol industry.

First, hydrocarbon producers benefited at the expense of CFC producers. The producers of HCs and HC-filled products benefited from the ban. In 1973–1974 HCs were used in 52 percent of aerosol fillings in the United States; by 1982 they comprised 89 percent (Johnsen 1981, p. 22). The producers of CFCs -11 and -12 and other chemicals used in conjunction with CFC propellants were temporary losers until markets for other uses of these CFCs developed.

Second, the aerosol filling industry is potentially more profitable because of consolidation and increased barriers to entry. Some independent fillers went out of business because they could not afford the capital investment required to convert to HC propellants. Reformulation costs, reflecting the need to accommodate the new propellants, may have also been a factor, although many fillers shared these costs with consumer products companies. Many consumer product firms that had run their own filling operations (captive fillers) began using independent fillers because they did not have the capital to switch propellants. By late 1981 independent fillers had a 58 percent market share, and captive fillers had a 42 percent market share. Before the ban, each had approximately a 50 percent market share (Johnsen 1981, p. 23).

The consolidation within the filler segment of the aerosol industry should result in lower costs because of economies of scale. The high costs of safety precautions required by hydrocarbons, including siting problems and insurance, are a barrier to entry for new firms. Firms within the filler segment were unable to reap the benefits of the consolidation and barriers to entry because the volume of fillings decreased in response to the ban; they should have become more profitable when the market for aerosols expanded.

Third, markets for environmentally safe products grew. Some consumer product firms capitalized on the demand for environmentally safe products that resulted from the ban. S. C. Johnson had been the nation's fifth largest manufacturer of aerosol sprays. In 1975 it increased its sales by eliminating CFCs in aerosols and advertising that its products were environmentally safe. In 1976 consumer product firms such as Gillette, Revlon, and Alberto-Culver announced that nonaerosol alternatives were available for all their products. In 1977 Bristol-Myers conducted a massive advertising campaign to promote its first non-CFC aerosol antiperspirant, Ultra Ban II (Ando and Marshall 1983, p. 20). Research and development also led to innovative and successful packaging forms, such as Grow Chemical's Enviro-Spray and Container Industries' Exxel propellantless system.

Aerosol fillings in the United States recently surpassed the record level of 2,823 million units established in 1973. According to the Chemical Specialty Manufacturing Association, fillings declined in anticipation of the ban to 2,231 million units, stabilized at that level until 1982, and have grown since then.

Finally, in the EEC nations, the aerosol ban was resisted because of the effects on the aerosol filling industry. One of the reasons that Great Britain and other EEC countries did not want to ban CFC-propelled aerosols is that many fillers were small operations that could not afford the transition costs to hydrocarbons (IAL Consultants 1986, sec. 5.10). Thus, the structure of the aerosol industry in the EEC was a reason for resistance to a ban.

Reactions after the Montreal Protocol

Substitute Development

After the Montreal Protocol was negotiated but prior to its implementation, a number of firms and industry associations took aggressive action to evaluate their CFC use, among them the Motor Vehicles Manufacturers Association (MVMA) and the Food Packaging Institute (FPI). The MVMA has participated in studies designed to establish standards for recycled refrigerants from automobile air-conditioners. These standards will facilitate the implementation of mobile recycling units known as vampires. Any equipment capable of recycling refrigerants of the required quality can be certified for use by automobile repair shops. This is an excellent example of voluntary cooperation to remove a technical barrier and forestall more draconian government action such as air-conditioner emission limits or bans on the use of CFCs.

The FPI represents firms that manufacture and distribute disposable food packaging used in fast-food restaurants. As public awareness of the threat of ozone depletion grew and media attention focused on the use of CFCs, disposable food packaging came under public scrutiny. Alternative non-CFC blowing agents are available for producing these products. Many of the cost-effective choices are hydrocarbons, which pose flammability, safety, and air pollution problems. A more expensive alternative is HCFC-22. FPI member companies realized that no firm would convert to HCFC-22 since it would lose either profits or market share because of increased costs. Conversion would have to be industry-wide to avoid economic bloodshed. Consequently the FPI, representing the industry, signed a voluntary conversion agreement with environmental organizations, including the Environmental Defense Fund.

Recently CFC prices have risen in response to the supply restrictions of the Montreal Protocol. The prices of CFC-11 and CFC-12 increased from $.60 and $.70 per pound to approximately $.80 and $.90 per pound during 1988. EPA estimates that prices may eventually rise as much as fivefold (Zurer 1989, p. 9). As would be expected, substitutes for CFCs are being developed. Du Pont estimates that it will take "five to seven years from establishment of a market incentive, such as the Montreal Protocol, until commercialization" (Du Pont 1988, p. 2). In addition, recycling is becoming economically feasible in some CFC markets such as auto air-conditioners.

Unfortunately, some of the potential substitutes for CFCs have environmental problems of their own. Since release of chlorine in the upper atmosphere is the cause of ozone layer depletion, two key factors determine the ozone depletion potential of CFCs: percentage by weight of chlorine and stability in the lower atmosphere. Hydrofluorocarbons (HFCs) and hydrochlorofluorocarbons (HCFCs) are two proposed substitutes for CFCs. Both are made by adding a hydrogen atom to the CFC molecule, which renders the molecule less stable so that it breaks down before reaching the upper atmosphere. Toxicity tests have not been completed on these compounds. A fraction of HCFCs will still reach the upper atmosphere and release chlorine (Zurer 1989, p. 12), which will be a problem if their use grows. In addition, these chemicals contribute to the pollution of the lower atmosphere. Hydrocarbons, the major substitute for CFC-propelled aerosols, have also been implicated as a major source of lower atmosphere pollution. A recent plan to improve urban air quality in the Los Angeles basin, released by the South Coast Air Quality Management District, proposes to ban the use of hydrocarbons as aerosol propellants.

Other possible substitutes for fully halogenated CFCs are CFCs with low ozone-depleting potential. An example is CFC-22, sometimes used in air-conditioning and refrigeration and not regulated under the Montreal Protocol. The problem with these CFCs is that some chlorine is still released in the upper atmosphere. Proposed substitutes for CFC-113 also have associated environmental problems. Methyl chloroform is a source of chlorine. Terpene, which one manufacturer expects to replace one-third of all CFC use in electronics components cleaning (EPA 1985, p. 21), is volatile and subject to explosion, and it may be a carcinogen. In addition, its heavy metal discharge will go into sewers. Methylene chloride, a substitute for CFCs in flexible foams and a flammability reduction agent sometimes placed in hydrocarbon-propelled aerosols, also has been implicated as a carcinogen.

One concern of industry is that CFC substitutes may be banned in the future. It is difficult for firms to justify large investments in the development of substitutes until toxicity and environmental testing has been completed and future regulations are predictable. As Du Pont's McCain said in relation to future regulation of HCFCs: "We have not decided to go forward in the alternative business. We are making small-scale plants. But if in a few years, when we have to get authorization for world-scale production facilities, we don't anticipate we can make money, we won't do it" (Zurer 1989, p. 13).

Environmental and toxicological evaluations are costly. Required testing can be a barrier to entry for firms with limited resources. In January 1988, more than a dozen U.S., European, and Japanese chemical firms announced a joint program to fund toxicity tests on selected fluorocarbon substitutes. This unprecedented collaboration is aimed at avoiding duplication of effort and shortening the completion time of testing. In addition to this testing effort, a second cooperative effort was begun (U.S. General Accounting Office 1989, pp. 27–28).

Corporate Strategy

The signatories of the Montreal Protocol agreed to cut back total CFC use over time; however, the agreement does not specify levels of reduction for particular CFC usages. It is expected that CFC uses with lower-cost alternatives will be eliminated first.

The success of international negotiations to restrict these chemicals has put users on notice. There are strong parallels between the efforts of hazardous waste generators and firms using ozone depleting chemicals. At a United Nations Environment Program–sponsored meeting in the Hague in October 1988, numerous industries and associations shared their experiences in reducing the use of CFCs. Northern Telecom, a large multinational that reduced CFC-113 by 25 percent over four months, described the preconditions for a successful source reduction program:

First of all, companies must adopt a fast-track management approach that provides their environmental experts and engineers with the mandate and resources to devise solutions. Second, companies must support their suppliers in the R&D battle to create new chemical formulations. Third, companies must foster better cooperation between their manufacturing process and environmental engineers—internally and through company-to-company links. And, finally we need more cooperation among nations to establish a positive international climate for carrying forward environmental protection measures. (Kerr 1988)

Other important organizational factors include direct access to and support of senior-level management and intimate involvement of product line managers.

This discussion incorporates the simplifying assumption that firms are fully aware of the management options open to them, but firms vary in their technical sophistication and availability of resources. Large firms are more likely to have greater internal resources. Consequently, a service analogous to the agricultural extension service would be helpful for small and medium-sized firms. Public sector resources have and should be invested in this context for technical assistance, including aid to less developed countries.

The difficulty firms have in coverting away from the use of CFCs depends, in part, on regulations that inhibit the market penetration of alternatives. For example, CFC-113 is written into military specifications for cleaning processes. Manufacturers wishing to demonstrate the high quality of their components are reluctant to adopt aqueous-based cleaning systems or other alternatives. Despite this constraint, the Digital Equipment Corporation now uses aqueous-based cleaning systems in its manufacturing process.

Effects on Industry Structure

There have been a number of effects on industry structure. First, firms are trying to capitalize on the market for environmentally safe products. As in the case of the U.S. aerosol ban, some companies are trying to capitalize on the demand for CFC-free products. Recently several Japanese auto manufacturers announced that they soon will no longer use CFCs in their automobile airconditioners.

Second, CFC producers are likely to obtain windfall profits. The effect of the Montreal Protocol on CFCs is similar to that of an effective oil cartel's restrictions: prices go up more than quantity demanded goes down, creating windfall profits for producers. These profits can be used to finance the development of substitutes and reduce the long-run cost of regulation for the CFC industry; however, in the United States, pending administrative or legislative proposals would capture any windfall by a tax on profits or by an auction of the transferable permits required in order to produce CFCs.

Third, markets for CFC substitutes are not likely to be very competitive because of high R&D costs. CFC producers are large chemical firms that have the resources to manage substitute development. The high research and development costs of bringing alternatives to the market are a significant barrier to entry, and existing producers are leading the charge. Because of the magnitude of the costs, however, some producers have banded together to do toxicity testing of more promising substitutes.

Fourth, many potential CFC substitutes are specialty chemicals whose markets are less competitive than for commodity chemicals. Unlike CFCs -11, -12, and -113, which are commodity chemicals, many potential CFC substitutes are specialty chemicals. The markets for commodity products are characterized by high volume and low price, while those for specialty products are characterized by low volume and high price. The profit margins on specialty chemicals are usually higher because of less competition.

Fifth, changes in the structure of CFC-user industries are likely to occur. The Montreal Protocol may create structural changes in CFC-user industries. CFC regulations will probably benefit large CFC-user firms at the expense of small CFC-user firms and lead to less competition. Suppliers will exert more control over most user industries because of the limited supplies of halogenated CFCs and because many substitutes will be specialty chemicals whose markets are less competitive. Some of the substitutes require process modification, and large firms may have cost advantages over small firms in making these modifications. And in cases where recycling is a cost-effective strategy, large firms may have a cost advantage over small firms because of economies of scale.

Table 5.7 presents some of the options available to reduce the use of CFC-11 in the manufacture of flexible slabstock foam. Methylene chloride can be substituted as a blowing agent for many slabstock foams. Recycling of CFC-11 is also possible. Although the cost of methylene chloride is lower than that of CFC-11 for many grades of slabstocks, quality control of soft foams blown with methylene chloride is more difficult and can lead to higher scrap rates. This is especially true for small manufacturing plants that do not have the technical expertise to use the chemical efficiently. Methylene chloride becomes economical for large plants at a CFC price of $.30 per pound, for medium-sized plants at a price of $.68 per pound, and for small plants at a price of $2.05 per pound. Notice also that recycling at large plants is more economical than conversion to methylene chloride is for small plants. Higher prices for CFC-11 will give large plants a significant cost advantage over small and medium plants. Because small and medium plants comprise 47 percent of the market, CFC regulations could promote significant structural changes in this industry. Studies of the options available to reduce the use of CFCs in other applications such as thermoformed polystyrene sheet, cleaning, and drying, depict the same pattern: large

Table 5.7
Technical Options to Reduce the Use of CFC-11 in the Manufacture of Flexible Slabstock Foam

Cost ($/pound)	Plant Size	Action Taken
.30	Large	Convert to methylene chloride
.68	Medium	Convert to methylene chloride
1.41	Large	Recycle
2.05	Small	Convert to methylene chloride

Source: Camm, et al. (1986).

plants have a cost advantage over small and medium-sized plants (Palmer, Mooz et al. 1980; Camm et al. 1986).

Finally, the treaty was difficult to negotiate because of concerns about the effect of regulations on the international competitiveness of domestic industries. CFC producers and users throughout the world were able to convince their representatives that unilateral regulations would place them at a disadvantage with competitors in other countries, which made drafting an international agreement very difficult. It was not until scientific evidence concerning ozone depletion was conclusive that many nations overcame their parochial interests and signed an international agreement designed to reduce CFC usage worldwide. In order to obtain the agreement, exceptions still had to be granted to some special interest groups, such as developing countries.

LESSONS FROM BUSINESS RESPONSE
TO CFC REGULATION

Several lessons can be derived from observations of firm and industry response to CFC regulation.

It is important for environmental policy to address all sources of a pollutant. The selective aerosol ban in the United States failed in the long run because it addressed only one use of CFCs. In the short run CFC usage significantly decreased in the United States. The ban achieved a quick, predictable reduction of CFCs, which bought some time for further development of atmospheric science concerning ozone depletion.

A production cap policy can be effective if it is set correctly. The EEC, however, set the cap at a level that did not constrain CFC usage.

A selective ban is potentially more costly than a production cap. Costs of reducing CFC usage vary by use, size of plant, and location of plant. Because firms adopt the least costly CFC reduction methods first, the unit cost of achieving any level of CFC reduction increases with the magnitude of the reduction. If all the burden of CFC regulation is borne by one industry, it is probable that all firms in that industry will be forced to use methods that are more costly than if the reduction requirement were spread among all user industries. (A detailed discussion of the economic consequences of bans and production capacity limitations is contained in Yarrow 1986a, 1986b.) As a result, the aerosol use ban produced considerable international friction in the early rounds of discussions preceding the Montreal Protocol.

Government policies should result in an increased cost of the pollutant to be reduced. Neither the aerosol ban in the United States nor the production ceiling in the EEC resulted in a significant price increase. Without a price increase, firms lacked an incentive to cut back total usage of CFCs. Ideally government policies would have caused CFC prices to rise, reflecting the increased scarcity of the ozone level and creating incentives for firms to develop substitutes and recycle. In fact, the ban in the United States initially created surplus production capacity of CFCs -11 and -12, which put downward pressure on prices. Attractive pricing maintained the performance-cost characteristics of CFCs and allowed manufacturers to expand markets such as refrigeration, foam, insulation, and solvents. Thus, government policies that were instituted to reduce CFC emissions may have increased emissions in the long run.

It is important to set policies correctly the first time. CFC producers were willing to cut back production capacity in anticipation of an aerosol ban but actually increased production capacity under the threat of regulation of non-aerosol uses. Apparently there was diminished political support for additional CFC regulation after the ban. This indicates the difficulty of expanding environmental regulations once they have been implemented. Policies are difficult to change unless a major catalyst for change, such as additional scientific evidence, is present.

Policy makers need to create policies that manage all pollutants simultaneously and take into account the consequences of substitution. Many substitutes for CFCs result in environmental problems. The history of environmental control is full of examples of environmental policies that attempt to solve one problem at the cost of creating another.

Government policy makers should recognize that scarcity is usually only a function of price. Industry resisted the regulation of CFCs by claiming that safe and effective substitutes did not exist; however, safe and effective substitutes have been found whenever industry had economic incentives to find them. This was true in the case of the aerosol ban and is true in the case of the Montreal Protocol. As the price of a polluting substance increases, an incentive is created for industry to find substitutes.

Government policies should focus on providing incentives for research and development and fostering industry cooperation, as in the case of CFC substitute toxicity testing. Research and development are expensive, and without adequate incentives, private industry may not undertake them. Because an individual firm often cannot capture all the benefits of its research and development, it has a tendency to underinvest even if it has the financial resources to absorb the cost and risk. The value of increased R&D is clear. The history of CFCs clearly indicates that the lack of available substitutes slowed the policy response.

The drive of business to find ways to benefit from regulation should be recognized by policy makers in the design of environmental policies. The history of the regulation of ozone-depleting chemicals indicates that firms and industries benefited from government policies and contributed to the solution of the CFC problem. Environmental policies differ in their ability to harness this creative energy of firms. The CFC aerosol ban was limited in this regard because it did not create incentives for businesses to reduce nonaerosol uses of CFCs. On the other hand, the production limits established by the Montreal Protocol do create such incentives.

Equity effects of environmental policies need to be recognized, but they can be better managed outside environmental policy. Although some firms and industries have benefited from CFC regulation, others have been losers. Governments' desire to protect firms and industries in environmental policies is one of the most important reasons for the slow response to the CFC problem.

Cooperative environmental strategies need to be developed among firms and among nations. Self-interest is an important force to harness in the cause of improving environmental quality, but so is cooperation. There have been instances in which firms within an industry have imposed voluntarily environmental restrictions on themselves. For example, the food plastics industry as a whole was willing to convert from the use of CFC-12 to the more costly but less polluting HCFC-22 in order to counter public censure resulting from both solid waste and ozone depletion concerns. In addition, it committed to a research program to develop non-CFC alternatives. Similarly the signing of the Montreal Protocol illustrates the ability of nations to overcome their parochial interests and to cooperate in the solution of global environmental problems that threaten survival.

APPLICATION TO OTHER ATMOSPHERIC POLLUTION PROBLEMS

Public attention on environmental issues is at a high-water mark. In the United States, this interest is focused on the reauthorization of the Clean Air Act. On July 21, 1989, President Bush broke a decade-old deadlock by introducing a set of proposals for managing acid rain, smog, and air toxins. Although some elements of these proposals are controversial, the acid rain program has drawn grudging praise from most combatants.

The administration's acid rain control program entails the most ambitious use of market-based methods ever proposed in environmental legislation. The plan would issue allowances, or marketable permits, to designated pollution sources. Each source is given the responsibility to bridge the gap between its current discharges of sulfur dioxide (SO_2) and the amount specified in the allowance. The key aspect of this plan is the flexibility it gives a source to reduce emissions by any means, including the purchase of permits from other sources. This emissions trading program would put utilities directly into the strategic context presented in this chapter.

At first glance, the gains from a market-based acid rain control strategy seem largely economic. Closer inspection reveals the powerful stimulus that economic gain provides for innovation in pollution-reducing strategies. These incentives are critical to achieving larger emissions reductions. Experience with the unit cost of emissions reduction indicates that it increases with the magnitude of reductions unless technical change occurs. Open-ended market policies give full credit for any technology, operating rule, or input change that results in emissions reduction. By not forcing utilities into a fixed set of control choices, the maximum incentive is provided to develop alternatives.

Chief among the options receiving new interest should be energy efficiency.

Since market-based programs shift the emphasis away from emission rate regulations to annual tonnage limitations, energy efficiency is given full play as a strategy to reduce emissions. Under emission rate–based systems, there is no incentive for a source to do anything other than comply precisely with the emission rate. Neither reducing the underlying demand for energy nor improving the efficiency of the generating process produces any advantage in achieving compliance. Under a market system operating on a currency of tons of SO_2 emissions, energy efficiency improvements result in fewer tons crossing the stack gas monitors. These reductions could then be applied to emission reduction obligations at other plants owned by the utility or sold on the general market.

As we look to more complex and potentially damaging atmospheric problems such as global climate change induced by greenhouse gases, these policy innovations become critical. Expanding the traditional base of regulatory control to include the millions of daily decisions to combust fossil fuels and discharge CO_2 is daunting. As in the case of acid rain, the issue is how to get polluters to take account of their pollution. Harnessing the power of the market is our best opportunity to influence this extremely decentralized arena, as well as to bring about international cooperation.

We stand at an important crossroads in the history of environmental policy, produced by the convergence of a unique set of political, economic, and environmental conditions. We have the opportunity to adopt innovative techniques. A new strategy—tapping market forces that are the source of creative entrepreneurial energies—offers improved environmental quality at reduced cost. The challenges that lie ahead in solving global atmospheric problems are extraordinary. But the lessons from the CFC experience are clear: give polluters the maximum incentive to gain from reducing their emissions, and they will be part of the solution, not the problem.

NOTES

Support for this study was provided by the Norman Foundation. The content of this chapter is the sole responsibility of the authors and does not represent the views of the Norman Foundation.

1. The JACA study was a partial analysis that emphasized only the cost to industry. That study did not evaluate changes in consumer well-being from the increased competition in personal care products spawned by the introduction of a much wider array of delivery systems such as pumps, roll-ons, sticks, and non-CFC aerosols. Further, the JACA study did not evaluate the benefits produced from reducing CFC emissions.

REFERENCES

Alliance for Responsible CFC Policy. 1986. "A Search for Alternatives to the Current Commercial Chlorofluorocarbons." Paper submitted to UNEP Economic Workshop on the Protection of the Ozone Layer, May.

Ando, Faith H., and Charles R. Marshall. 1983. "The Economic Impact of Regulating

Chlorofluorocarbon Emissions from Aerosols: A Retrospective Study." EPA 560/4-83-001. April.

Bevington, C. F. P. 1986. "Chlorofluorocarbons: Production, Use, Trade, and Current Regulations in the European Economic Community." Metra Consulting Group, London. Paper submitted to UNEP Chlorofluorocarbon Workshop.

Camm, F., T. H. Quinn, A. Bamezai, J. K. Hammitt, M. Meltzer, W. E. Mooz, and K. A. Wolf. 1986. "Social Cost of Technical Control Options to Reduce Ozone Depleters in the United States: An Update." Working draft, Rand Corporation, Santa Monica, Calif., prepared for the U.S. Environmental Protection Agency, Washington, D.C., February.

Daly, John. 1984. "New Propellants for Aerosol Fragrances." *Aerosol Age* (September).

Daly, John. 1988. "Emerging New Propellant Blends." *Aerosol Age* (October).

Dudek, Daniel J. 1986. *Stratospheric Ozone Depletion: The Case for Policy Action."* New York: Environmental Defense Fund, July.

Dudek, Daniel J. 1987. *Chlorofluorocarbon Policy: Choices and Consequences.* New York: Environmental Defense Fund.

Dunn, Donald. 1988. "New Propellants Respond to Regulatory Developments." *Aerosol Age* (January).

Du Pont. 1987. "Fluorocarbon/Ozone Update" (March).

Du Pont. 1988. "Fluorocarbon/Ozone Update" (January).

Farhad, Niloofar, and Lloyd M. Elkin. 1985. *Integrated Solvents Analysis: Production of Fluorocarbons 11 and 12 from Carbon Tetrachloride.* Office of Pesticides and Toxic Substances, U.S. Environmental Protection Agency, Washington, D.C.

Giovanni, Michael San. 1980. "Self-Pressuring Packages Are Back!" *Aerosol Age* (March).

IAL Consultants Ltd. 1986. "Possible Effects of Additional Control Measures of CFC's in the U.K. Aerosol Industry." Paper submitted to the UNEP Socioeconomic Workshop, May.

ICF Incorporated. 1986. "An Analysis of the Economic Effects of Regulatory and Non-regulatory Events Related to the Abandonment of Chlorofluorocarbons as Aerosol Propellants in the United States from 1970 to 1980, with a Discussion of Applicability of the Analysis to Other Nations." Paper submitted to UNEP Economic Workshop on the Protection of the Ozone Layer, May.

Johnsen, Montford. 1981. "Why Aerosol Contract Packaging for Cosmetics." *Aerosol Age* (September).

Kerr, Margaret G. 1988. "The CFC Challenge: Conservation and Elimination." Paper presented to the UNEP Conference at the Hague, October 20.

Lagow, Richard. 1987. "Draft: Finding of the Chlorofluorocarbon Chemical Substitutes International Committee." EPA Contract 68-02-3994, U.S. Environmental Protection Agency, Washington D.C., September.

Mooz, William E., Kathleen A. Wolf, and Frank Camm. 1986. "Potential Constraints on Cumulative Global Production of Chlorofluorocarbons." Rand Corporation, Santa Monica, Calif., prepared for U.S. Environmental Protection Agency, Washington D.C., May.

Palmer, Adele R., William E. Mooz, Timothy H. Quinn, and Kathleen A. Wolf. 1980. "Economic Implications of Regulating Chlorofluorocarbon Emissions from Non-aerosol Applications." Rand Corporation, Santa Monica, Calif., prepared for U.S. Environmental Protection Agency, Washington D.C., June.

Pearce, David W. 1986. "The European Economic Community Approach to the Control of Chlorofluorocarbons." Prepared for the Second Part of UNEP Workshop on the Control of CFCs, Washington, D.C., September.

Porter, Michael E. 1980. *Competitive Strategy*. New York: Free Press.

U.S. Environmental Protection Agency. 1985. "Analysis of Issues Concerning a CFC Protocol." Washington D.C., February.

U.S. General Accounting Office. 1989. "Stratospheric Ozone: EPA's Safety Assessment of Substitutes for Ozone Depleting Chemicals." Washington, D.C., February.

Yarrow, George. 1986a. "The Economic Consequences of a Ban on Chlorofluorocarbon Use in Aerosols." Oxford: Hertford College.

Yarrow, George. 1986b. "The Economic Consequences of a Production Capacity Limitation for Chlorofluorocarbons." Oxford: Hertford College.

Zurer, Pamela S. 1988. "Search Intensifies for Alternatives to Ozone-Depleting Halocarbons." *Chemical and Engineering News*, February 6, p. 1720.

Zurer, Pamela S. 1989. "Producers, Users Grapple with Realities of CFC Phaseout." *Chemical and Engineering News*, July 24, pp. 7–13.

Water in the United States: Balancing the Law and Ethics of Environmental Protection and Economic Growth

RICHARD A. WEHMHOEFER

As water has become scarcer across the United States due to drought and population growth and as water quality has declined due to pollution from both point and nonpoint sources, several legal and ethical questions have arisen about the adequacy of our current water laws to address the protection of this scarce resource while providing for sustained economic growth throughout the country. First, does current law provide the necessary ethical and legal guidance to determine who has a right to this limited resource? Second, how does the law of water balance environmental protection of this resource and economic growth, which necessarily affects both the quantity and quality of water? Finally, are the current public policy, legal, and ethical frameworks adequate to deal with the future? This chapter addresses these questions. It is intended to serve as a starting point for understanding some of the pressing conflicts concerning water that have found their way into the courts and legislatures. Some public policy, legal, and ethical outcomes are suggested for policy makers to consider while attempting to achieve economic growth and a reasonable quality of life for residents in the United States.

SETTING THE STAGE

Litigation surrounding water rights has tended to be prevalent in the United States. This is so because conflicts generally arise when there are several competing demands for water accompanied by shortages and a declining quality brought on by multiple uses. In addition, the United States has a supportive legal system that allows for the resolution of these disputes in a judicial arena.

In the East, continued population growth and concentration have placed severe stress on the quantity and quality of drinkable water, and drought has exacerbated these problems, which are expected to continue well into the next century.

In the West, water problems are as old as the history of the region. Historically the name of the lands lying west of the one hundredth meridian was the "Great American Desert."[1] This region often receives less than 20 inches of average annual precipitation, compared with up to 40 inches in the East.[2] This scarcity makes life and farming virtually impossible without water storage, diversion, and irrigation.

In fact, over 80 percent of all irrigation in the United States takes place in the West, where over 90 percent of the available water resources goes for agricultural purposes.[3] In addition, with the recent rapid population growth in parts of the West, conflicts between urban and rural areas over water allocation and use, as well as the environmental degradation that arises with increased use, have become inevitable.

Thus, both the East and the West share common problems of trying to maintain sustained economic growth while struggling to protect their limited water supply—a supply that is essential in order to ensure any type of economic growth into the future.

SURFACE WATER LAW: A LEGAL AND ETHICAL OVERVIEW OF RIPARIAN RIGHTS

Surface water, which most water users generally rely on, is divided into two legal categories: riparian and prior appropriation.

In the East, where water has historically been quite plentiful, the riparian water rights doctrine developed. The construction of the doctrine has been best summarized as

one who owned lands touching upon a stream was entitled to have the full flow of the stream come by his place undiminished in quantity and unimpaired in quality, except that each landowner was entitled to make reasonable use of the water upon his own lands, provided: (1) that he returned the stream to its natural channel before it left his lands, so as not to deprive succeeding lower riparian owners of their rights; and, (2) that use on his land was reasonable in respect to the corresponding rights of other riparian owners lying below [rule of reasonable use].[4]

This principle of law was the rule of decision used by most states before 1850; it still is the law exclusively in all the states east of the Mississippi River and in the tier of states just to the west of it. Riparian rights permitted use of water in quantities sufficient to satisfy most domestic needs.

This law supports the utilitarian notion that the greatest good can be achieved by allowing all persons living on or near watercourses an adequate supply of water so long as these users do not unreasonably diminish the supply or quality of the water for downstream users.

Under the riparian doctrine, the "right" to use water is considered real property, but the water itself is not the property of the landowner. Rather, the riparian water right is a "natural right," a public good and merely an appurtenance, or appendage, of the land. A riparian water right is a property that enters materially into the value of the estate; it may not, however, be separately transferred, sold, or granted to any other person than the owner of the land along the stream or watercourse.

While it is generally held that such water rights are natural rights and appurtenant to the land because these rights are public goods, the water is subject to state regulation. In effect, rights of individual landowners are subordinate to the public interest. Thus, the eastern states, exercising their police power, may subject riparian water rights' owners to reasonable regulation for the benefit of the greatest public good.

Reasonable regulation generally focuses on water uses that are necessary to the sustenance of life and enjoyment of the property. A hierarchy of uses has been recognized by the courts. First priority is given to water used for drinking, cooking, and stock watering. Second priority is to industrial and irrigation uses. Third priority is to water transported away from the land directly contiguous to the stream.

In situations where there is a conflict among owners over the amounts of water withdrawal for reasonable uses, it has been determined that when the conflict is over domestic uses, all owners must bear the burden of the shortage equally in times of short supply. When there is a conflict between upper owners for domestic uses and lower owners for a secondary purpose (e.g., industrial), the lower owners have to forgo their rights. When the conflict is between lower and upper owners for the same secondary use, then the upper owners have a claim senior to that of the lower owners.

Owners of riparian water rights also have certain responsibilities, the logical results of the law of riparian water rights. If every owner is entitled to the full flow of the stream diminished only by the necessary withdrawals of the upper owners for reasonable purposes and to the water in its natural state of purity, it logically follows that a riparian owner may not obstruct the stream by building dams or use the water in such a way as to leave it unreasonably polluted.

As a rule of decision, the riparian law is not even fully effective in the achievement of its own ends. First, a judicial decision on a riparian water right holds only so long as another judge does not interpret the law or the facts differently. Thus, a landowner is never certain of his or her rights until a judicial determination has been made on a specific set of facts. In addition, as fact situations change, a new case may arise for the same landowner, resulting in a new decision. Under this system, a landowner's investment is not always stable or secure.

In the light of modern knowledge and economic conditions, there are more serious defects in this riparian system. First, the doctrine presents no logical basis or framework for efficient water allocation, use, or environmental management. As court-made and self-enforced law, it cannot because utilitarian analysis is subject to differing cost-benefit analysis models. Further, interpretation of the concept of the greatest good for greatest number often depends on the facts of each specific situation, as well as the values of the decision maker.

Second, the rule of reasonable use requirement of the doctrine tends to encourage waste or nonuse by upstream landowners so as not to create an expectation in the minds of downstream users that they can expect an increased supply of water for their use. The "greatest good" for upstream landowners may be to continue inefficient uses or practices because the costs to conserve often provide little benefit for these owners even though conservation measures may result in savings for downstream landowners.

Third, the allowance of the law for certain reasonable degradation of the supply serves to discourage care given by upstream landowners to sustain or improve the quality of water that finds its way back to the stream for use by downstream riparian water rights' owners. Like wasteful use, there are often no incentives for upstream owners to spend additional resources to improve on allowances for reasonable degradation.

Because of these weaknesses in the riparian system, the courts or the state riparian water management program cannot evolve beyond a series of common law cases and reliance on historical diversions and environmental degradation. Thus, the utilitarian notion that water in a stream can be reasonably shared in such a way as to maximize the greatest good for the greatest number of water users while preserving the water's quality has often proved to be impractical and unworkable.

SURFACE WATER LAW: A LEGAL AND ETHICAL OVERVIEW OF THE PRIOR APPROPRIATION DOCTRINE

In the western United States, the needs and subsequent water laws have been significantly different from the riparian system. Most important, this area has been consistently dry so that water remains in relatively short supply. As the population in the West has grown, the use and reuse of this scarce resource have risen dramatically. In addition, the value system and traditions in the West are affected by a long historical line of Indian, Spanish, and Mexican cultures, all with different legal and ethical views, values, and customs with respect to the exploitation of natural resources.

The early unwritten law with respect to gold and silver finds closely parallels the existing water laws of the West. With respect to these rare and precious materials, the tradition, as formalized into law, reads:

He who first discovers gold [or other precious metal], if he develops a claim within a reasonable period of time, and continues his development diligently, may have the benefits of his labor. If he fails to develop and work the claim diligently, his rights [to the precious metal] are forfeited.[5]

When questions of water rights arose in the West, the same general rule prevailed. This procedure and its rule acquired the name prior appropriation doctrine. As the western territories became states, most states rejected the riparian doctrine even to the point of repudiating it in their state constitutions. Some of the states used their constitutions as a means of declaring state water policy specifically to be prior appropriation, and some states employed the constitution to establish the machinery for state administration of the prior appropriation doctrine.

Appropriation statutes generally follow the mining camp principle for gold prospecting. Perhaps the best definition of the doctrine is the following description from the *Report of the President's Water Resources Policy Commission:*

The appropriation doctrine . . . rests on the proposition that beneficial use of water is the basis, measure and limit of the appropriative right. The first in time is prior in right. Perfected only by use, the . . . right is lost by abandonment. . . . An appropriative water right is not identified by ownership of riparian lands. Its existence and relationship to other rights on the same stream are identified in terms of time of initiation of the right by start of the work to divert water [from the stream] coupled with an intent to make beneficial use of it and the diligence with which the appropriator prosecutes to completion his diversion works and actually applies the water to beneficial use.[6]

Although details vary greatly, this statement is the essence of water law in the West. Throughout appropriation law, the elements of "first-in-time, first-in-right," "due diligence," "beneficial use," and "water conservation" play important roles, because in these states water has historically been scarce.

Prior appropriation law supports an egoist notion that the "self-interest" of the water user is protected by the individual's staking a claim to a given volume of water. The prior appropriator must prove he or she arrived at the stream first and then perfected the claim by devoting due diligence (i.e., time, effort, and resources) to divert the water to a beneficial use, including applications such as domestic use, irrigation, mining, stock watering, or industrial use.

Under the prior appropriation doctrine, the volume of water itself becomes the real property of the claimant. The water is a property separate and apart from the land. The water right can be transferred, traded, sold, or granted to other users along with the perfected priority date of appropriation. The water right can be leased or exchanged, its diversion point can be moved, and its beneficial use can be changed from one use (e.g., stock watering) to another (e.g., domestic).

Just as with mineral rights, the prior appropriation water right can be severed from the land to which it had been historically applied and moved hundreds of miles away. The water right is a private good to be used as the private owner sees fit subject to state regulation governing the use of the water in such a way as not to harm other claimants' priority rights on the same stream or watercourse.

In stark contrast to the riparian water rights system, rights of individual owners in the prior appropriation system are supreme; however, just as with the riparian water rights system, states following prior appropriation concepts have recognized that the scarcity of the resource, combined with the growing multiplicity of owners and competing uses on the same stream, necessitates the need for some regulation to protect the quantity and quality of this resource.

The concept of self-interest pervades the prior appropriation system, however, which often serves to create a much more vigilant attitude on the part of water rights' owners themselves in this system compared with the riparian water rights' system. Because the users of water in the prior appropriation system are also the owners of the scarce resource, they are necessarily concerned about preserving the quantity and quality of their investment. Rather than the water simply being a public good that individuals have a right to share and use, water in the prior appropriation system is private property, a personal investment the owners want to see appreciate in value. In particular, the owners of prior appropriation water rights want to see the quality and quantity of water in the whole stream basin protected because they may one day desire to sell their water rights to down-stream users; change their use of the water from one use to another, such as agricultural or industrial use to municipal use (which necessarily means owners do not want to see the quality on any point in the stream degraded in any way); or move their point of diversion from one point on the stream to a different point. In sum, the owners of water rights in this system must remain constantly on guard so that no point on the stream unreasonably declines in water quality.

In addition, a state adopting a prior appropriation concept carries out its role of protecting society's health, safety, and welfare by acting to preserve and protect not only the quantity of water in the stream but also the quality of the resource. In effect, the state acts to ensure that private property rights are preserved and protected.

COMPARING THE TWO SYSTEMS

Comparison of the major features of riparian water rights and prior appropriation laws shows that the utilitarian theory of the riparian system is often inferior to the self-interest notion exemplified in the prior appropriation system. Although such an observation may seem surprising, the prior appropriation system provides an ethical and legal framework to prevent abuses of water that one might otherwise expect when thinking of the notions of self-interest and egoist ethics.

In determining water rights in the prior appropriation system, disputes are settled by state judicial agencies called water courts. These courts, composed of judges well versed in water issues for a given stream or river basin, act to ensure that the prior appropriative water right is a permanent, exclusive right guarantee-ing security of investment for the owner of the right.

Prior appropriation laws reflect the implementation of a beneficial use policy. This means that waste, nonuse, and nonbeneficial uses can be prohibited. Although the prior appropriation right itself is monopolistic, it is so only in terms of beneficial use.

The water courts are also empowered to work with state water agencies to make and enforce rules and regulations governing the management of the re-source. The administrative agency frames its regulations in terms of beneficial use, and the rules can be based on sound scientific and hydrological principles. With scientists and water resource engineers participating in rulemaking, there is a greater likelihood that the law will keep up with the knowledge of hydrology.

It appears that comprehensive and effective management of watercourses probably could occur only when a state adopts the major principles of the prior appropriation system. In fact, in response to the stated strengths of the prior appropriation doctrine, riparian states are beginning to adopt elements of prior appropriation. For example, the riparian system is now increasingly based on permitting, in which water users are granted a permit specifying a volumetric amount of water for their use provided they meet the requirements of the permit with respect to water quantity and quality. In effect, the permit acts in much the same manner as the perfected water right in the prior appropriation system. Therefore, when both systems are compared, the prior appropriation system generally gets higher marks.

WHAT DOES THE FUTURE HOLD?

Americans once saw clean and inexpensive water as a kind of national entitlement that was all but inexhaustible.[7] Today, however, water has become relatively scarce, and conflicts among competing users are commonplace.

Clearly several past and current actions jeopardize future generations' access to fresh water that will meet quantitatively and qualitatively derived standards. Such actions include surface water diversions on an excessive scale; pollution and contamination of surface water supplies by toxic and other discharges; and ongoing local, state, national, and international debates about the politics of water (who gets the water that is available, when, where, and in what quantity and quality?). As these actions affect our water supply, chances for sustained economic growth may be seriously undermined.

Edith B. Weiss has argued that there are three principles that can ensure our children and grandchildren enough good water: the conservation of options, conservation of quality, and equitable access and use.[8]

Conservation of options means that we should retain as wide a variety of freshwater sources as possible along with available points for diversions. This means getting away from the "big is better" mentality of big dams and big water projects that benefit only the few at the expense of the many. As federal deficit pressures grew in the 1980s, we began to see federal government reluctance to fund the building of such projects, which may have the unintended consequence of preserving conservation of options for future generations.

Conservation of quality means a ban on persistent toxic contamination of streams and lakes and of aquifers linked hydrologically to streams. This means a more vigorous stance by federal, state, and local governmental agencies in passing and enforcing strict water quality standards and water pollution laws, including dealing with the issue of acid rain. If recent statements are any predictor, President Bush's promise to be an environmental president lends credence to the conservation of quality argument.

Issues of equitable access and use arise both among generations and among members of the same generation. As the riparian system has begun to adopt attributes of the prior appropriation doctrine, the issue of equitable access and use may gain national acceptance. In addition, conservation of options and of quality is intended to ensure that all generations will have an equal relationship to the resource.

MANAGING FOR FUTURE GENERATIONS

Preventing actions that deplete water resources or degrade water quality will be far more effective and less costly for economic growth than will remedial efforts or attempts to impose liability for damages after the fact. This means that policy makers must give priority to identifying dangers, assess the likely effects of proposed actions, monitor the consequences of actions already taken, and consult among affected parties. It also means increasing the efficient use of water, including recycling it for different uses. Whether all of these priorities can be accomplished depends in large measure on the capability and capacity of water users themselves, working with legislatures, courts, and water management policy makers to adapt to changing conditions and needs.

Changes in policy will have to be made to address these issues. In particular, all levels of government must act now to adopt elements of the prior appropriation system along with concepts of self-interest in order to get the users of water more focused on the preservation of the quantity and quality of water in their respective stream basins. Without protecting this scarce resource, the likelihood of any sustained economic growth for future generations may be unattainable. It is clear that the utilitarian concept of riparian water rights does not adequately address the issues of quantity or quality of water, particularly for downstream users.

Historically, policy makers, legislatures, courts, and water users themselves have generally risen to the occasion, making changes when needs have arisen. If history is to be our guide, it is likely that water laws and concepts of prior appropriation will continue to be adopted to account for changing needs and public uses. Because water is so vital to our survival, such flexibility has been, and will continue to be, a necessary component of water law in the United States.

NOTES

1. *California v. United States,* 438 U.S. 646, 648 (1978).
2. U.S. Department of Interior, Geological Survey, *National Atlas* (Washington, D.C.: U.S. Government Printing Office, 1970): p. 97.
3. Ibid.

4. C. Busby, "Water Rights and Our Expanding Economy," *Journal of Soil and Water Conservation* 9 (March 1954): p. 68.

5. Ibid.

6. *Report of the President's Water Resources Policy Commission* (Washington, D.C.: U.S. Government Printing Office, 1950): p. 156.

7. Kent A. Price, "A Water Crisis?" *Resources* 83 (Spring 1986): 1.

8. Edith B. Weiss, "In Fairness of Future Generations," *Resources* 83 (Spring 1986): 4.

Administrative Behavior, Ethics, and Environmental Policy: The Norfolk, Massachusetts, Solid Waste Dispute

FREDERIC A. WALDSTEIN

The purpose of this case study is to examine the factors that do and ought to play a role in evaluating the behavior of administrators in the environmental policy process. The central issue involves a dispute between the town of Norfolk and the Massachusetts Department of Environmental Quality Engineering (DEQE) concerning financial liability for the cost of constructing an impervious liner to the town's sanitary landfill. All parties to the dispute recognized that the liner was necessary to ensure against contamination of the groundwater supply by leachate.[1] Questionable ethical behavior by the DEQE was raised during the dispute resolution process and serves as a springboard for a more general review of ethics in public administration. The result of this review is applied to the evaluation of the DEQE's administrative behavior in the dispute.

HISTORY OF THE DISPUTE

On August 9, 1983, DEQE had directed Norfolk to construct an impervious liner at the base of the proposed expansion to the Town's refuse disposal facility. This liner would prevent groundwater pollution by collecting leachate, a liquid waste formed when rainwater percolates through deposited trash. Norfolk herein seeks reimbursement from the Commonwealth for the direct cost and service obligations which it has incurred in complying with DEQE's liner requirement.[2]

The Disputants

On July 1, 1975, the Executive Office of Environmental Affairs (EOEA) was created in response to the demands of an environmentally sensitive public to develop a highly visible, comprehensive agency to coordinate the state's environmental agenda. The EOEA serves as the primary agency responsible for improving the quality of the environment and protecting the natural resources of the state. To fulfill its responsibilities, the EOEA has overall fiscal, policy, planning, and legal decision-making authority concerning environmental matters.

Within the EOEA is the Department of Environmental Quality Engineering (DEQE). Its primary responsibilities are to protect public health and safety by regulating industrial, commercial, and municipal activities that pollute air, water, and soil. DEQE was the principal party representing the state in the dispute.

The towns of Norfolk, Hull, and Boxford were the municipalities that requested payment from the state to cover the costs of the environmental improvements they made to their respective landfills. Norfolk was the initial claimant against the state. All parties stipulated and agreed that the Hull and Boxford claims were similar and that the decision on Norfolk's claim would also apply to their own. The only difference among the three claims was the amount of payment requested.

The Division of Local Mandates (DLM) in the Office of the State Auditor was the original adjudicatory setting for the dispute between the DEQE and the three towns. It was created as a special unit within the auditor's office to act as a liaison between the commonwealth and its municipalities and to play an adjudicatory role in disputes between the state and municipalities in cases alleging state-imposed mandates on communities where financial liability is at issue. The Norfolk Superior Court assumed appellate jurisdiction.

The Legal Issues

In 1971 Massachusetts set standards and regulatory procedures pertaining to the proper disposal of solid waste in existing and future sanitary landfills. It states in part that no person, including a town or a private party, can establish a landfill without submitting plans to DEQE and receiving DEQE approval. Part of the approval process must take into consideration the effect of the facility on public health.

In conjunction with carrying out its mandate to protect the public health, the DEQE adopted portions of the Federal Clean Water Act (33 U.S.C. secs. 1251, et seq.) that required the installation of certain equipment to protect groundwater. Potential or actual polluters were controlled by the best conventional pollution control technology (BCT) standard.[3] In conjunction with imposing the BCT standard, DEQE had required several landfill operators to install impervious liners to protect against contamination of the groundwater by leachate.

Referendum Question 2, or Proposition 2½, and its progeny became part of the Massachusetts General Laws (MGL) as Chapter 29, section 27C. The relevant portion reads:

Any administrative rule or regulation taking effect on or after January first, nineteen hundred and eighty-one which shall result in the imposition of additional costs upon any city or town shall not be effective until the general court has provided by general law and by appropriation for the assumption by the Commonwealth of such cost, exclusive of local administration expenses, and unless the general court provides by appropriation in each successive year for such assumption.

In short, any costs to municipalities mandated by the state based on rules or regulations not in effect prior to 1981 are the responsibility of the state.

The Dispute

The DEQE directed the town of Norfolk to install an impervious liner at the base of a proposed extension to its landfill to prevent leachate from polluting surrounding groundwater.[4] Norfolk complied with the requirement to obtain approval for the extension. In 1985 it petitioned the DLM for financial relief from the $162,527.50 in expenses incurred in the construction of the liner. The town based its claim on MGL Chapter 29, section 27C, which says in part that any costs imposed on municipalities by the state that result from new regulations are the state's liability. Norfolk argued that the liner requirement constituted an administrative rule or regulation that had not been in effect prior to 1981.

DEQE responded to the claim by stating that the liner requirement was not a new regulation under the terms stipulated by Chapter 29, and therefore the DLM had no jurisdiction to decide the case. While stipulating that MGL Chapter 150A made no specific reference to liners, the DEQE nonetheless argued that in the interest of groundwater protection, it could, as a matter of policy, require land-fills to construct liners under the 1971 provisions of that law as the need arose.[5] In support of this position, DEQE said that liner requirements had been imposed on many municipalities and private operators since the late 1970s. The 1971 law required the department to control leachate and prevent groundwater protection, claimed DEQE, and liners are one form of leachate control. In any case, DEQE held that it had informed town officials that a liner would be required for the landfill extension prior to 1981.

Finally, DEQE held that Norfolk was not required to own or operate a landfill; therefore the DEQE liner policy was not a mandate. That is, it was the town's choice to have a landfill, and DEQE was only ensuring that it be operated properly through capital upgrading to meet the state's BCT standard. If it felt the costs were too great, the town could close its landfill and contract with some other municipality or private firm to dispose of the town's waste.

Judgment

On April 29, 1985, the DLM handed down its decision. It rejected DEQE's jurisdictional claims and found in favor of Norfolk that the liner requirement constituted a post-1981 rule or regulation for which the state was financially liable. It did not, however, award the full amount requested by Norfolk; it disallowed $18,500 for venting, testing, and similar costs because DLM held that they would have been incurred under the 1971 regulations, independent of the liner requirement. The state was ordered to pay those costs that were directly attributable to the new policy. Furthermore, any future expenses resulting from this or other regulatory decisions would also be the responsibility of the state.

The commonwealth appealed the DLM decision to Norfolk Superior Court. All parties agreed that the court's ruling would apply to similar cases pending between the DEQE and the towns of Hull and Boxford. In July 1988, Judge William H. Welch upheld the DLM decision in its entirety. In his decision, Judge Welch stated, "It would seem in the exercise of intellectual honesty DEQE should acknowledge if [the liner requirement] has now become their policy even though this might require them to pay for the cost of such liners."[6] A motion for reconsideration in September 1988 was denied.

INTELLECTUAL HONESTY AND ETHICAL BEHAVIOR

Judge Welch was not subtle in expressing his belief that DEQE was being intellectually dishonest by using semantic sleight of hand in an effort to evade its responsibility to pay for the cost of the landfill liner. The judge's position was that DEQE acted unethically if we accept the definition that ethics in this context means behavior "professionally right or befitting; conforming to professional standards of conduct."[7] Implicit in this definition is the existence of professional standards that serve as a useful guide to public administrators as they execute their substantive duties. If these standards do not exist, there can be no determination of ethical conduct other than according to subjective, idiosyncratic criteria about which there is little or no public agreement. A case may be made that this is indeed the predicament for public administrators in general and for those involved in environmental policy in particular.

PUBLIC ADMINISTRATION AND THE ISSUE OF ETHICS

The Traditional Conception of Professional Ethics

Public administration, to use the language of Frank Goodnow at the turn of the century, represents one of two distinct governmental functions: politics and administration. "Politics has to do with policies or expressions of the state will [policy formulation]. Administration has to do with the execution of these policies [policy implementation]."[8] Although no one seems to know quite where to draw the line between the two spheres, the dichotomy between policy formulation and policy implementation has had profound implications for what is perceived as appropriate professional conduct in each. The traditional perspective is that policy is decided by elected officials who represent the will of the people in the democratic tradition. The unelected bureaucrat is perceived as a non-democratic functionary tolerated to the extent necessary to execute the will of the people as expressed through the democratic process. We may identify this as the policy-administration dichotomy.

Under the traditional model, a high premium is placed on constraining the discretionary behavior of the public administrator. Indeed, for some the entire issue of ethical behavior in public administration focuses on the responsibility of the bureaucracy and the elected officials to minimize discretionary behavior by individual administrators.[9] Others believe that administrative discretion can best be reduced through formal laws that govern bureaucratic behavior.[10] Herbert Simon, in his celebrated work *Administrative Behavior,* divides decisions into two categories: those that are driven by "facts" and those that are driven by "values" or "ethics":

If it is desired to retain the terms "policy" and "administration," they can best be applied to a division of the decisional functions. . . . While not identical with the separation of "value" from "fact," such a division would clearly be dependent upon that fundamental distinction.[11]

According to Simon, the ethical premises describe the objective of the organization in question, and in the public sphere these should be defined by the legislature. Taken to its logical conclusion, the implication is that the ethical administrator deals only with facts as defined by the value choices of the policy makers, who are duly elected representatives of the people.

An Alternative Conception of Professional Ethics

In 1936 Pendelton Herring challenged the concept that the American bureaucracy was essentially antidemocratic in nature:

We conclude, then, that the purpose of the democratic state is the free reconciliation of group interests and that the attainment of this end necessitates the development of a great administrative machine. Thus, paradoxical as it may seem to Jeffersonian Democrats, the liberal democratic state must be sustained by a huge bureaucracy. This viewpoint, however, has not won general acceptance.[12]

Indeed, this viewpoint has not won general acceptance more than fifty years after Herring offered it. But an increasing number of public administration theorists are exploring the concept of administrative behavior as an integral part of the democratic process that includes a policy-making role.[13]

A principal motivation for adopting this approach to analyzing administrative behavior is rejection of the belief that the public administrator need merely perform a well-defined task clearly articulated by elected representatives of the public. Simon and others assume that "facts" or knowledge are static, objective, and easily obtainable. But knowledge is evolving and subjective: "Our information is always incomplete, bad or just unavailable. Yet life goes on. Decisions have to be made. . . . Where no consensus or norm exists, anything that can be accepted as 'fair' in some ways is at a premium."[14] Thus, problem solving for the public administrator is more than just technical; it is also political. And it would be useful to develop a professional ethic that takes this into account. In its absence, public administrators are left in the precarious position of exercising political control de facto (a state of affairs perceived by traditionalists as un-ethical) with no ethical code to guide them. Consequently potential ethical issues are rarely considered.

In short, one may posit that public administrators are dissuaded from concerning themselves with ethical issues as they execute their responsibilities because the existing professional ethic is irrelevant to the extent it does not address political reality. These assumptions underlie the following discussion of environmental policy, particularly as it pertains to the dispute between Norfolk and the DEQE.

ETHICAL ADMINISTRATIVE BEHAVIOR AND ENVIRONMENTAL POLICY

For several reasons, environmental policy is an area with few axiomatic parameters available to guide the public administrator. First, it is a relatively new field of public policy. Laws explicitly pertaining to environmental protection as the first priority were virtually unknown until the 1960s. The principal administrative agency responsible for environmental management in Massachusetts, the Executive Office of Environmental Affairs, was not created until 1975. Both the legal and the administrative apparatuses to address the issue are relatively new.

Second, many early environmental laws were passed by elected officials more sensitive to public demand for environmental protection than to environmental protection itself. Laws were passed with little knowledge of either their implications once implemented or the technological feasibility of implementing them in the first place.[15]

Third, and most important, the complexity of the environment is so great that our understanding of what constitutes environmentally sound policy is undergoing continual revision. For example, sanitary landfills were hailed throughout the 1960s and 1970s as ecologically safe; within the last decade we have realized the potentially grave threat they pose to the groundwater supply. An alternative to landfilling that has been advocated is burning trash in waste-to-energy facilities, but our lack of knowledge about their potential contribution to the greenhouse effect and uncertainty about health risks from potentially carcinogenic materials such as dioxin that are released when using this technology have caused many to revise their opinion that this is the optimal solution to our waste disposal needs. In short, it is impossible to predict what we will learn about environmental protection even in the short term. There are few, if any, objective facts that administrators can rely on. Rather, administrators must have flexibility to adopt policy with political consequences in order to take advantage of the constant flow of new information pertaining to the environment. How should they do this?

The Consequences of Relying on the Traditional Model

One way to answer the question is to adopt the incremental strategy the DEQE used. The arguments raised before the DLM appear to be petty and disingenuous, based on a narrow reading of technical terminology. But extrapolating from Fred Eidlin's thesis, this may be the inevitable result of reliance on the traditional policy-administration model. Eidlin argues that viewing public policy problems as technical rather than political tends to take them out of the realm of political discourse and into the realm of technical application.[16] This constrains the administrators to rely on conservative models of social change because they are excluded from the political realm. Thus, in attempting to justify a policy decision with important political ramifications, DEQE was limited to reliance on technical arguments that appeared to be less than intellectually honest. But because there are no professional standards upon which DEQE or any other administrative agency in Massachusetts can rely when engaged in political issues, such judgment may be inappropriate. But arguing that it is inappropriate to judge DEQE unethical for the way it attempted to justify its position is not to exonerate its behavior. What is needed is a different context for considering the dispute.

Interpreting DEQE Behavior from a Political Perspective

DEQE was engaged in dialogue and negotiation with the town of Norfolk with respect to the technical design and development of the sanitary landfill liner. Their relationship did not change until the politically charged question of fiscal liability reared its head. At this point both parties developed an adversarial relationship, in part because the sole dispute resolution mechanism, the DLM, was adjudicatory.

Perhaps a more constructive approach would have been to avoid the adjudicatory process by maintaining a dialogue from the outset that included frank discussion about financial liability. It may be that Norfolk would have been willing to absorb some of the costs of constructing the liner had the issue been raised in the appropriate forum at an earlier stage of the process. A greater political sensitivity on the part of DEQE would have allowed it to perceive the fiscal liability problem. During early phases of the project, DEQE may have been able to negotiate with Norfolk based on some combination of coercion or mutual agreement. For example, Norfolk needed DEQE and other permits before it could modify its landfill. The permitting process can serve as a powerful incentive for communities to cooperate with state government agencies. But these are political, not technical, concerns. And DEQE, like most other administrative agencies, is grounded in the traditional policy-administration model that perceives such issues as professionally inappropriate in theory.

SUMMARY

The tradition out of which professional standards and ethics have evolved for public administrators is based on a dichotomy between political representatives who are expected to reflect the will of the people in a democracy, on the one hand, and the administrators who are expected to execute that will, on the other. A small but growing body of literature suggests that the dichotomy does not accurately depict the world of the administrator, who is constantly confronted with political questions in an ever-changing policy environment. Consequently administrators lack adequate professional standards to cope with their working environments. Given this context, DEQE behavior in the Norfolk dispute may not be appropriately described as unethical. What is needed is a set of professional standards that can be applied to the political activity in which administrators become engaged. This will provide a sounder foundation for determining the ethical nature of politically related acts.

NOTES

I acknowledge support for research on solid waste as an environmental policy issue by the Charles A. Lindbergh Fund, the Fried Foundation, Mrs. James D. Newton, and Bentley College.

1. As rainwater percolates through landfills, it filters out harmful chemicals and other toxins. The resulting mixture is referred to as leachate that merges with the groundwater supplies.

2. *In Re Town of Norfolk and the Massachusetts Department of Environmental Quality Engineering: Policy Concerning Sanitary Landfill Design and Construction (310 CMR 19.00 et seq.),* Determination No. DLM 85-1 (Boston: Office of the State Auditor, Division of Local Mandates, April 29, 1985), p. 1.

3. Geri Lambert, "Ground Water Protection: The Policy Crisis of Solid Waste Management in Massachusetts" (master's thesis, Tufts University, 1986), p. 52.

4. The accounts of the dispute are taken from official records of the Division of Local Mandates in the Office of the State Auditor and copies of decisions rendered by the Norfolk Superior Court.

5. The Massachusetts Supreme Judicial Court has recognized a distinction between policy decisions and regulations. The former have been interpreted to be exempt from certain parts of the Massachusetts Administrative Procedures Act, while the latter are not. Justification has been the need to give agencies the flexibility necessary to implement legislative law effectively and efficiently.

6. William H. Welch, "Memorandum on Motion for Summary Judgement," No. 85-1312, p. 3.

7. Henry C. Black, *Black's Law Dictionary,* 5th ed. (St. Paul: West, 1979), p. 496.

8. Frank J. Goodnow, "Politics and Administration," in Jay M. Shafritz and Albert C. Hyde, *Classics of Public Administration,* 2d ed. (Chicago: Dorsey Press, 1987).

9. Ernst Freund, *Administrative Power over Persons and Property* (Chicago: University of Chicago Press, 1928), pp. 97–103.

10. John Dickenson, *Administrative Justice and the Supremacy of Law in the United States* (Cambridge: Harvard University Press, 1927), pp. 105–56.

11. Herbert Simon, *Administrative Behavior,* 3d ed. (New York: Free Press, 1976), p. 58.

12. E. Pendelton Herring, "Public Administration and the Public Interest," in Shafritz and Hyde, *Classics of Public Administration,* p. 75.

13. For example, see John P. Burke, "Reconciling Public Administration and Democracy: The Role of the Responsible Administrator," *Public Administration Review* 49(2) (March–April 1989): 180–85, and Kathryn G. Denhardt, "The Management of Ideals: A Political Perspective on Ethics," *Public Administration Review* 49(2) (March–April 1989): 187–93.

14. Fred Eidlin, "Ethical Problems of Imperfect Knowledge in the Policy Sciences," *Public Administration Quarterly* 11(4) (Winter 1988): 414–15.

15. Charles O. Jones, "Speculative Augmentation in Federal Air Pollution Policy-Making," *Journal of Politics* 36 (May 1974): 438–64.

16. Eidlin, "Ethical Problems," p. 412.

8

Promoting Source Reduction Strategies in the Massachusetts Jewelry Manufacturing Industry: The SE Project

CHARLES BAXTER

The traditional roles of business and government as they pertain to controlling environmental pollution have been evolving as our understanding of the environment, pollution, and pollution control has grown. The role of government has grown from arbitrating disputes regarding environmental nuisances to protecting public goods. Throughout the changing roles, government has resisted the temptation to tell businesses how best to operate. Rather, government has dictated end-of-the-pipe standards that limit the amount of pollutants businesses are allowed to discharge to the environment, thereby leaving them free to run their operations as they wish. As the understanding of the hazards associated with the management of some industrial wastes has increased, so has the cost of properly managing those wastes. Source reduction, or the elimination of waste at the source of generation, has emerged as a key strategy in the management of hazardous substances. Unlike traditional end-of-the-pipe controls, however, it requires a change in the actual manufacturing processes of business. As a result, if government wants to promote the implementation of source reduction, there will need to be a change in the traditional roles of government and industry. This chapter presents a case study of a pilot project that provides an alternative approach to government's role in reducing environmental pollution.

SOURCE REDUCTION

As the management of waste has become more expensive and the environmental consequences of improper waste management are better understood, more attention is being focused on reducing the waste stream rather than handling, shipping, and managing the waste. Source reduction offers many benefits, including reduced waste management costs and lower liability risks, and because it often means upgrading or modifying production process lines, it typically improves efficiency and productivity.[1]

Source reduction is the concept of not creating a waste; one does not have to manage what one does not generate. A source reduction strategy includes good housekeeping practices, input substitution, product reformulation, and/or process modification. Other terms used to describe this preferred method of managing wastes include *waste reduction, waste prevention, waste abatement, waste minimization, waste avoidance, waste elimination,* and *toxic use reduction. Source reduction* is favored over the other terms because it focuses on the production process itself rather than the management or control of waste. The following definition for hazardous waste source reduction was developed by the Massachusetts Department of Environmental Management (DEM) and shall be the accepted definition for the purposes of this chapter: "Any steps taken by a generator to minimize hazardous wastes before they are generated through changes in raw materials or in the manufacturing process."[2]

Planning for and facilitating the safe and efficient management of hazardous waste in Massachusetts is the responsibility of the DEM.[3] DEM began promoting source reduction in 1983, when approximately 65 percent of Massachusetts waste was managed at facilities located in other states.[4] Source reduction was and is viewed as a hazardous waste management strategy that could help bridge the gap between the rate at which hazardous waste is generated in Massachusetts and the available in-state capacity. No experts in the field believe that hazardous waste can be eliminated; there will continue to be the need for hazardous waste treatment and disposal facilities into the foreseeable future.

DEM's initial efforts to promote source reduction were in the realm of technology transfer through conferences and technical seminars on industry-specific source reduction techniques. Although the conferences and seminars were well attended, the implementation rate of source reduction strategies was unimpressive. Despite the obvious economic and environmental advantages associated with source reduction, few companies took full advantage of waste reduction opportunities. Barriers that have been identified include institutional inertia, lack of knowledge about opportunities, and a lack of understanding of the associated benefits.[5]

DEM decided to expand its promotion of source reduction by providing direct technical assistance to companies regarding source reduction strategies. Its objectives for the technical assistance program included the following:

1. Identifying source reduction technologies and techniques being used within an industry sector.

2. Assessing the effectiveness of these technologies and techniques in reducing waste generation.

3. Assessing the impact of source reduction on company operations.

4. Promoting source reduction as a cost-effective waste management strategy to industry.

5. Promoting increased long-term compliance with all state and federal environmental regulations.[6]

Because of the logistical problems with coordinating a statewide program, DEM decided to conduct a limited pilot project. It selected the project based on the spatial distribution of the industry, the types and quantity of wastes generated by the industry, industry support for the project, opportunity to apply experience learned from the project elsewhere, and the ability to increase compliance with environmental regulations within the industry.[7] The jewelry manufacturing industry, which is concentrated in southeastern Massachusetts, was chosen as the target industry for the pilot project.

The jewelry manufacturing industry was subject to a series of increasingly stringent environmental regulations affecting all forms of waste generation. The industry uses a myriad of hazardous materials, which has resulted in regulatory restrictions on waste management practices, as well as air and water discharges. The types of wastes generated by the industry are some of the most toxic hazardous wastes generated by any other industry. They include cyanide, heavy metals, chlorinated solvents and acid, and alkaline cleaners.[8]

As government placed more and more regulatory restrictions on water discharges, industry responded by developing end-of-the-pipe treatment technologies to remove the metals and destroy the cyanide. These wastewater treatment processes generate metallic sludge that must be handled as a hazardous waste. The Hazardous and Solid Waste Amendments of 1984 (HSWA) mandated land bans on a variety of categories of hazardous wastes. Land bans, or the prohibition on the disposal of the waste in hazardous waste landfills, while necessary, reduced the industry's hazardous waste management options and resulted in dramatic increases in the cost of managing their wastes. The land bans affected the primary wastes generated by the jewelry industry, including used solvents and most types of sludge generated by the end-of-the-pipe wastewater treatment works.

The Massachusetts jewelry industry was under added pressure due to a joint program of the U.S. Environmental Protection Agency and the Massachusetts Department of Environmental Protection designed to clean up the Ten Mile River. (The majority of the industry is concentrated along the river and its tributaries.) A study completed as part of the program contained a finding that the river would not meet its designated uses unless the level of pollutants was significantly reduced. Based on this study, new permits were issued that dramatically reduced the allowable discharges of heavy metals and other toxic pollutants, in many cases below levels that could be obtained with conventional end-of-the-pipe technologies. Many smaller shops were going out of business or risking noncompliance with environmental regulations.

THE PILOT PROJECT

DEM began putting together the Southeastern Massachusetts Jewelry Platers' Project (SE Project) in 1986. The original proposal for the project contained three phases. Phase I was the data collection and information dissemination phase. During this initial phase DEM staff were to visit shops that chose to participate in this voluntary program, to complete an inventory of the companies' hazardous materials management systems, and to make recommendations on possible source reduction strategies for the companies. Phase II, currently underway, was designed to provide detailed engineering and economic analyses of source reduction strategies for selected shops. Phase III was not detailed in the original proposal but was envisioned to be the implementation phase, where DEM, working with the companies, would try to fund one or more projects proposed in phase II.[9]

DEM surveyed the jewelry industry in southeastern Massachusetts and identified eight primary Standard Industrial Code (SIC) categories that adequately characterized the industry. Using those SIC codes as a screening tool, DEM identified 102 companies within the study area.[10] The size of the companies ranged from three employees in several small shops to over five thousand at a major manufacturer. All of the companies identified during the survey were invited to participate in on-site source reduction inventories.

DEM efforts to solicit industry's participation in the SE Project were greatly enhanced by the support of two major industry trade associations: the Manufacturing Jewelers and Silversmiths of America and the American Electroplater and Surface Finishers. When DEM started approaching companies, there was an understandable level of apprehension. By disseminating information through the trade associations and continually stressing that it was not a regulatory agency, DEM was able to allay most companies' fears regarding exposure to additional regulatory pressure. Additionally the regulatory agency (Department of Environmental Protection) had indicated that it considered participation in the project as a showing of good-faith effort and would consider it in any enforcement actions.

After completing a training program designed to familiarize them with the industry and the concepts of source reduction, graduate students working in two teams under the direction of the DEM project manager began conducting on-site inventories at participating shops. During phase I (February 1987–July 1988) project staff visited over fifty shops, and the teams of graduate students completed twenty-one source reduction inventories.

The inventories provided valuable data to DEM on the management practices of the companies and formed a basis for reports prepared for the company. The reports summarized each company's manufacturing processes and its hazardous materials management practices and contained recommendations regarding source reduction strategies that would be cost-effective for the company to implement.

Concurrent with the on-site inventories, a series of technology transfer workshops were held at the local chamber of commerce. During phase I there were fourteen workshops and a two-day trade fair. Fifty-two companies participated in at least one of the workshops, and the average attendance for all of the workshops was twenty-six individuals. The workshops played a significant role in the success of the SE Project not only because of the information they provided but also from the dialogue they initiated among the various companies. The workshops had the added benefit of allowing some companies still leery of government agencies to meet the project staff in a nonthreatening environment.

PRELIMINARY FINDINGS

DEM asked the companies that received on-site inventories to provide quantitative information on water, material, and dollar savings associated with source reduction strategies implemented in conjunction with the SE Project. Seven companies provided some quantitative results (table 8.1).

In summary phase I of the pilot project was successful in fulfilling the objectives of the technical assistance program. The conclusions of this phase can be summarized as follows:

- DEM was able to identify proved source reduction technologies or techniques capable of reducing hazardous waste generation, reducing or eliminating water discharges, and reducing air emissions. (Phase II of the project should provide additional information on

Table 8.1
Summary of Reported Savings from Source Reduction Strategies Implemented by Participants in Phase I

Water conservation	
Quantity saved	26,920,000 gallons per year
Dollars saved	incomplete [a]
Metal recovery	
Dollars recovered	225,000 [b]
Solvent substitution	
Quantity replaced	1,233 gallons per year
Dollars saved	20,000

[a]Two companies reported a combined savings of $35,000. The other companies that responded did not list monetary values.
[b]The dollar amount reported reflects only the actual value of the precious and base metals that were recovered and sold. The avoided disposal costs of sludge that would have been generated through the use of conventional treatment technology were not calculated.

Source: information in this table was taken from DEM's Preliminary Report on Phase I Source Reduction Activities: Southeast Jewelry Platers' Project.

different types of source reduction technologies and their adoption by the jewelry industry.)

• Companies successfully implemented source reduction strategies without adversely affecting product quality.

• Companies that chose to implement source reduction strategies realized economic benefits of material and water savings, as well as reduced waste management costs.

• Several companies were able to reduce their regulatory burden through reducing their waste streams.

One of the objectives of the pilot project was to design a project to serve as a model for a broader technical assistance program. The ability to duplicate the success of the SE Project is yet to be determined. Similar projects in Massachusetts and Rhode Island should offer insight into the transferability of the model.

The SE Project clearly demonstrated that government can and should provide technical assistance to industry regarding source reduction. A program that increases the implementation of source reduction benefits the state by reducing the need for solid and hazardous waste management capacity, lowering pollutant loading in the environment, and providing business with an economic advantage over companies employing conventional pollution control technologies.

Because the project was so comprehensive, it is difficult to identify the critical elements that allowed it to succeed. It is important to ask what elements of it were key to its success because that analysis may identify how government can most efficiently target its technical assistance resources. Further research is needed to study the results of the project and survey the industry to identify the elements of the project that most attracted industry.

NOTES

The author was a research associate with the Office of Safe Waste Management, Department of Environmental Management, and served as the project manager for the SE Project during phase I. The views and information presented in this chapter are those of the author and are neither based on nor necessarily reflect those of DEM or DEP.

1. Office of Safe Waste Management, *Hazardous Waste Management in Massachusetts: 1988 Statewide Environmental Impact Report* (Boston: DEM, 1989), p. 35.

2. Lee Dane, "One State's Source Reduction Program: The Massachusetts Perspective," in *Third Annual Massachusetts Hazardous Waste Source Reduction Conference Proceedings* (Boston: DEM/ASME, 1986), p. 18.

3. Massachusetts, like most other states, divides the responsibility for environmental protection among many different agencies. The responsibility for hazardous substances used and discharged into the environment resides in the Department of Environmental Protection (DEP) and the Department of Environmental Management (DEM). DEP is the environmental regulatory agency.

4. DEM, *Hazardous Waste Management in Massachusetts: 1983 Statewide Environmental Impact Report* (Boston: DEM, 1984), p. 3.7.

5. Office of Safe Waste Management, *Hazardous Waste Management in Massachusetts: 1988,* p. 34.

6. DEM, "The Southeast Project: A Technical Assistance Project to Assist the Southeast Jewelry Platers," proposal submitted to the Massachusetts Executive Office of Environmental Affairs (Boston: DEM, 1986).

7. Dane, "One State's Source Reduction Program."

8. Gary E. Hunt, "Hazardous Waste Minimization: Part IV Waste Reduction in the Metal Finishing Industry," *Journal of Air Pollution Control Association* 38(5) (May 1988): 672.

9. DEM, *Southeast Project.*

10. The study area included the communities of Attleboro, North Attleboro, Taunton, Norton, Dighton, Fall River, and Plainville.

_9

Morality, Money, and Motor Cars

NORMAN BOWIE

Environmentalists frequently argue that business has special obligations to protect the environment. Although I agree with the environmentalists on this point, I do not agree with them as to where the obligations lie. Business does not have an obligation to protect the environment over and above what is required by law; however, it does have a moral obligation to avoid intervening in the political arena in order to defeat or weaken environmental legislation. In developing this thesis, several points are in order. First, many businesses have violated important moral obligations, and the violation has had a severe negative impact on the environment. For example, toxic waste haulers have illegally dumped hazardous material, and the environment has been harmed as a result. One might argue that those toxic waste haulers who have illegally dumped have violated a special obligation to the environment. Isn't it more accurate to say that these toxic waste haulers have violated their obligation to obey the law and that in this case the law that has been broken is one pertaining to the environment? Businesses have an obligation to obey the law—environmental laws and all others. Since there are many well-publicized cases of business having broken environmental laws, it is easy to think that business has violated some special obligations to the environment. In fact, what business has done is to disobey the law. Environmentalists do not need a special obligation to the environment to protect the environment against illegal business activity; they need only insist that business obey the laws.

Business has broken other obligations beside the obligation to obey the law and has harmed the environment as a result. Consider the grounding of the Exxon oil tanker _Valdez_ in Alaska. That grounding was allegedly caused by the fact that an inadequately trained crewman was piloting the tanker while the captain was below deck and had been drinking. What needs to be determined is whether Exxon's policies and procedures were sufficiently lax so that it could be said

Exxon was morally at fault. It might be that Exxon is legally responsible for the accident under the doctrine of respondent superior, but Exxon is not thereby morally responsible. Suppose, however, that Exxon's policies were so lax that the company could be characterized as morally negligent. In such a case, the company would violate its moral obligation to use due care and avoid negligence. Although its negligence was disastrous to the environment, Exxon would have violated no special obligation to the environment. It would have been morally negligent.

A similar analysis could be given to the environmentalists' charges that Exxon's cleanup procedures were inadequate. If the charge is true, either Exxon was morally at fault or not. If the procedures had not been implemented properly by Exxon employees, then Exxon is legally culpable, but not morally culpable. On the other hand, if Exxon lied to government officials by saying that its policies were in accord with regulations and/or were ready for emergencies of this type, then Exxon violated its moral obligation to tell the truth. Exxon's immoral conduct would have harmed the environment, but it violated no special obligation to the environment. More important, none is needed. Environmentalists, like government officials, employees, and stockholders, expect that business firms and officials have moral obligations to obey the law, avoid negligent behavior, and tell the truth. In sum, although many business decisions have harmed the environment, these decisions violated no environmental moral obligations. If a corporation is negligent in providing for worker safety, we do not say the corporation violated a special obligation to employees; we say that it violated its obligation to avoid negligent behavior.

The crucial issues concerning business obligations to the environment focus on the excess use of natural resources (the dwindling supply of oil and gas, for instance) and the externalities of production (pollution, for instance). The critics of business want to claim that business has some special obligation to mitigate or solve these problems. I believe this claim is largely mistaken. If business does have a special obligation to help solve the environmental crisis, that obligation results from the special knowledge that business firms have. If they have greater expertise than other constituent groups in society, then it can be argued that, other things being equal, business's responsibilities to mitigate the environmental crisis are somewhat greater. Absent this condition, business's responsibility is no greater than and may be less than that of other social groups. What leads me to think that the critics of business are mistaken?

William Frankena distinguished obligations in an ascending order of the difficulty in carrying them out: avoiding harm, preventing harm, and doing good.[1] The most stringent requirement, to avoid harm, insists no one has a right to render harm on another unless there is a compelling, overriding moral reason to do so. Some writers have referred to this obligation as the moral minimum. A corporation's behavior is consistent with the moral minimum if it causes no avoidable harm to others.

Preventing harm is a less stringent obligation, but sometimes the obligation to prevent harm may be nearly as strict as the obligation to avoid harm. Suppose you are the only person passing a 2-foot-deep working pool where a young child is drowning. There is no one else in the vicinity. Don't you have a strong moral obligation to prevent the child's death? Our obligation to prevent harm is not unlimited, however. Under what conditions must we be good samaritans? Some have argued that four conditions must exist before one is obligated to prevent harm: capability, need, proximity, and last resort.[2] These conditions are all met with the case of the drowning child. There is obviously a need that you can meet since you are both in the vicinity and have the resources to prevent the drowning with little effort; you are also the last resort.

The least strict moral obligation is to do good—to make contributions to society or to help solve problems (inadequate primary schooling in the inner cities, for example). Although corporations may have some minimum obligation in this regard based on an argument from corporate citizenship, the obligations of the corporation to do good cannot be expanded without limit. An injunction to assist in solving societal problems makes impossible demands on a corporation because at the practical level, it ignores the impact that such activities have on profit.

It might seem that even if this descending order of strictness of obligations were accepted, obligations toward the environment would fall into the moral minimum category. After all, the depletion of natural resources and pollution surely harm the environment. If so, wouldn't the obligations business has to the environment be among the strictest obligations a business can have?

Suppose, however, that a businessperson argues that the phrase "avoid harm" usually applies to human beings. Polluting a lake is not like injuring a human with a faulty product. Those who coined the phrase *moral minimum* for use in the business context defined harm as "particularly including activities which violate or frustrate the enforcement of rules of domestic or institutional law intended to protect individuals against prevention of health, safety or basic freedom."[3] Even if we do not insist that the violations be violations of a rule of law, polluting a lake would not count as a harm under this definition. The environmentalists would respond that it would. Polluting the lake may be injuring people who might swim in or eat fish from it. Certainly it would be depriving people of the freedom to enjoy the lake. Although the environmentalist is correct, especially if we grant the legitimacy of a human right to a clean environment, the success of this reply is not enough to establish the general argument.

Consider the harm that results from the production of automobiles. We know statistically that about 50,000 persons per year will die and that nearly 250,000 others will be seriously injured in automobile accidents in the United States alone. Such death and injury, which is harmful, is avoidable. If that is the case, doesn't the avoid-harm criterion require that the production of automobiles for profit cease? Not really. What such arguments point out is that some refinement of the moral minimum standard needs to take place. Take the automobile example. The automobile is itself a good-producing instrument. Because of the advantages of automobiles, society accepts the possible risks that go in using them. Society also accepts many other types of avoidable harm. We take certain risks— ride in planes, build bridges, and mine coal—to pursue advantageous goals. It seems that the high benefits of some activities justify the resulting harms. As long as the risks are known, it is not wrong that some avoidable harm be permitted so that other social and individual goals can be achieved. The avoida- ble-harm criterion needs some sharpening.

Using the automobile as a paradigm, let us consider the necessary refinements for the avoid-harm criterion. It is a fundamental principle of ethics that "ought" implies "can." That expression means that you can be held morally responsible only for events within your power. In the ought-implies-can principle, the over- whelming majority of highway deaths and injuries is not the responsibility of the automaker. Only those deaths and injuries attributable to unsafe automobile design can be attributed to the automaker. The ought-implies-can principle can also be used to absolve the auto companies of responsibility for death and injury from safety defects that the automakers could not reasonably know existed. The company could not be expected to do anything about them.

Does this mean that a company has an obligation to build a car as safe as it knows how? No. The standards for safety must leave the product's cost within the price range of the consumer ("ought implies can" again). Comments about engineering and equipment capability are obvious enough. But for a business, capability is also a function of profitability. A company that builds a maximally safe car at a cost that puts it at a competitive disadvantage and hence threatens its survival is building a safe car that lies beyond the capability of the company.

Critics of the automobile industry will express horror at these remarks, for by making capability a function of profitability, society will continue to have avoida- ble deaths and injuries; however, the situation is not as dire as the critics imagine. Certainly capability should not be sacrificed completely so that profits can be maximized. The decision to build products that are cheaper in cost but are not maximally safe is a social decision that has widespread support. The arguments occur over the line between safety and cost. What we have is a classical trade-off situation. What is desired is some appropriate mix between engineering safety and consumer demand. To say there must be some mix between engineering safety and consumer demand is not to justify all the decisions made by the automobile companies. Ford Motor Company made a morally incorrect choice in placing Pinto gas tanks where it did. Consumers were uninformed, the record of the Pinto in rear-end collisions was worse than that of competitors, and Ford fought government regulations.

Let us apply the analysis of the automobile industry to the issue before us. That analysis shows that an automobile company does not violate its obligation to avoid harm and hence is not in violation of the moral minimum if the trade-off between potential harm and the utility of the products rests on social consensus and competitive realities.

As long as business obeys the environmental laws and honors other standard moral obligations, most harm done to the environment by business has been accepted by society. Through their decisions in the marketplace, we can see that most consumers are unwilling to pay extra for products that are more environmentally friendly than less friendly competitive products. Nor is there much evidence that consumers are willing to conserve resources, recycle, or tax themselves for environmental causes.

Consider the following instances reported in the *Wall Street Journal*.[4] The restaurant chain Wendy's tried to replace foam plates and cups with paper, but customers in the test markets balked. Procter and Gamble offered Downey fabric softener in concentrated form that requires less packaging than ready-to-use products; however the concentrate version is less convenient because it has to be mixed with water. Sales have been poor. Procter and Gamble manufactures Vizir and Lenor brands of detergents in concentrate form, which the customer mixes at home in reusable bottles. Europeans will take the trouble; Americans will not. Kodak tried to eliminate its yellow film boxes but met customer resistance. McDonald's has been testing mini-incinerators that convert trash into energy but often meets opposition from community groups that fear the incinerators will pollute the air. A McDonald's spokesperson points out that the emissions are mostly carbon dioxide and water vapor and are "less offensive than a barbecue." Exxon spent approximately $9,200,000 to "save" 230 otters ($40,000 for each otter). Otters in captivity cost $800. Fishermen in Alaska are permitted to shoot otters as pests.[5] Given these facts, doesn't business have every right to assume that public tolerance for environmental damage is quite high, and hence current legal activities by corporations that harm the environment do not violate the avoid-harm criterion?

Recently environmentalists have pointed out the environmental damage caused by the widespread use of disposable diapers. Are Americans ready to give them up and go back to cloth diapers and the diaper pail? Most observers think not. Procter and Gamble is not violating the avoid-harm criterion by manufacturing Pampers. Moreover, if the public wants cloth diapers, business certainly will produce them. If environmentalists want business to produce products that are friendlier to the environment, they must convince Americans to purchase them. Business will respond to the market. It is the consuming public that has the obligation to make the trade-off between cost and environmental integrity.

Data and arguments of the sort described should give environmental critics of business pause. Nonetheless, these critics are not without counterresponses. For example, they might respond that public attitudes are changing. Indeed, they point out, during the Reagan deregulation era, the one area where the public supported government regulations was in the area of environmental law. In addition, *Fortune* predicts environmental integrity as the primary demand of society on business in the 1990s.[6]

More important, they might argue that environmentally friendly products are at a disadvantage in the marketplace because they have public good characteristics. After all, the best situation for the individual is one where most other people use environmentally friendly products but he or she does not, hence reaping the benefit of lower cost and convenience. Since everyone reasons this way, the real demand for environmentally friendly products cannot be registered in the market. Everyone is understating the value of his or her preference for environmentally friendly products. Hence, companies cannot conclude from market behavior that the environmentally unfriendly products are preferred.

Suppose the environmental critics are right that the public goods characteristic of environmentally friendly products creates a market failure. Does that mean the companies are obligated to stop producing these environmentally unfriendly products? I think not, and I propose that we use the four conditions attached to the prevent-harm obligation to show why not. There is a need, and certainly corporations that cause environmental problems are in proximity. However, environmentally clean firms, if there are any, are not in proximity at all, and most business firms are not in proximity with respect to most environmental problems. In other words, the environmental critic must limit his or her argument to the environmental damage a business actually causes. The environmentalist might argue that Procter and Gamble ought to do something about Pampers; I do not see how an environmentalist can use the avoid-harm criterion to argue that Procter and Gamble should do something about acid rain. But even narrowing the obligation to damage actually caused will not be sufficient to establish an obligation to pull a product from the market because it damages the environment or even to go beyond what is legally required to protect the environment. Even for damage actually done, both the high cost of protecting the environment and the competitive pressures of business make further action to protect the environment beyond the capability of business. This conclusion would be more serious if business were the last resort, but it is not.

Traditionally it is the function of the government to correct for market failure. If the market cannot register the true desires of consumers, let them register their preferences in the political arena. Even fairly conservative economic thinkers allow government a legitimate role in correcting market failure. Perhaps the responsibility for energy conservation and pollution control belongs with the government.

Although I think consumers bear a far greater responsibility for preserving and protecting the environment than they have actually exercised, let us assume that the basic responsibility rests with the government. Does that let business off the hook? No. Most of business's unethical conduct regarding the environment occurs in the political arena.

Far too many corporations try to have their cake and eat it too. They argue that it is the job of government to correct for market failure and then use their influence and money to defeat or water down regulations designed to conserve and protect the environment.[7] They argue that consumers should decide how much conservation and protection the environment should have, and then they try to interfere with the exercise of that choice in the political arena. Such behavior is inconsistent and ethically inappropriate. Business has an obligation to avoid intervention in the political process for the purpose of defeating and weakening environmental regulations. Moreover, this is a special obligation to the environment since business does not have a general obligation to avoid pursuing its own parochial interests in the political arena. Business need do nothing wrong when it seeks to influence tariffs, labor policy, or monetary policy. Business does do something wrong when it interferes with the passage of environmental legislation. Why?

First, such a noninterventionist policy is dictated by the logic of the business's argument to avoid a special obligation to protect the environment. Put more formally:

1. Business argues that it escapes special obligations to the environment because it is willing to respond to consumer preferences in this matter.
2. Because of externalities and public goods considerations, consumers cannot express their preferences in the market.
3. The only other viable forum for consumers to express their preferences is in the political arena.
4. Business intervention interferes with the expression of these preferences.
5. Since point 4 is inconsistent with point 1, business should not intervene in the political process.

The importance of this obligation in business is even more important when we see that environmental legislation has special disadvantages in the political arena. Public choice reminds us that the primary interest of politicians is being reelected. Government policy will be skewed in favor of policies that provide benefits to an influential minority as long as the greater costs are widely dispersed. Politicians will also favor projects where benefits are immediate and where costs can be postponed to the future. Such strategies increase the likelihood that a politician will be reelected.

What is frightening about the environmental crisis is that both the conservation of scarce resources and pollution abatement require policies that go contrary to a politician's self-interest. The costs of cleaning up the environment are immediate and huge, yet the benefits are relatively long range (many of them exceedingly long range). Moreover, a situation where the benefits are widely dispersed and the costs are large presents a twofold problem. The costs are large enough so that all voters will likely notice them and in certain cases are catastrophic for individuals (e.g., for those who lose their jobs in a plant shutdown).

Given these facts and the political realities they entail, business opposition to environmental legislation makes a very bad situation much worse. Even if consumers could be persuaded to take environmental issues more seriously, the externalities, opportunities to free ride, and public goods characteristics of the environment make it difficult for even enlightened consumers to express their true preference for the environment in the market. The fact that most environmental legislation trades immediate costs for future benefits makes it difficult for politicians concerned about reelection to support it. Hence it is also difficult for enlightened consumers to have their preferences for a better environment honored in the political arena. Since lack of business intervention seems necessary, and might even be sufficient, for adequate environmental legislation, it seems business has an obligation not to intervene. Nonintervention would prevent the harm of not having the true preferences of consumers for a clean environment revealed. Given business's commitment to satisfying preferences, opposition to having these preferences expressed seems inconsistent as well.

The extent of this obligation to avoid intervening in the political process needs considerable discussion by ethicists and other interested parties. Businesspeople will surely object that if they are not permitted to play a role, Congress and state legislators will make decisions that will put them at a severe competitive disadvantage. For example, if the United States develops stricter environmental controls than other countries do, foreign imports will have a competitive advantage over domestic products. Shouldn't business be permitted to point that out? Moreover, any legislation that places costs on one industry rather than another confers advantages on other industries. The cost to the electric utilities from regulations designed to reduce the pollution that causes acid rain will give advantages to natural gas and perhaps even solar energy. Shouldn't the electric utility industry be permitted to point that out?

These questions pose difficult questions, and my answer to them should be considered highly tentative. I believe the answer to the first question is "yes" and the answer to the second is "no." Business does have a right to insist that the regulations apply to all those in the industry. Anything else would seem to violate norms of fairness. Such issues of fairness do not arise in the second case. Since natural gas and solar do not contribute to acid rain and since the costs of acid rain cannot be fully captured in the market, government intervention through regulation is simply correcting a market failure. With respect to acid rain, the electric utilities do have an advantage they do not deserve. Hence they have no right to try to protect it.

Legislative bodies and regulatory agencies need to expand their staffs to include technical experts, economists, and engineers so that the political process can be both neutral and highly informed about environmental matters. To gain the respect of business and the public, its performance needs to improve. Much more needs to be said to make any contention that business ought to stay out of the political debate theoretically and practically possible. Perhaps these suggestions point the way for future discussion.

Ironically business might best improve its situation in the political arena by taking on an additional obligation to the environment. Businesspersons often have more knowledge about environmental harms and the costs of cleaning them up. They may often have special knowledge about how to prevent environmental harm in the first place. Perhaps business has a special duty to educate the public and to promote environmentally responsible behavior.

Business has no reticence about leading consumer preferences in other areas. Advertising is a billion-dollar industry. Rather than blaming consumers for not purchasing environmentally friendly products, perhaps some businesses might make a commitment to capture the environmental niche. I have not seen much imagination on the part of business in this area. Far too many advertisements with an environmental message are reactive and public relations driven. Recall those by oil companies showing fish swimming about the legs of oil rigs. An educational campaign that encourages consumers to make environmentally friendly decisions in the marketplace would limit the necessity for business activity in the political arena. Voluntary behavior that is environmentally friendly is morally preferable to coerced behavior. If business took greater responsibility for educating the public, the government's responsibility would be lessened. An educational campaign aimed at consumers would likely enable many businesses to do good while simultaneously doing very well.

Hence business does have obligations to the environment, although these obligations are not found where the critics of business place them. Business has no special obligation to conserve natural resources or to stop polluting over and above its legal obligations. It does have an obligation to avoid intervening in the political arena to oppose environmental regulations, and it has a positive obligation to educate consumers. The benefits of honoring these obligations should not be underestimated.

NOTES

The title for this chapter was suggested by Susan Bernick, a graduate student in the University of Minnesota philosophy department.

1. William Frankena, *Ethics,* 2d ed. (Englewood Cliffs, N.J.: Prentice-Hall, 1973), p. 47. Actually Frankena has four principles of prima facie duty under the principle of beneficence: one ought not to inflict evil or harm; one ought to prevent evil or harm; one ought to remove evil; and one ought to do or promote good.

2. John G. Simon, Charles W. Powers, and Jon P. Gunneman, *The Ethical Investor: Universities and Corporate Responsibility* (New Haven, Conn.: Yale University Press, 1972), pp. 22–25.

3. Ibid., p. 21.

4. Alicia Swasy, "For Consumers, Ecology Comes Second," *Wall Street Journal,* August 23, 1988, p. B1.

5. Jerry Alder, "Alaska after Exxon," *Newsweek,* September 18, 1989, p. 53.

6. Andrew Kupfer, "Managing Now for the 1990s," *Fortune,* September 26, 1988, pp. 46–47.

7. I owe this point to Gordon Rands, a Ph.D. student in the Carlson School of Management. Indeed the tone of the chapter has shifted considerably as a result of his helpful comments.

II

PUBLIC ATTITUDES AND INVOLVEMENT IN ENVIRONMENTAL ISSUES

"I Am No Greenpeacer, But . . . " or Environmentalism, Risk Communication, and the Lower Middle Class

MARK SAGOFF

Car and Driver, a magazine popular among macho motorists, has come out for "the global environment."[1] For two decades, the magazine railed against "safety twits,"[2] Ralph Nader,[3] the Clean Air Act,[4] eco-fascists,[5] endangered species programs,[6] seat belts and air bags,[7] speed limits,[8] welfare cheats,[9] and all regulations devised by "the bloated civil service, the feeders at the public trough" who "still thrive in all their pompous, isolated, self-serving, over-stuffed glory."[10] In the November 1988 issue, however, Brock Yates, who for years assailed the bureaucracy, wrote:

Like it or not, our beloved car is an irksome source of pollution, urban congestion, and excessive fossil-fuel consumption. Calls for an end to the CAFE [corporate average fuel economy] standards—recently heard from no less an eminence than General Motors president Robert Stempel—seem selfish and simple-minded. I am no Greenpeacer, but I believe we face larger problems on this globe than the search for more horsepower-per-cubic-inch or the financial welfare of the auto industry.[11]

In the August 1989 *Car and Driver,* William Jeannes, a columnist who historically echoed Yates's diatribes against environmental regulations, joined the bandwagon: "If you are concerned about planet Earth and the cars you drive on it," he wrote, "you understand that an efficient automobile is one that . . . contributes as little carbon dioxide as possible to fuel the greenhouse effect."[12]

Tough-minded, hard-working American men, the kind who know how to strap a twelve-gauge shotgun on the back of a pickup, could always count on a few magazines—*Sport Truck, Car and Driver,* and *Motor Trend,* for example—to stand up against doomsaying environmental and bureaucratic wimps. These magazines, which have long defended the oil and automotive industry against the likes of Ralph Nader and the Sierra Club, have now gone over to the enemy. The

November 1989 issue of *Sport Truck* calls on Detroit to provide technology that is friendly to the environment. "Even if performance has to be compromised by clean air legislation," an editorial concedes, "we're just going to have to bite the bullet. Because when our enthusiasm butts heads with our health, something has to give."[13]

FOUR RULES FOR RISK COMMUNICATION

In supporting CAFE standards, *Car and Driver* did not lose all the old-time religion.[14] It still fulminates volcanically against governmental efforts to improve safety of any kind, especially highway safety. Brock Yates recently praised "Peach State libertarian marksmen" who potshotted unattended radar units "Smokey" had set up to slow down Georgia drivers.[15] In rhetoric his readers have come to expect, Yates celebrated "the latent anarchism of the American people,"[16] who will pick up a rifle before letting anyone tell them how fast to drive their cars.[17]

Car and Driver, which out-Herods the *American Rifleman* in trying to keep the government off our backs, nevertheless has adopted an environmentalist image.[18] Why? Why are environmental restrictions acceptable when all other regulations, especially safety regulations, remain anathema to this popular journal? How can such a macho magazine extol risk taking and at the same time speak for the trees?

Readers of *Car and Driver* were quick to pose these questions. "An endorsement of tighter CAFE standards from the magazine obsessed with performance and freedom from government regulation. What gives?" wrote a man from Conyers, Georgia, in a letter in the October 1989 issue. "When it comes to breaking the speed limit and opposing radar detector bans, you're right there. Now you become de facto Naderites by endorsing a regulation that threatens the lives of Mustangs, ZR-1s, etc."[19]

Readers may rest assured that *Car and Driver* continues to oppose paternalistic regulations, such as air bag and seat belt requirements, that try to make driving less dangerous. CAFE standards, however, do not attempt to limit one's personal freedom to drive as one likes. Rather, these standards seek to protect nature from pollution and, perhaps, to make America less dependent on the Organization for Petroleum Exporting Countries (OPEC). Accordingly, in calling for tougher CAFE standards, *Car and Driver* does not necessarily endorse safety regulations but supports nature, nationalism, patriotism, and so on. These values are right up there with breaking speed limits and ignoring radar detector bans.

Readers of *Car and Driver* are not, in general, risk averse. They oppose speed limits and air bags. That they may court danger personally implies nothing, however, about their attitude toward nature and the environment. You do not have to be risk averse to favor policies that promote energy independence or protect the integrity and beauty of the natural environment. You do not have to be a "safety twit" to want fuel economy; people who drive fast can brake for animals.

A person who owns a fast car and drives it that way—a person who likes to take risks—may be as concerned about nature as someone who drinks Perrier and watches birds for fun. This concern is likely to lie in a moral, cultural, or even religious respect for nature rather than in a quest for personal safety. This environmental ethic has little to do with risk assessment, risk management, and risk perception. Rather, it lies in a collective sense of moral responsibility many of us feel toward each other and toward the natural world.

In this chapter, I examine political attitudes among lower-middle-class Americans, particularly white men, who, according to public opinion surveys, are swelling the ranks of the environmental movement. I want to use what some people may describe as "the greening of the rednecks" as an occasion to propose four theses as cardinal rules of risk communication:

1. Risk communicators need to address concerns, values, and problems that may have little to do with risk.
2. Risk communicators have to communicate about risk primarily in ethical, not economic, terms.
3. Nature is more important than the environment.
4. Law can be a powerful legitimating instrument.

The first thesis—that risk communication may have less to do with risk than is commonly thought—will not sound paradoxical to those who know the literature. The literature of risk analysis distinguishes between risk as an objective physical property of events (one may call this the magnitude of a risk) and risk as a social construct (the meaning of a risk).[20] Thus, the risks involved, say, in jumping and being pushed from the same window may carry exactly the same objective magnitudes but have entirely different meanings. Indeed, the meaning of a risk, which arises from its social and moral circumstances, can depend as little on its objective magnitude as its objective magnitude depends on its social meaning.

Efforts at risk communication (I believe many experts will agree) cannot succeed if they address only the objective magnitude of various technological risks. Rather, the decisive concerns may lie in the relationships of power, culture, and mutual respect or disrespect among various participants within a political process.[21] These participants may argue over the objective assessment of risk, but the deeper conflict often lies in political disagreements—that is, in differing conceptions of our national goals and the way we should achieve them. One may express doubts, for example, about the safety of genetic engineering but be concerned more fundamentally about the moral character of "artificial" animals or "man-made" life.[22]

The second rule follows as a corollary from the first. Many experts, even those who urge the relevance of economic risk-benefit calculations, concede that ethical and cultural factors are often more decisive than economic ones in making people accept or resent various hazards. Arguments over the objective magnitude of a particular hazard, indeed, may skirt the main question, which is whether the risk, whatever its magnitude, is politically and ethically acceptable. Risk communicators have to be able to discuss hazards in ethical and cultural rather than just in economic and scientific terms. The objective magnitude of a risk, within wide limits, may not really matter.

In 1969 Chauncey Starr pointed out that a lot of moral factors influence the acceptability of a risk, "the most obvious being the difference by several orders of magnitude in society's willingness to accept 'voluntary' and 'involuntary' risk."[23] The concepts of voluntary and involuntary are themselves open to a great deal of interpretation, moreover, and may implicate many other values. Accordingly, scholars have described scores of ethical concerns besides voluntariness that endow hazards with different meanings—reasons that explain why some hazards remain culturally acceptable while others are not, even if their costs and benefits are the same.[24] These values include the familiarity of a risk, its connection (however slight) to something dreadful, like cancer, the remoteness of its source, and the uncertainty surrounding it. Pollution, which is primarily an aesthetic or cultural rather than a scientific concept, particularly engages ethical and political sentiments, whether it is dangerous or not.[25] We may resist or resent pollution more because of aesthetic and cultural revulsion than any kind of fear, even if we continue to talk about pollution in the technical context of risk.

To see this possibility, imagine that you spit continually into a large glass, which you keep in the refrigerator, until it is full. Now imagine that someone asks you to drink it down, explaining that must be perfectly safe since you swallow your spit all the time. You may not relish drinking it even though it is safe, and you might even resent being told you are irrational for not swigging it down. Perhaps we are irrational, in a sense, to decide what we are willing to eat, drink, or breathe on grounds other than those of objective safety and health. Yet it also seems foolish to dismiss as irrational the cultural, aesthetic, and moral distinctions on which social life may ultimately depend.

NATURE, LAW, AND THE ENVIRONMENT

We now come to the third rule, which emphasizes the importance of nature as distinct from environment. The concept of nature suggests our common birthright or the legacy of the past—perhaps a gift from God. The concept of the environment, on the other hand, refers to surroundings that we may manipulate according to our interest and profit. Thus, we may perceive nature as an object of love and respect, while we regard the environment as a collection of resources to be managed prudently and efficiently over the long run. In that event, moral concerns we may have about the preservation of nature may not be well expressed in the context of managing, say, the environmental commons.

Consider, for example, the way Exxon handled its public relations after the recent unpleasantness in Prince William Sound. The corporation pointed out, correctly I assume, that the environment would bounce back after a few years. Natural resources (fishing, for example) would sustain no long-term damage, and

Exxon promised to compensate those who suffered short-term economic loss. Exxon could not understand what upset people so much, since stocks of fish would return to normal levels in a few years and everyone would be paid off for interim losses.

This response ignored what many Americans, on seeing the dead otters on television, may have perceived as the most serious crime: the crime against nature. Many Americans felt Exxon should have recognized and apologized for the sin of defiling the beauty, integrity, and innocence of nature on such a large scale. That recognition and that apology never came. Moral concepts like sin and forgiveness may be central to our culture and history as a people. These concepts may not always be available, however, to corporate executives. They may speak the positive language of economics; they may be less comfortable with the concepts of good and evil than the concepts of benefits and costs.[26] The American people, however, are not afraid of—and may even expect—normative or ethical discourse. Americans are not embarrassed by talk about good and evil; they are not hesitant to discuss moral judgments in moral terms.

At one time, perhaps, the concepts of economics—risk-benefit analysis, efficient allocation of resources, and so on—might have carried a normative significance. In the years prior to the New Deal, for example, environmentalism coincided generally with conservationism, a movement, represented, for example, by Gifford Pinchot, which sought to make efficient use of resources in order to maximize the long-run benefits nature offers people.[27] Pinchot and others argued that society would be happier or somehow better off if it maximized in this way the production of goods and services that consumers wanted to buy. A literature of environmental economics developed during the 1960s that extended this normative argument to pollution control and other problems of environmental policy.[28]

During the New Deal and after, however, the environmental movement returned to its roots in Puritanism and romanticism, as represented, for example, by Henry David Thoreau, Ralph Waldo Emerson, and John Muir, to emphasize the religious idea that humanity is rich in relationship to the number of things it can afford to leave alone.[29] During the 1970s and 1980s, environmentalists argued that consumption is not itself a value and that societies that maximize consumption or consumer satisfaction do not become better off in any morally meaningful sense. Money, after basic needs are met, does not buy happiness. Environmentalists argued that we will be happier, healthier, and wiser if we try to live in respectful harmony with nature rather than exploit it, however efficiently that is done.

Readers of magazines like *Sport Truck* and *Car and Driver* may also tend to make judgments in moral terms—in terms of some ethical or cultural rule or principle—rather than according to academic theories. *Car and Driver* does not print risk-benefit calculations about seat belts and speed limits because it knows its readers regard these as matters not of prudence but of principle. Arguments framed in terms of resource economics—analyses of costs, benefits, efficiency, social discounting—are likely to appall rather than to appeal to environmentalists who view obligations to nature in ethical rather than in economic terms. The protection of nature seems to them to be a question of principle, not just a question of prudence.[30]

Finally, industry would be much better served, I shall argue, if it looked on pollution control law as an opportunity to protect nature in cost-effective ways. Industry now pays high costs associated with pollution control policies that are proved failures. Industry now has the opportunity to join the political mainstream in developing a regulatory system that will work incrementally and efficiently to decrease wastes and emissions. The conservativism of industry, however, may lead it to oppose rather than to propose legislation that could make more environmental progress at lower costs. Industry might rather bear those ills it has, in other words, than to rush to others that it knows not of.

In the past, corporations have enjoyed a strong bargaining position with the government under statutes—the Clean Air Act is a good example—that are so cumbersome that they are nearly impossible to enforce.[31] Statutory amendments now under consideration (the permitting requirements of President Bush's proposed Clean Air Act, for example) may be easier to enforce and therefore are more likely to lead to the environmental improvements the public expects. Industry might do well to support rather than to oppose more cost-effective and more enforceable statutes, including permit systems, that will work to reduce waste and pollution. By helping to frame and to enact these statutes—statutes that not only promise but also can deliver a cleaner environment—industry could join the political mainstream and reap the legitimacy and credibility that comes with supporting environmentally sound regulation.

The alternative will involve deeper dousing in strict and joint-and-several liability schemes and the prospect of even tougher criminal sanctions. Thus, business leaders have every reason to join with environmentalists and other Americans generally in getting behind statutes that will give us progress and not just promises in protecting nature and improving the environment.

DO REAL AMERICANS CARE
ABOUT THE ENVIRONMENT?

At the time *Car and Driver* announced for "the global environment," the *London Economist* cited a speech by Margaret Thatcher "that marked her conversion from Iron Lady to Green Goddess":

Hard on her heels trod Mikhail Gorbachev, who made the environment a theme of an address to the United Nations; George Bush, who built part of his election campaign on a promise to clean up America; and the EEC Commission, trying to outdo its member governments in greenery. Never have so many politicians seized so quickly on one idea.[32]

Politicians, according to the *Economist,* "are responding to an extraordinary shift in public opinion, apparent all over the world."[33] Public opinion polls amply document this trend, at least in the United States. A *New York Times*–CBS poll in June 1989 found 80 percent of those polled agreed while 14 percent disagreed with the statement, "Protecting the environment is so important that requirements and standards cannot be too high, and continuing environmental improvements must be made at all costs."[34] These results show an increase since 1981, when yeas and nays were nearly equal.[35]

What may strike us as surprising about the rush of politicians to the environment is that they need not (and they do not) change their other political colors when they paint themselves green. President Bush, for example, planted trees in Spokane, yet he spoke against gun control and for a constitutional amendment against desecrating the flag.

A pro-environment position, then, seems not to imply anything about any other salient political issue. In defending the environment, therefore, the president did not have to become more liberal with respect, say, to the death penalty, abortion rights, or the drug problem. The environmental bandwagon—unlike gun control or abortion rights—apparently has room for everybody. Environmentalism plays as well in Peoria as on Martha's Vineyard.

Where, then, does environmentalism fit in the political spectrum? Some have argued that environmentalism fits best within upper-middle-class suburban liberalism, particularly in its opposition to laissez-faire capitalism and its support for paternalism and the welfare state.[36] Social scientists, however, have described environmental concern as a belief system strongly held by the American public but only weakly constrained by or integrated in broader political ideologies.[37] As two researchers put this thought, environmentalism is "an issue in search of a home."[38]

A lot may depend on how one characterizes or measures the concept of environmental concern.[39] Scholars have long observed a tension, even an antagonism, between a prudential conservation ethic or gospel of efficiency, which endorses long-run, cost-benefit accounting, and a moral environmental ethic, which rebels against utilitarian thinking and might be associated historically with Aldo Leopold and John Muir. This distinction can be drawn politically today between prudential and ethical environmentalism or, roughly, those who seek to protect nature for the sake of exploiting resources efficiently and those who wish to protect nature for its own sake.[40]

The distinction between prudential and ethical environmentalism may help to explain an anomaly that has long puzzled social scientists. Environmentalism has become an overwhelming political force even though "traditional American values and beliefs pose barriers to the development of a strong pro-environment orientation."[41] According to this analysis, as Americans squared off against the apparently limitless natural frontier, they formed a "dominant social paradigm" (to use Dennis Pirages's term) around values like materialism, unfettered progress, and personal liberty.[42] Researchers have established that in many aspects, this dominant social paradigm (e.g., support for laissez-faire government, insistence on property rights, faith in science and technology, commitment to individual liberty, and faith in economic growth and material abundance) relates

strongly, but negatively, to environmental concerns.[43] Environmentalists themselves have called for a paradigm shift away from "the basic values which have
built our society" and lie "at the root of the ecological crisis."[44]

Social scientists and analysts even today reason that since lower-middle-class
Americans—the "silent" or "populist" majority—strongly share the dominant
social paradigm and since this paradigm conflicts so deeply and thoroughly with
a protective approach to nature, the lower middle class has to oppose laws
protecting the environment. Only upper-middle-class suburban professionals,
who prefer the welfare state over the dominant paradigm, could favor environmental protection. "This reaffirms the importance of liberalism as a component
of the broader ideological systems from which environmental attitudes are
drawn."[45]

As candidate Reagan campaigned for the White House, his advisers, following
this plausible analysis, construed environmental concern as a crochet of upper-
middle-class professionals, mostly suburbanites, who sought to protect the
amenities they enjoyed. These advisers aimed the campaign, then, at farmers,
workers, businessmen, and lower-middle-class whites who, they thought, sought
to be free from environmental constraints.[46] Swept into office by this constituency, President Reagan entered the White House intent on rolling back environmental regulations.[47]

During the early Reagan years a group of writers made explicit what his
campaign implied: environmentalism represented the "conservativism of the
liberals" and expressed itself as a suburban agrarianism in opposition to industry,
farming, business, and other forms of production that might swell the numbers of
the privileged class.[48] In short, environmentalists constituted a new aristocracy,
opposed to traditional American values, who sought to maintain their privileged
status against economic and social growth.[49] "Having made it to the top, they
become far more concerned with preventing others from climbing the ladder
behind them, than in making it up a few more rungs themselves."[50]

Several social scientists in the 1970s, aware of this political analysis,[51] tested
whether environmental concern was indeed rooted in the upper-middle-class
intelligentsia.[52] These writers quickly dismissed conclusions drawn from evidence that "environmental groups . . . have an upper middle-class membership."[53] Rather, these scientists have reached a virtual consensus that "the
link between the upper-middle class and environmental activism is a link between socioeconomic status and factors of political activism, rather than a link
between the upper-middle class and environmental concern."[54] Indeed, as one
writer notes, the most vocal, coordinated opposition to environmentalism comes
from the top levels or corporate management; therefore, "the *opponents* of
environmentalism come closer to being an elite than do core environmentalists."[55]

Recent studies and public opinion polls point unambiguously to the conclusion
that "support for environmentalism is diffuse in the population as a whole."[56]
These studies, according to one review article, "are showing that environmental

concern is broad-based in American society, cutting across nearly all so-cioeconomic categories."[57]

The question arises, then, why environmentalism plays as well in Peoria as on Martha's Vineyard. Are the issues the same? Are lower-middle-class workers, farmers, and small businessmen in Birmingham and Baton Rouge defending the same environment as well-to-do liberals in Brookline and Bethesda? Are political constituencies that disagree on nearly everything else truly united behind one environmental banner? Are environmentalists motivated primarily by prudential concerns about safety, health, and the coming ecological crisis? Have long-standing religious and ethical beliefs, which may be consistent with the dominant social paradigm, in contrast, brought the lower middle class into the environmental consensus?

It is reasonable to conjecture that if Americans in the dominant paradigm are optimistic, freedom-loving, risk-taking, wealth-seeking individualists, then they would tend to scoff at warnings about the so-called ecological crises. The scientific evidence, for example, about the greenhouse effect remains uncertain and even contradictory; why, then, listen to a lot of nattering nabobs of negativity? If Americans were secure in their local communities—if the air they breathe and the streams in which they fish remained the same—they might not worry about purveyors of doom who prognosticated global change.

Faced with persistent ecological and environmental degradation in their own immediate communities, however, Americans may not so quickly dismiss concerns about the global environment. Love of community belongs to the dominant social paradigm. People within that paradigm may regard the continuity of nature as necessary for the maintenance and identity of communities to which they belong. When communities are threatened by large technological, economic, and political changes, therefore, people may find predictions of environmental disaster more credible. Security of a moral and visceral sort requires that nature—in a romantic and religious sense, not merely as a collection of resources—remain intact. It should be no surprise, therefore, that the environment has become a populist issue throughout the world.

ENVIRONMENTALISM AND THE LOWER MIDDLE CLASS

To examine more closely the place of environmentalism in the political spectrum, let us turn to the *Farm Journal,* in which, during the 1970s, farmers voiced resentment against "government controls" that "engulf our every move."[58] An Indiana farmer writing in the *Journal* in January 1976 described an attitude then prevalent toward environmental regulations among farmers:

EPA is another non-elected, self-perpetuating group with awesome power. No one dares question them. Congressmen. How can Russell Train be permitted to use dirty tricks, scare tactics and unproven theories to influence people to support him?[59]

The following month, the *Farm Journal,* in an editorial titled "'Organic Foods': Today's Big Rip-Off," notes that "only ignorance of nature leads one to label as 'artificial' fertilizers which are mined from the earth or made from 'natural' gas."[60] In the following issue, an article titled "Will You Go to Jail over Erosion?" inveighs against agricultural zoning regimes that prevent farmers from selling their land to developers. According to the article, environmentalists "want to preserve open land because they like to look at it, but they're trying to preserve the farms without preserving the farmers."[61]

How does the *Farm Journal* view environmentalism today? At about the same time *Car and Driver* started speaking for the trees, the *Farm Journal* also greened. In the June–July 1989 issue, the editors proudly introduced a regular column, titled "Environment Today," to let farmers know, for example, that the overapplication of fertilizers by corn growers accounts for the bulk of groundwater nitrate problems.[62] In 1976 the *Journal* castigated organic foods; in 1989 it praised organic and low-input farming as the ways farmers may make themselves less dependent on the chemical industry.[63] In 1976 a typical *Journal* article carried the title "Coming: A New Wave of Hard-Hitting Insecticides."[64] Twelve years later, a representative title reads, "Are Pesticides Losing Their Punch?"[65]

For one explanation of this change, look in the January 1989 issue, where an editorial breaks ranks with the past.[66] "Before I say anything else," the author, Gene Logson, begins, "understand that I eat red meat; red, white and medium rare. I know which side my bread is buttered on, because I spread it a quarter-inch thick." Logson establishes his credentials as a two-fisted cattleman with no patience for "diet dillies, organic nuts, and Bambi lovers" and others overconcerned about risk. "Having said that," he continues, "allow me to say a good word for animal rightists." The good word is that animal rights advocates threaten not the independent family livestock farmer but animal megafactories. Logson believes that if factory farm practices continue, competition may drive the world's egg production into four counties in Arkansas. All beef will be fed in five counties in Colorado and Texas. All hogs will be born in Missouri and fattened in Iowa:

If large-scale animal factories continue to have their way, you will slowly be pushed out of the hog and beef business just as happened to 95% of the chicken farmers.

On the other hand, if animal rightists have their way, the livestock industry will return to smaller, family-sized farms.[67]

This argument takes up a familiar populist theme: the resentment small and middle-sized farmers direct against larger, better-capitalized operations that use economies of scale to undersell them. It also relates a love-of-nature issue, animal rights, to concerns about protecting the economic viability of small farmers and farming communities.

Similarly articles in which the *Farm Journal* reversed its view of organic farming do not argue that low-input methods will produce a safer or a more nutritious product. Rather, the *Journal* advocates low-input farming just insofar as it liberates farmers from their dependence on chemicals and thus allows them to keep the money that would otherwise pass through to the chemical industry. The argument for low-input farming, if it concerns health at all, concerns the economic health of farming communities. To protect the land, to maintain traditional technologies, and to engage in labor-intensive husbandry makes sense economically for small farmers who want to stay in business. Without the environmental brake, the technological treadmill in agriculture would lead quickly to the industrialization of production and therefore to the demise of the small operator. Farmers have good reasons to side with environmentalists against this process.

A century ago, southern populists excoriated corporations and trusts that, "in their insatiate greed" plundered the wealth of America and drove farmers into poverty.[68] The ethical and political sentiments that united farmers in the West and South against the trusts a century ago may be alive and well today. When large agrichemical businesses show big profits, farmers may treat them with suspicion, especially when those farmers, who grow the crops, have nothing to show for their pains but debt. Environmentalism is a populist issue; the protection of nature could become a rallying call today as free silver was a hundred years ago.

Exactly a century ago, when the populist movement in the United States grew to its height, the People's party formed in the South. By 1896 the party established a coalition with the Democrats, representing farmers, workers, and members of the lower middle class who "looked around them and saw what seemed to them an unhealthy growth of big business, monopolistic industries brought into existence by the demands of Civil War technology, saw changing mores and class alignments, [and] saw a breakneck pace of national life that seemed to be leaving the farmer and his ways behind."[69]

The populist fusion party lost the presidential election in 1896 but not by a large margin. In later political campaigns, this alliance did help to elect presidents, including the two Roosevelts, who combined the reform of capitalism and the protection of nature in one program. Teddy Roosevelt was elected as both a conservationist and a trust-buster; Franklin Roosevelt stood strongly for environmental protection and the regulation of industry. Thus, it may be a cyclical event—it surely seems to be an American tradition—that political movements arise that combine distrust of big business and a desire to protect nature and the environment. Analogies may be drawn between populism historically and the environmental movement today.

The central ideological commitment of populism in the past, as one commentator has said, follows from the "deification of nature."[70] He continues:

The natural/artificial dichotomy, one suspects, also underlies much of the emotional reaction of populism to such things as banks, gold, Eastern manners, lace cuffs, tie wigs, and foppery of all kinds. . . . The impression is conveyed that everything good, decent, homely, simple, honest, in a word *natural,* is about to be felled, murdered, raped, crucified by something phony, mannered, effete, superfluous, in a word artificial.[71]

Sentiments of this sort mix easily with the resentments of the small against the great—resentments small farmers, small businessmen, and those who live in small towns direct against the rich and powerful who live in distant cities. These beliefs reflect, in a way, problems with the way power (not just risk) is distributed in society. If technologies, whether represented by railroads, banks, or factories, confer too much power on too few people, if the many have no sense of participating in the decisions the few make about how these technologies are used, then the many are likely to regard these technologies as nefarious.

The populist crusade in America stands as well on a second principle: egalitarianism and the ethic of hard work. This idea, again a Jeffersonian theme, sees virtue as residing in the simple people, who make up the overwhelming majority of Americans, and in their collective traditions. The simple people are continually victimized, according to this populist mythology, by greedy and evil persons who control finance, industry, and technology. These captains of industry are not to be trusted. As Woody Guthrie put the thought, they rob you not with a gun but with a fountain pen.[72]

Small-town and lower-middle-class Americans of the kind who joined the populist cause, moreover, have little tolerance for theories and analyses. They trust the tangible and the immediate; they think more in anecdotes than in abstractions. President Reagan caught this aspect of his constituency perfectly. These Americans, moreover, tend to read moral meanings into events. The idea that good or bad things could happen by chance—that there might be disasters for which no one is morally responsible—might seem absurd to them. There must be a hero or villain; there is someone to repay or someone to blame.

It is no accident that the dumping of hazardous waste (as at Love Canal) became the primary battleground on which lower-middle-class Americans first sided with environmentalists. Waste (whether hazardous or not) imposes the excrescence of technology and industry on nature; once this kind of waste is produced, it can never be gotten rid of.[73] Only nature can degrade waste—return it to nature—but the rubbish produced by technology today, such as radioactive wastes, may not be degraded in the foreseeable future. Waste of this sort constitutes a stain on nature that will not wash out.

Risk assessment cannot address this conceptual or moral problem. If chemical wastes, as at Love Canal, constitute a stain, they are morally perverse, and, therefore, as the residents of Love Canal concluded, they must be hurting adults and children in the community, whatever any report may say. When natural and human communities are presumed to have an integrity that has been violated, the resulting political issues cannot be discussed persuasively in risk-benefit or even scientific terms.

Americans who made up the bulk of the Reagan majority sought to preserve the moral sentiments and ideals they cherished against an attack from the government and from the liberal intelligentsia they thought owned the government. It may be fair to say that the locus of this grievance has now shifted from the government to large-scale technologies, which seem to be intruding, through their economic and environmental effects, on the integrity of nature and the viability of local communities. If so, environmental regulations, particularly in their insistence that interventions in nature be *safe,* give otherwise powerless Americans a weapon with which to protect their communities and their ways of life. And any technology thought to threaten those ways of life, along with the conception of the natural on which they are based, cannot possibly be safe enough.

WHAT SORT OF STATUTES SHOULD INDUSTRY SUPPORT?

Environmental law began to reflect the force of environmentalism as a populist issue starting in about 1980 after Love Canal, the dumping of kepone in the James River, and several other unfortunate episodes led many Americans to believe (correctly) that statutes enacted in the 1970s were not working. Public resentment and a growing conviction that something had to be done forced Congress to restructure environmental legislation from prospective command-and-control strategies to regulations based in retroactive liability and criminal penalties. Industries were put on notice not to contaminate or pollute except in permissible ways—or face severe legal penalties after the fact. In previous legislation, industry was permitted to do anything it was not prohibited from doing. More recent laws reverse the approach, making industry strictly liable for any environmental problem it was not permitted to create.

During the 1970s, most federal environmental laws were prospective; that is, they told industry what sorts of pollution control technology to install. Economists and others criticized such command-and-control approaches as inefficient since industry itself, rather than the government, is in the best position to manage pollution. Congress acted on this criticism with a vengeance, probably not in the way the critics intended, by enacting a series of laws that assigned liability retroactively to any corporation that might be involved in causing a pollution problem.[74] Under strict liability statutes, as one commentator points out, "responsible parties are liable for environmental contamination regardless of individual degrees of fault," and, one may add, regardless of the extent of the risk or hazard the contamination creates. According to this environmental lawyer:

The effect of these laws is to shift much of the responsibility for planning for a dangerous and uncertain environmental future to that segment of society most capable of finding innovative and efficient solutions—the private sector. Regardless of its perceived fairness, if carried through, this approach will result in a quantum leap in the effectiveness of environmental laws.[75]

Which kind of statutes should industry support?[76] The old command and control had the advantage, for industry, that they did not work; they were far too cumbersome to implement or enforce. Their unenforceability, however, led to an even greater disadvantage: the public demanded something tougher. And so we have liability-based laws that are tougher—they may hurt industry a lot more—but may not help us make progress toward a cleaner, more healthful, more natural environment.

It seems plausible to suppose that industrial associations such as the Chemical Manufacturers Association and the American Petroleum Institute should use their considerable power and expertise to support laws that work to clean up the environment in cost-effective ways. Laws of this kind may require industry to pollute only with a permit; they may also have to empower citizens' groups to enforce compliance with those statutes through the courts. At the same time, these laws would allow industry, for example, through the use of permit trading schemes and other market incentives, to ratchet down pollution to lower levels by the most efficient and least costly methods. Industry, bureaucracy, environmentalists, and the public are ready to support laws that get results rather than laws that simply appeal to particular ideologies. Industry should now support workable and enforceable legislation that will ratchet down the amount of waste and pollution in the most cost-effective ways.[77]

Representatives from industrial and from environmentalist associations now have many interests in common. The primary common goal must be to find a regulatory framework that will work to control and eventually decrease emissions. Industry must support laws that make this kind of progress in cost-effective ways or face further toughening of liability-based and criminal sanctions, which, in the continued absence of progress, will become vindictive. Environmentalists, who may now be weary of making the best the enemy of the good, no longer insist on statutes that promise the moon but are so unrealistic that they defeat all prospects of progress. Environmentalists must desire a regulatory framework that gives us efficient improvement, even if it does not, for example, solve the ozone problem in Los Angeles in five years.

If environmentalists and corporate executives have these strong interests in common, why don't they work together? Part of the reason is cultural: these groups have a long history of suspicion and antagonism. Another problem arises from the growth of industries that live off this antagonism. Public relations firms, for example, must describe environmentalists as fire-breathing dragons in order to get large retainers from industry to slay or tame them. If environmentalists and executives worked together for common legislative purposes, they would overcome the distrust that makes business for public relations firms. There would be no dragon to slay.[78]

If environmentalists and corporate executives cut a political deal, for example, to pursue workable statutes, they would eliminate much of the work not only of public relations experts but also of experts in risk assessment, risk analysis, risk management, risk communication, and so on. The idea behind workable laws is to make the environment safer, cleaner, and more natural in enforceable but cost-effective ways. We can do this without supporting an establishment of theorists to answer questions—like "how safe is safe enough?"—that no one will ever answer because they always require more research.[79]

It is time for business leaders and environmental leaders to deal directly with one another, without the benefit of academic and public relations experts who have made a niche for themselves by forcing these two sides further apart. We have the necessary experience with environmental law—we have learned enough by trial and error, which is the only way—to write statutes that work. This kind of experience, if we rely on it, can turn opposition to cooperation between industry leaders and environmental groups in restructuring environmental law.

NOTES

The research reported in this chapter received support from a grant from the Ethics and Values Studies Program of the National Science Foundation, Grant BBS 8619104. The views expressed are those of the author only and not necessarily those of any institute or agency.

1. Brock Yates, *Car and Driver* 35(2) (August 1989): 16.

2. William Jeannes, "Eye of the Road," *Car and Driver* 34(1) (July 1988): 11.

3. See, for example, "The Rise and Fall of Ralph Nader," *Car and Driver* 28(3) (September 1982): 64–71. "To the Naderites, the automobile and the corporations that foist it off on the innocent public are nothing less than public enemy number one" (p. 64).

4. "Driver's Seat," *Car and Driver* 26(2) (August 1980): 5–6.

5. Ibid. "Before long, thanks to Ed [Muskie], our cars will produce fewer pollutants than our peonies. . . . Unfortunately, it begins to look as though automobile exhaust was never the villain Ed Muskie and the California Air Resources Board and the Eco-Fascists made it out to be."

6. Ibid. "The American Ornithological Union, the National Audubon Society, and the Friends of the Earth have vowed to use federal money to keep the condors alive and miserable for as long as possible."

7. *Car and Driver* has inveighed relentlessly against passive restraints and other safety devices as decidedly nonmacho; see, for example, Patrick Bedard, "Stalking the Wild Bureaucrat," *Car and Driver* 24(10) (April 1979): 17.

8. Virtually any issue, but for a recent example, see Brock Yates, "Miscellaneous Fulminations," *Car and Driver* 34(10) (April 1989): 20.

9. Patrick Bedard, "Take an Endangered Species to Lunch," *Car and Driver* 25(10) (April 1980): 16: "No matter how strapped, Uncle Sam can always come up with a little something for the loonies, losers, and lunkheads of this country."

10. Brock Yates, "Say 'Cheese,' " *Car and Driver* 33(9) (March 1988).

11. Brock Yates, "Would You Draw to This Pair," *Car and Driver* 34(5) (November 1988): 23.

12. William Jeannes, "Eye on the Road," *Car and Driver* 35(2) (August 1989): 7.

13. *Sport Truck* (November 1989): 18.

14. Brock Yates, "I Take Pen in Hand," *Car and Driver* 35(2) (August 1989): 16 (an open letter to American carmakers defending CAFE standards as necessary "to reduce automobile carbon-dioxide emissions, a significant contributor to the greenhouse effect

and global warming"). See also William Jeannes, "Eye on the Road," *Car and Driver* 35(1) (July 1989): 5 (conceding that "the buying public *must* somehow be talked out of buying too-large cars").

15. Brock Yates, "Say 'Cheese'," *Car and Driver* 33(9) (March 1988): 25.

16. Ibid.

17. Brock Yates, *Car and Driver* 34(8) (February 1989): 19.

18. Patrick Bedard, "The Gipper Boots Big Brother off Our Dashboards," *Car and Driver* 28(4) (October 1982): 14 (conceding, however, that "President Reagan has yet to achieve his campaign promise of getting big government off our backs").

19. Letters to *Car and Driver* 35 (4) (October 1989): 10. The editors responded by printing another letter from a California man who wrote: "The only way to cut down on the global production of CO_2 is to drastically reduce the amount of fuel being burned." This reader continues: "I'm an enthusiast, and I like to drive as fast as you guys, but let's face it: we keep this up and nobody's going to be left alive to drive anything."

20. For the distinction between the study of risk as a physical fact and as a social construct, see H. J. Otway and K. Thomas, "Reflections on Risk Perception and Policy," *Risk Analysis* 2(1982): 69–82.

21. People need to discuss and clarify the meaning of a technology—what it expresses about their relationship to industry and to the larger community—as much as they need to understand its magnitude. When they ask about the meaning of a risk, however, they may be told, in reply, more and more about its magnitude, so they challenge what they are told. These people are irrational. They asked for bread and were given a stone.

22. For discussion, see Usher Flesing, "Risk and Culture in Biotechnology," *Trends in Biotechnology* 7(March 1987): 56.

23. Chauncey Starr, "Social Benefit versus Technological Risk," *Science,* September 19, 1969, p. 1235.

24. See, for example, W. C. Clark, "Witches, Floods, and Wonder Drugs: Historical Perspectives on Risk Management," in *Societal Risk Assessment: How Safe Is Safe Enough?* ed. R. C. Schwing and W. A. Albers (New York: Plenum, 1980), pp. 287–313; J. Conrad, "Society and Risk Assessment: An Attempt at Interpretation," in J. Conrad, ed., *Society, Technology, and Risk Assessment* (New York: Academic Press, 1980), pp. 241–76; and S. Raynor, "Disagreeing about Risk: The Institutional Cultures of Risk Management," in *Risk Analysis, Institutions, and Public Policy,* ed. S. G. Hadden (Fort Washington: Associated Faculty Press, 1984), pp. 150–68.

25. See, for example, Mary Douglas and Aaron Wildavsky, *Risk and Culture* (Berkeley: University of California Press, 1982).

26. One might be reminded of the closing chapters of the *Great Gatsby,* in which Gatsby's girlfriend (with him in the car) hits a woman, killing her, and drives away. Gatsby's only concern is whether he will be caught and how much it will cost to buy everyone off. The moral dimensions of the situation completely elude him. It is unclear in the text whether this accident, like that of the *Valdez,* involved drunk driving.

27. For a good account of this utilitarian interpretation of environmental concern, see Samuel Hays, *Conservation and the Gospel of Efficiency* (Cambridge, Mass.: Harvard University Press, 1968).

28. For a useful bibliography of this literature, see Anthony Fisher and Frederick Peterson, "The Environment in Economics: A Survey," *Journal of Economic Literature* 14(1976): 1–33.

29. For an account of the current form of the environmental movement and its history, see Samuel Hays, *Beauty, Health, and Permanence* (New York: Cambridge University Press, 1987).

30. By raising the possibility that prudence and morality may come to different conclusions about the environment, I mean to emphasize the logical difference between them. The former is directed to individual or community self-interest, the latter to individual or community self-respect. If the former has to do with what sells, what satisfies consumer interests and preferences whatever those wants happen to be, the latter concerns what is objectively good or bad, right or wrong, and consistent or inconsistent with the ideals and aspirations our society has expressed in public law.

Prudence or instrumental rationality, as Kant pointed out, is hypothetical. It has to do with the relation between means and ends. Thus, if I want my car to work properly, I have to give it gas, oil, and basic maintenance. An instrumental or prudential rationality assumes ends (or "preferences") as given and judges only the means needed to achieve those ends (or "satisfy" those preferences). Thus, if I want my car to function, I ought (prudentially) to give it the gas, oil, and maintenance it needs.

Morality, in contrast, is categorical. This means it arises as an imperative based simply on the circumstances of an action or a decision. If I see a person drowning whom I can easily rescue at no great inconvenience or risk to myself, I ought to do so, for this is what morality demands in such a situation. Similarly commonplace imperatives of moral duty—thou shalt not kill, steal, and so on—tell us that in certain circumstances, certain kinds of behavior are morally appropriate or inappropriate, quite apart from rational self-interest (e.g., quite apart from the question whether one can get away with an immoral action without getting caught).

Sometimes it may seem as if the counsels of prudence and the counsels of morality coincide rather than pull in opposite directions. With respect to the AIDS epidemic, for example, President Reagan said that morality and prudence teach the same lesson: chastity before marriage and fidelity after it. But morality and prudence rarely, if ever, teach the same lesson. They depend on entirely different reasons for acting and thus indicate entirely different courses of action. President Reagan apparently believes that morality counsels chastity and fidelity—and this is at least an arguable position. But prudence does not argue for chastity, even in the age of AIDS; rather, it teaches safe sex, not abstinence, and it permits as much promiscuity and adultery as one can manage with the proper technical safeguards.

Robert Fullinwider, illustrating the difference between prudence and morality, writes: "Warning young people that premarital sex risks disease and pregnancy—the two evils most commonly invoked—does not warn them away from sex; it warns them away from risky sex. It gives them no reason to avoid sex when the dangers of pregnancy and disease are not present. Now, it is important to teach young people to be prudent and this is not an easy thing to do. But their lessons in prudence should not be mixed up with their lessons in morality. If chastity is morally required, then it remains so even if the dangers of sex disappear. Vaccinations for AIDS, herpes, and syphilis will change the prudential status of promiscuity but not its moral status." Robert Fullinwider, "AIDS and Moral Lessons," *Baltimore Evening Sun*, September 10, 1987, p. A17.

Those who would teach moral lessons often use prudential terms. Be faithful to your spouse—or you might pick up a disease. Do not lie or steal—or you might get caught. Be polite and respectful to others—so that you may gain preferment. In teaching morality or virtue in this way, we suggest that the reasons to be faithful, to be honest, and to be respectful of others are instrumental reasons. We imply that there is no such thing as an ethical justification for an action or a choice.

Moral reasons for protecting nature—like moral reasons for restraining promiscuity or telling the truth—depend on notions of integrity, dignity, self-control, and responsibility. These reasons more likely arise from a love of nature, a respect for natural history, and a sense that everything valuable does not depend on profitability or willingness to pay. The love of nature, respect for the past, and care for the integrity of the environment may express virtues that stand on their own bottoms. They do not guarantee one a place in heaven or, for that matter, a heaven on earth.

31. For a discussion of how and why the Clean Air Act proved too cumbersome to implement and enforce, see, for example, R. Shep Melnick, *Regulation and the Courts: The Case of the Clean Air Act* (Washington, D.C.: Brookings, 1983); David Schoenbrod, "Goals Statutes and Rules Statutes: The Case of the Clean Air Act," *UCLA Law Review* 30 (1983): 720–828; and William Pedersen, "Why the Clean Air Act Works Badly," *University of Pennsylvania Law Review* 129 (1981): 1059–1105.

32. "The Politics of Posterity," *Economist,* September 2, 1989, p. 3.

33. Ibid.

34. *New York Times,* July 2, 1989, p. 1.

35. Similarly, a September 1988 Gallup Poll found that 84 percent of Americans are very concerned about water pollution—a 36 percentage point increase since 1970. In April 1989, the *Washington Post* and ABC News completed a survey that found that nine Americans in ten ranked "taking stronger action to clean up the nation's air and water" as a top priority for government and business leaders. According to recent Roper and Cambridge Research studies, a majority of Americans favor tougher environmental laws and regulations—up from a less than 30 percent minority in the late 1970s. A National Opinion Research Center survey found that almost two-thirds of all Americans believe that the country spends too little to protect the environment; a Harris Poll in February 1989 determined that a greater than two-thirds majority favors increased government spending to control acid rain and toxic waste dumping even if it means higher taxes. Several other surveys confirm the same trend: that Americans are willing to pay as much as a thousand dollars each in higher taxes, for example, to clean up toxic wastes. For documentation of these surveys, see Louis Harris, et al., *The Rising Tide: Public Opinion, Policy and Politics,* Section 5 (Washington, D.C.: Sierra Club Press, 1989).

36. For a review of the sources of this popular belief, see D. L. Sills, "The Environmental Movement and Its Critics," *Human Ecology* 3(1975): 1–41.

37. For an early discussion, see P. Converse, "The Nature of Belief Systems in Mass Society," in D. Apter, ed., *Ideology and Discontent* (New York: Macmillan, 1964), pp. 206–61.

38. J. F. Springer and E. Costantini, "An Issue in Search of a Home," in S. Nagel, ed., *Environmental Politics* (New York: Praeger, 1974), pp. 195–224.

39. For analysis, see Kent D. Van Liere and Riley Dunlap, "Environmental Concern: Does It Make a Difference How It's Measured?" *Environment and Behavior* 13(6) (1981): 651–76).

40. This distinction, its history, and the remarks I make about it in the next paragraph represent standard fare in discussions of environmental ethics. For more sophisticated renderings of this distinction, see, for example, Holmes Rolston, *Environmental Ethics*

(Philadelphia: Temple University Press, 1988), and Eugene Hargrove, *Foundations of Environmental Ethics* (Englewood Cliffs, N.J.: Prentice-Hall, 1989).

41. Riley E. Dunlap and Kent D. Van Liere, "Commitment to the Dominant Social Paradigm and Concern for Environmental Quality," *Social Science Quarterly* 65(4) (1984): 1023. These authors add (p. 1025): "Our results suggest that the traditional values and beliefs constituting our society's dominant social paradigm are important sources of opposition for environmental protection."

42. Dennis C. Pirages, "Introduction: A Social Design for Sustainable Growth," in D. C. Pirages, ed., *The Sustainable Society* (New York: Praeger, 1977), pp. 1–13.

43. For a recent review of these studies, see Diane M. Samdahl and Robert Robertson, "Social Determinants of Environmental Concern," *Environment and Behavior* 21(1) (1989): 57–81.

44. James A. Swan, "Environmental Education: One Approach to Resolving the Environmental Crisis," *Environment and Behavior* 3(1971): 225. For similar views, see William Ophuls, *Ecology and the Politics of Scarcity* (San Francisco: Freeman, 1977), and Dennis Pirages, *The Evolution of Societies* (Englewood Cliffs, N.J.: Prentice-Hall, 1977).

45. Samdahl and Robertson, "Environmental Concern," p. 61.

46. Environmentalists "presented a serious challenge to agriculture, labor, and business, which turned on them with alarm." Samuel P. Hays, *Beauty, Health, and Permanence: Environmental Politics in the United States, 1955–1985* (New York: Cambridge University Press, 1987), p. 287.

47. See ibid., pp. 491–526.

48. William Tucker, *Progress and Privilege: America in the Age of Environmentalism* (Garden City, N.Y.: Doubleday, 1982).

49. For excellent analysis and debunking of this view, see Denton E. Morrison and Riley Dunlap, "Environmentalism and Elitism: A Conceptual and Empirical Analysis," *Environmental Management* 10(5) (1986): 581–89.

50. Tucker, *Progress and Privilege*, p. 15. According to this interpretation, the liberal middle class directed a series of policies against the interests of lower-middle-class people during the 1970s. These policies included forced integration (well-off liberals live in or can move to white suburbs not implicated in busing); affirmative action (the members of the privileged classes are unlikely to be the marginal applicants who lose their jobs to blacks); and urban renewal or "removal" (gentrifying ethnic communities). According to this account, environmentalist policies to limit economic growth, such as through pollution control and energy conservation, also served the interests of the upper against those of the lower middle class. These policies created jobs in high-paying professions for the college educated at the expense of farmers, blue-collar workers, small business people, and others who strove to improve themselves by producing wealth rather than by entering privileged professional castes.

Several political scientists–Aaron Wildavsky is a prominent example—interpreted ecological doomsaying, even more prevalent in the 1970s than today, as a scare tactic through which liberal elites tried to control social progress and cut off or abort the economic growth that would make others equally well off. See, for example, S. Epstein, *The Politics of Cancer*, rev. ed. (Garden City, N.J.: Anchor Press, 1979); James Ridgeway and Alexander Cockburn, *The Politics of Ecology* (New York: Dutton, 1971); and John Whitaker, *Striking a Balance* (Washington, D.C.: AEI-Hoover Institute, 1976).

"Restriction is coercion," Wildavsky wrote. "Doubt it? Ask an environmentalist about the consequences of running out of energy (the very word suggests losing strength): immediately you will hear about getting rid of 'gas-guzzling' automobiles, walking or riding a bicycle to work, residing in closer and more self-contained communities, and otherwise doing what comes naturally. Before your eyes, an entirely new way of life will unfold out of a seemingly small restriction on fossil fuels." Aaron Wildavsky, "No Risk Is the Highest Risk of All," *American Scientist* 67 (January–February 1989): 36. Wildavsky has elaborated his views, especially in *Risk and Culture,* coauthored with Mary Douglas (Berkeley: University of California Press, 1982). Wildavsky and (possibly to a lesser extent) Douglas argue that environmentalists promote various fears—just as anti-Semites produced the fear that the Jews were poisoning the wells—as a form of social control and criticism (p. 7). These authors argue, for example, that the reason environmentalists inveigh against asbestos rather than sunbathing as a cause of cancer is that the asbestos risk "justifies a particular anti-industrial criticism," whereas "there is no obvious way in which the incidence of skin cancer caused by leisure-time sunburn can be mobilized for criticism of industry, and so we hear less of it" (p. 7).

51. According to this analysis, on one side of a deep political divide stand those "who, largely as a result of having passed through the higher levels of the educational system, make their living in . . . the 'knowledge industry' "—which is to say education, entertainment, publishing, communication, research, government and corporate bureaucracy, and other occupations "where it is expected that people have 'ideas.' " Peter Berger, "The Greening of American Foreign Policy," *Commentary* 61(3) (March 1976): 23.

Environmental organizations such as the Sierra Club drew much of their membership from this suburban professional class, which tended to be democratic and to favor a liberal social agenda and an activist government. On the other side of the political divide stand those, often in the lower middle class, who make their living by manipulating things rather than symbols. This group includes operators of small businesses, farmers, blue-collar workers, and Americans in the rural South and Midwest who tend to resist the liberal social agenda, such as forced integration ("busing"), affirmative action, redistributive programs ("welfare"), prison reform, gun control, speed limits, and, in general, the intrusion of the federal government in their lives. This group contributed proportionally fewer members to activist environmental organizations and, indeed, to activist political groups generally.

Since the Vietnam War, the Republican party has explicitly based its electoral strategy on identifying Democrats with the liberal eastern intelligentsia or, more derisively, with those who are soft on defense, indulge flag burners, furlough criminals, coddle drug addicts, condone homosexuality, and cater to welfare cheats while taxing working-class Americans and telling them how they ought to live. This strategy has proved enormously successful in accumulating votes. *Car and Driver,* after all, has a larger circulation than, say, the *New York Review of Books.*

52. The most significant social science studies include F. H. Buttel and W. L. Flinn, "The Structure of Support for the Environmental Movement, 1968–1970," *Rural Sociology* 39(1974): 56–69; F. H. Buttel and W. L. Flinn, "The Politics of Environmental Concern: The Impacts of Party Identification and Political Ideology on Environmental Attitudes," *Environment and Behavior* 10 (1978): 17–36; and J. A. Honnold, "Predictors of Public Environmental Concern in the 1970s," in M. E. Dean, ed., *Environmental Policy Formation* (Lexington, Mass.: Lexington Books, 1981), pp. 63–76. For a good

review article, see K. D. Van Liere and R. E. Dunlap, "The Social Basis of Environmental Concern: A Review of Hypotheses, Explanations and Empirical Evidence," *Public Opinion Quarterly* 44 (1980): 181–97.

53. For an example of this kind of argument, see B. J. Frieden, *The Environmental Protection Hustle* (Cambridge, Mass.: MIT Press, 1979). For example, Frieden writes (p. 131): "Highly educated professionals and executives can usually afford the high cost of a house in an established, desirable suburb with an attractive environment. Their opposition to home building is usually opposition to someone else's opportunity to buy a moderate-cost home. And the environment they protect is an environment they can afford to enjoy."

54. Paul Mohai, "Public Concern and Elite Involvement in Environmental-Conservation Issues," *Social Science Quarterly* 66 (14) (1985): 820–38. This article reviews a large number of studies that test relevant hypotheses.

55. Morrison and Dunlap, "Environmentalism and Elitism," p. 583.

56. Ibid.

57. Mohai, "Public Concern and Elite Involvement," p. 836. The article concludes (p. 837): "Thus the upper-middle class link with environmental activism can be seen as a link between that class and the factors of political activism rather than a link between the upper-middle class and environmental concern as has often been asserted by past literature and popular belief."

58. Bill Copeland, "We Don't Elect Those Who Control Us," *Farm Journal* (January 1976): 17.

59. Ibid.

60. Editorial, "'Organic Foods': Today's Big Rip-Off," *Farm Journal* (February 1976): 66.

61. Laura Lane, "Will You Go to Jail over Erosion?" *Farm Journal* (Mid-February 1976): 23.

62. *Farm Journal* (June–July 1989): 20.

63. Darrell Smith, "Organic Grower Farms It 'His Way': Innovative and Intensive Management Help Del Akerlund Farm without Chemicals," *Farm Journal* (September 1989): E-8. See also "Taking the Low Road," *Farm Journal* (December 1988): 15–17 (reporting favorably on the low-input farming of Don Elston of Ohio who "joined a movement of unconventional farmers who are driven by a desire to reduce production costs and protect the environment" [p. 15]).

64. *Farm Journal* (October 1976): 20.

65. Darrell Smith, "Are Pesticides Losing Their Punch?" *Farm Journal* (Mid-January 1989): 16. The article begins: "There are strains of lambsquarters, velvetleaf and pigweed that can take a bath in atrazine or Bladex and laugh at the fool who sprayed them. And there are microorganisms in some fields that, given a choice, probably would order some insecticides from room service."

66. Gene Logson, "Maybe the Animal Rights Movement Is Good for Us," *Farm Journal* (January 1989): 26-D.

67. *Farm Journal* (December 1988): 4 prints this letter from Iowa farmers Mark and Brenda Dagel: "Lately we've been annoyed about all the corporate hog farms being built: National in Nebraska now wanting to expand to Colorado, Smithfield planning to build 100 units with 1,000 sows to produce two million hogs per year. (That will replace 666 family operations of 150 sows each.)

"We have felt that the animal welfare people were fighting us, threatening to take our farrowing crates and gestation stalls. Maybe we should join them. It might be the only way to stop corporate hog farms. Wouldn't it be fun to watch the big corporations farrow pigs in open pens that would have to be bedded and cleaned out?"

68. Bruce Palmer, *"Man over Money"*: *The Southern Populist Critique of American Capitalism* (Chapel Hill: University of North Carolina Press, 1980), p. 9.

69. George McKenna, *American Populism* (New York: Putnam, 1974), p. 85.

70. Ibid., p. 3.

71. Ibid., p. 4.

72. For a discussion of populism in this context, see Margaret Canovan, *Populism* (New York: Harcourt Brace Jovanovich, 1981), esp. chap. 1.

73. This is an aesthetic and conceptual thesis; it has nothing to do with technology. To make waste conceptually something different, one must perceive it differently. This is what happens when junk becomes identified as antiques or when hideous slums are converted, by an act of perception and a little gentrification, into glorious heritage. For an excellent study of the conceptual boundaries among useful object, waste, and art, see Michael Thompson, *Rubbish Theory* (New York: Oxford University Press, 1979).

74. Before 1980 the government found its capacity to implement pollution control statutes severely limited by the difficulties it faced in identifying environmental problems and in creating workable and enforceable regulations to deal with them. Laws enacted after 1980, for example, the Hazardous and Solid Waste Amendments of 1984 and the Superfund Amendments and Reauthorization Act of 1986, shift the burden of identifying and solving problems to the private sector. These statutes provide the necessary incentives by establishing joint and several liability, as well as criminal penalties for any problems that industry might create and might be identified later on.

75. Adam Babich, "Restructuring Environmental Law," *Environmental Law Reporter* 19 (February 1989): 10057.

76. It would be irresponsible for industry not to lobby for or against any policy or program, that is, to abandon the field to environmentalists and other lobbies. One reason, of course, is that environmentalists have again and again made the best the enemy of the good and in the statutory quest for environmental perfection have squandered opportunities for environmental progress. Environmentalists have shown their enthusiasm for ideology (e.g., a minimal risk or no-risk society) and, with it, their inability to deal with reality (the economic, political, and technological realities that quickly turn laws consistent with this ideology into fictions honored in the breach rather than in the observance). If we are going to have laws that work to clean up the environment—rather than laws that announce noble aspirations but are utterly unenforceable—we need to have input from industry, as well as from agency bureaucrats and environmentalists. Laws that industry did not help to write, I fear, it will find ways to ignore. For further argument along these lines, see Mark Sagoff, *The Economy of the Earth: Philosophy, Law, and the Environment* (New York: Cambridge University Press, 1988), esp. chap. 9.

77. I believe that the permitting program (Title IV) of the Clean Air Act President Bush has proposed has these virtues. The Chemical Manufacturers Association has supported (or at least does not oppose) this strategy. The American Petroleum Institute (API) has come out against it. The only reason I can imagine the API opposes a permitting program is that such a program is far more enforceable than state implementation plans as they are now set up. The API apparently does not want an enforceable law even if that law, being based on a marketable permit scheme, allows industry to control pollution in the most cost-effective ways.

78. I recently visited a large public relations firm as part of a seminar on risk assessment in biotechnology. The panel of public relations experts represented the environmentalist lobby, led primarily by the National Wildlife Federation, as ideological and religious fanatics with great powers of controlling Congress. This is nonsense. The National Wildlife Federation and environmental groups generally have taken very moderate and responsible positions. (These groups are not to be confused with Jeremy Rifkin, American author and activist, who has his own agenda.) It seemed to me that these experts have a built-in conflict of interest with the corporations they serve. To get corporate business, they must represent environmentalists as much more unreasonable and antagonistic than they really are.

79. For an interesting critique of the literature of risk analysis, see Judith A. Bradbury, "The Policy Implications of Different Conception of Risk," *Science, Technology, and Human Values* 14(4) (1989): 380–99. Bradbury singles out for criticism *Risk Communication, Risk Statistics, and Risk Comparisons: A Manual for Plant Managers*, by V. T. Covello, P. M. Sandman, and P. Slovic, a manual published in 1988 by the Chemical Manufacturers' Association (Washington, D.C.). According to Bradbury (pp. 386–89), this manual epitomizes all the vices that ensure the failure of political discourse between business and environmental groups. Bradbury writes that the manual presents "an almost-classic example of . . . the 'individual-blame' bias of linear communication models." Bradbury writes (pp. 386–87): "Nor does it discuss ways the public might be involved in making decisions about risk, rather than being passive recipients—the 'target audience' (Covello, Sandman, and Slovic 1988, p. 9)—for technical spokespersons' messages. Rather, the manual focuses on risk communication as an act rather than a process and stresses ways to enhance the technical manager's presentation of probabilistic risk concepts. Effective communication is conceived in the limited sense of the manager's ability to explain risk concepts clearly."

11

Environmentalism as a Humanism

ROBERT C. SOLOMON

Does environmentalism have to be explained? Is the visible and olfactorily obvious deterioration of the soil, air, and water around us and the now widespread anxiety (bordering on panic in some quarters) for the quality of these necessities of life a problem whose social significance is really worth pondering, at just the time when we now have the numbers to cooperate and mobilize for some serious reform? With the emergence of a new consensus and a hitherto unknown solidarity on these vital matters, do we really want to "understand" this social phenomenon in the divisive language of moral self-righteousness, class ideologies, and ressentiment? This is what Mark Sagoff, it seems, wants us to do.

One of the themes—perhaps the main theme—of my own work in business ethics is the self-defeating nature of those overly antagonistic dichotomies between self-interest and altruism, between business values and ethical values, between the bottom line and social responsibility, between money and morals. On the subject of corporate policy and environmental ethics, we are talking about one internally complex system of interlocking values and not two antagonistic forces. The polemical distinctions—between the love of nature and the exploitation of nature ("reverence" and "utilitarianism"), for instance—distort and disguise the complex issues of environmentalism and make mutual understanding and cooperation impossible. For example, those "deep" ecologists who wage war against one another and play "more Mao than thou" in their competition to reject technology and all conceivable technological solutions to environmental problems do the environmental movement no favors but only isolate environmentalism from the very possibility of cooperative reforms.[1] It is in response to such divisive polemicizing that the reactionary accusations of environmentalists as elitists gain plausibility.[2] To attack exploitation may also be to reinforce it and to provoke the belligerence rather than invite the cooperation of those who are identified as the exploiters. But competition for the high moral ground and James Watt–type ad hominem arguments are not the way to environmental reform. Cooperation and consensus, embracing the interests of the largest corporations as well as the concerns of the ordinary citizen, is the only avenue.

Some of this rage for cooperation and synthesis might be laid at the doorstep of my infatuation with Hegel and Hegelianism, following the great nineteenth-century philosopher in his own attempts to integrate a divided world at war and recapture our already lost rapport with nature. (It was Hegel who first advanced the optimistic conception of "the end of history" to summarize this grand sense of synthesis.) But in my more practical, paracorporate life, this emphasis on cooperation and consensus serves a vital purpose: to reject the rather belligerent antibusiness prejudices of many of my colleagues (as well as the antiacademic attitudes of the executives I work with) in order to recognize the absolutely essential role of the multinational corporations along with more idealistic reformers in any conceivable solution to the urgent environmental problems that confront us and to acknowledge the importance of shared concerns and solutions. This is not to deny that some giant corporations are part of the problem, but it will do no good to promote self-righteously the myth of endemic corporate irresponsibility, even if there are significant instances of such, and turn solvable practical problems into irresolvable differences in ideology. I thus find myself very much at odds with Sagoff even while I agree with and heartily endorse and appreciate many of his insights and, especially, his central observation that environmentalism is no longer an issue for isolated eccentrics but one of the most powerful populist issues of our times.

POPULISM AND ELITISM: "THE MORAL SUPERIORITY OF THE UNINVOLVED"

When I was younger, I was an avid reader of *Car and Driver*. The feel of a fast car on the open road seemed to me then, as it still seems to me now, one of the great joys of living in a technological, open society. And what I could not afford to drive, I read about in *Car and Driver*. I do not remember reading the editorials—like most other readers I concentrated on the pictures and the "specs"— but I do remember rather distinctly that, even then, I was not hysterically opposed to government regulation of the roads, give or take ten or twenty miles per hour or so, and though radar detectors were not yet available, I am sure that I would have had one if they were. I also seem to remember joining the American Civil Liberties Union and campaigning against the death penalty. I even enjoyed watching birds, though the fetish for imported water was not yet with us. Reading Sagoff's essay, however, one would certainly think that every reader of *Car and Driver* was a liberal-bashing, libertarian redneck. The love of technology gets played off against the love of nature, philistine enthusiasms against effete, innocent pleasures. Is there any reason to give credence to such contrasts?

I do not dispute Sagoff's report of those editorials that I never read, but I do question the use of intentionally loud-mouth monthly columnists to gauge the mood of the country. Indeed, the use of such research to make the populist point is, I think, to betray an indefensible distance from the very people Sagoff pretends to understand. It is as if, in accordance with one of our rather long-standing philosophical traditions, he were looking at society (especially the masses) down the wrong end of a rather long telescope, from a great impersonal distance. There is a very real problem of perspective in his analysis, the distance—and with it the disdain—from which he seems to view the people he talks about—drivers, farmers, utilitarians, businessmen (of course), the wrong kinds of environmentalists, lower-middle-class citizens who become environmentally concerned only out of immediate self-interest, the liberal intelligentsia, and the undifferentiated populace of populism in general. Against our new and certainly welcome shared enthusiasm for the protection of the environment, Sagoff casts suspicion on our motives as so much self-interest, so much mere utility and risk aversion, so much hype and political bandwagoneering. In contrast, he insists on taking the "high road" of ethics and morals, explicitly distinguishing this elevated route from mere prudentialism, exploitative utilitarianism, and risk-cost-benefit analysis.

These distinctions reflect what Chemical Bank president Tom Johnson has nicely described as "the moral superiority of the uninvolved." It is all too comfortable to chastise the mean, practical motives of those who have to live with the responsibility and the consequences from a position of considerable abstraction and advantage. But the truth is that the fine distinctions so often belabored by philosophers find virtually no application in day-to-day life, and the distinctions between prudence and morality, self-interest and altruism all but collapse when we look at even the most ordinary case of a working person doing his or her job, whether as a factory worker, a secretary, or a chief executive officer.[3] It is worth reminding ourselves that we find few such distinctions in the classic writings of Plato and Aristotle, who were concerned with the harmonious behavior of citizens rather than the artificial divisions between schools of philosophy. These distinctions may be of some philosophical importance, but I believe that they lead to nothing less than disaster in the ongoing dialogue of public interest groups, industry, and government that constitutes the promising context of today's environmentalism.

ENVIRONMENTALISM AND EXPLOITATION: ON LEAVING "NATURE" ALONE

In his defense of a particularly moral, reverential environmentalism, Sagoff attacks or at least disparages all merely utilitarian and instrumental attitudes toward nature. Nature is not just there for our use and exploitation, he reminds us. And to be sure, those of us who still enjoy a daily walk in the woods would agree, but to what is this notion of "exploitation" opposed—the use of our little patch of nature as a garbage dump? Isn't our enjoyment of nature for its own sake also an aspect of our use of it? And from a long evolutionary perspective it is also a kind of exploitation. Our very footsteps alter the natural ecology, not to mention our efforts to protect and reserve the woods as is. Aesthetic enjoyment is a kind of use, and the setting aside of an acre or a half-continent for our enjoyment is (by the classical definition of utility) just as utilitarian as our use of it as an oil field. I am not arguing the perverse thesis that all use is exploitation, of course, but I do want to argue that the overly self-righteous distinction between utility and reverence is an insidious one that gives a false sense of moral superiority to the leisurely observer and wrongly condemns or belittles all of those whose job it is to provide the material preconditions that make that leisure possible (e.g., the electricity to run Sagoff's PC).

But if one insists on taking the larger view, ignoring the necessities and preconditions of human civilization as we know it, could it not be argued that even our benign insistence on saving a species from extinction is itself a willful and anthropocentric manipulation of nature? After all, millions have become extinct with no help from us. What we consider natural is just what we in our short tenancy have become used to and, perhaps, remember with a certain fondness.[4] If we insist on enlarging the scope of the argument to cosmic proportions, we must also be careful not to confuse our limited view of life on planet earth with mere nostalgia.

Greg Easterbrook has recently written, perversely but wisely, I think, that we do not need to take care of nature; nature is and always will be capable of taking care of itself. It is an old Sartrian point: nature cannot be destroyed. What falls under the heading of destruction is only what we (or some other conscious beings, including God or gods) have come to care about. What concerns us, in other words, is the conservation of a peculiarly human habitat, a world in which we can live comfortably and in harmony with those aspects of nature we choose to privilege. And even there the division between nature and human nature is particularly self-serving. Consider Frederick Turner, echoing David Hume two centuries before:

The theory of evolution implies that human history is also a part of nature, and that nature itself has always been a mess: everything interfering with everything else, everything changing, everything being used up, everything irreversible, waste everywhere—the good old second law of thermodynamics. Life is a mess—sucking, secreting, competing, breeding, dying—and human beings—desirous, aspiring, quarrelsome, proud, acquisitive, and embarrassingly self-conscious—are what nature produced when it had the chance to do so.[5]

Whatever else it may be, environmentalism should not be an antihumanism—a rejection of the human perspective—but rather an appeal to what is best and most human in us—our aesthetic sensitivities, our ability to step back from our projects and our prejudices and plan, our capacity to empathize and cooperate.

Rather than take such a large, suprahuman view of nature or an overly down-to-earth *Car and Driver* view of our complex interaction with nature, Sagoff insists on a quasi-religious (almost millenarian) vision of reverence for and love of nature (which he rather oddly couples with "respect for community and reverence for the past"—a very different set of concerns, I think, and not at all supportive of the kind of environmentalism he applauds). Such phrases are edifying, and no doubt even as we pronounce them you see before your inner eyes one of those glorious images of the unspoiled Alaskan wilderness, though probably not the equally natural swarming of life in an algae pond. But what commerce (I use this word not just ironically) can there be between the merely utilitarian view, so vulgarly stated, and the reverent vision of nature for its own sake? Does either of them provide us with a plausible view of our life in the midst of (and as an integral part of) nature? Is the answer to the environmental crisis a deep ecology in which we literally (and no doubt impossibly) reject our entire way of life, or is rather a much more superficial sense of solidarity in which we mutually negotiate our differences and mutual disadvantages? (It is often suggested that we should live more like the original native Americans, conveniently forgetting the rather dramatic difference in populations, the enormous suffering endured by those pretechnological peoples, and the often violent, even genocidal confrontations between them. But I think that this neo-Rousseauian romanticism of our own noble savages is a study that deserves some attention as a symptom of a certain self-hatred.)[6]

Such considerations do not constitute an argument against environmentalism but only an attack on a false deification of nature in the name of what is (but is rarely recognized as) a particularly virulent form of antihumanism. Current calls for the self-sacrifice of our species for the benefit of nature are only the most extreme version of this virulence. I have heard, hardly believing my ears, that the extinction of the human species (perhaps by way of AIDS) would be quite a good thing. It would not only give the waters, the air, and the ozone a chance to replenish themselves, but it would allow the continued existence of thousands of species that might otherwise become extinct in the continued presence of Big Human Brother.[7] I hope such suggestions inspire as much horror in you as they do in me but without for a moment suggesting that environmentalism as such requires any such species sacrifice or radical reversion to some fantasied more "natural" life-style. Some serious changes are no doubt in order, but as so often, the most radical suggestions are those that guarantee that those necessary changes will be put off indefinitely as cooperation and consensus are eclipsed by self-righteousness and nonsense.

UTILITARIANISM, HUMANISM, MORALITY, AND RISK

In the context of environmentalism—as in many other contexts both social and religious—the culturally contrived antagonism between nature and culture promotes prejudice and warfare and provokes insults and mutually defensive, typically vicious and unproductive arguments. But so too in philosophy—as in social and religious contexts too—the academically inspired opposition of morality and mere utility produces far more conflict and confusion than understanding. Sagoff's juxtaposition of moral reverence and utilitarianism does damage to his own environmental aims as well as to moral philosophy. In a symposium filled not with ideologues but a mixed audience of sincerely concerned businesspeople and academic ethicists, does such a split between utilitarianism and morality make any sense? To be sure, so-called utilitarian justifications of pollution and other antisocial actions are sometimes incredibly shortsighted and self-serving, but do we have to promote an overly abstract and often impractical notion of morality to compensate for the occasional deficiencies and short-sightedness of a vulgar pragmatism and a fraudulent appeal to utility? Indeed, how emaciated a conception of utilitarianism one would have to have in order to eliminate from consideration both the long-term view and all spiritual joys of reverence and aesthetics. John Stuart Mill would turn over in his grave. Utilitarianism, after all, was not originally promoted just as a defense of cost-benefit analysis. It was, and still is, a conception of moral philosophy.[8] Utilitarianism is, and continues to be, first and foremost a version of humanism (by which I do not mean to question its legitimate employment, from Jeremy Bentham to Peter Singer, in a defense of animals). Humanism, in contrast to many religious and political ideologies (but equally in harmony with others), is the insistence that people's interests and well-being, their pleasures, their pains, their happiness, and not some more abstract criteria—whether the will of God or the bottom line—should dictate our concerns and our actions.

I do not accuse Sagoff of being an antihumanist, but I do think that the concept of humanism is seriously distorted in his essay, as in many other recent diatribes for and against the environment. One essential aspect of humanism and the human is surely respect for our various biological and basic social needs, as well as our more large-minded values, including the ethics of equitable distribution that generally gets misplaced under the heading of economics. Corporations are neither inhuman nor unnatural but an obvious outgrowth of what is most human and most natural about us: our need to affiliate, cooperate, and organize in sizable groups. True, purely economic utilitarianism carves out a very one-sided view of human motivation, and the cost-benefit "rational strategies" of *homo economicus* are surely not definitive of what we mean or ought to mean by utility. Some of our interests may be so readily measured and quantified, but most of our more human concerns, such as love and affection, creativity, personal pride and living well, liberty and the pursuit of happiness, are not, and it is nonsense and inhuman to treat them as bits of irrationality and/or as "irregularities in the market." But though *homo economicus* may be inhuman, our economic interests constitute an essential element in human life. Demeaning the bottom line in favor of some "higher" ideal always carries with it the danger that both the high ideal and the bottom line will end up so much the worse for the conflict. Whatever our conception of environmentalism, it will inevitably have its utilitarian and its purely economic aspects, and to deny or dismiss this is to reject the possibility of any successful environmental reform whatsoever.

What Sagoff calls "moral," as opposed to merely utilitarian, is very Kantian (though more of the third *Critique* than the second) and equally narrow and limited. Is detached reverence and hands-off respect really our only proper attitude toward nature? (Is that the way the Indians did it? Or was engagement in nature, including a good deal of killing, an essential part of their reverence?) There is something absurd about a conception of morality that preaches respect for human dignity but abstains from action on the behalf of actual human beings and disdains the actual conversations and compromises in which the substance of morality gets actualized. So, too, there is something absurd about conceiving of environmentalism through the eyes of those armchair romantics whose occasional walks in the woods (as opposed to working in the fields or even puttering around the garden) stimulate occasional reveries. Environmentalism involves living and working in nature, not just appreciating it, and morality is nothing if not the way we deal day to day with each other and our environment. To separate these into convenient but antagonistic packages—moral reverence on the one hand and mere utility on the other—demeans the discussion.

One especially hateful aspect of utilitarianism, according to Sagoff, is the notion of risk and risk assessment, which he also juxtaposes with the moral. The hazards of risk and cost-benefit analysis have often been trumpeted in the philosophical literature on business ethics; the most famous perversions of this sort of thinking have become something of a touchstone for the profession—the infamous Ford Pinto case, for example, and more recent bad behavior on the part of Audi. But risk is not just an actuarial concept; it is also an ethical one. Sagoff rightly comments that it is the meaning of risk, as well as its magnitude, that has to enter into our deliberations. In fairly recent works, Bernard Williams and Martha Nussbaum have talked at length about the all-important concept of "moral luck," and Mary Douglas and Aaron Wildavsky—whom Sagoff rather one-sidedly chastises in his notes—have given an admirably balanced view of the cultural determinants of risk and its meaning in their *Risk and Culture*.[9] One need not defend or exonerate Exxon, for example, in order to note that the company was the victim (the only sense in which Exxon was the victim) of bad moral luck in its recent Alaskan spill disaster. (Its follow-up performance, however, has already become the paradigm example of corporate irresponsibility and the self-defeating substitution of public relations for concerted action.) But the recognition that "there but for the Grace of God . . ." ought to be an essential part of the humility that forms the frame of ethical criticism, and the tragedies that accompany technology and the manipulation of vast natural resources should not be subjected to that armchair Manicheanism that so readily divides the world into good guys and bad. For most of us, too, our integrity is to at least some extent a matter of moral luck. This is not to say that we have not been caught in our transgressions (small as they may be) but rather that we have not been caught up in those circumstances where our flaws and failings are very likely to undermine us, not to mention put us on the front page of the *New York Post*. It is rather to say that risk is an essential part of virtually every human endeavor, and our reaction to disaster should thus be one not only of blame but of instantaneous response and cooperation. Calculations of risk are not opposed to moral considerations; they are an essential part of moral preparation.

The ancient Greeks talked a great deal about moral luck, and in particular that form of bad luck which they (and we) call tragedy. The Greek concept of fate is much less in favor today (as the result of a very different paradigm of personal responsibility emerging from the Judeo-Christian tradition, I would argue, exemplified by the story of the Fall). But the related concept of an accident is still very much with us, and I think that Sagoff is wrong when he so easily juxtaposes risk and religion, "chance and moral concern." It may be true that Americans are too quick today to judge that someone must be at fault, but I see this as a recent perversion of our notions of morals, responsibility, and luck and detrimental to both our notions of civil liability and our concern for the environment. The result is that we get lawsuits instead of cooperative action, a mess in the courts in addition to the mess on the beaches. Moreover, our fetish with finding fault is philosophically quite opposed to the rather Stoical attitude of reverence for nature and to the dominant paradigm that Sagoff so often alludes to.

POPULISM AND IDEOLOGY

I have always been suspicious of philosophical and political analyses of populism and diagnoses of other phenomena in terms of populism. It sounds at first so innocent—"populism" like "popular"—but it is clearly a mass reference term with only barely hidden contemptuous overtones. (There is no question, for example, what an academic is saying when he accuses a colleague of "popularization" or what kind of snarled expression we expect of a music critic when he or she refers to "popular music.") Sagoff's examples, as well as the overall theme of his essay—environmentalism as ressentiment—makes quite clear the nature of the bias that lies behind his sociological analysis. Why should it be a puzzle how environmentalism ties in with ideology unless the point is to undermine its credibility? Why should a real issue have to be part of what Marx rather contemptuously called an ideology (that is, any self-defensive political position other than one's own, and it is only fitting that Marx's own views soon became the paradigm case of an ideology in just that same contemptuous sense)? I do not get the problem that seems to motivate much of Sagoff's essay. What presumption of self-interest and political fanaticism is suggested in the question, "Why should environmentalism have become so popular among the rednecks?" Why the use of the very term *redneck?* What about the absurdly naive view, which I mention only with some embarrassment, that environmentalism has become a widely shared, even populist issue just because, in the past few years, it has become so obviously important even to the most unobservant and self-absorbed citizens, not just to heavy-breathing citizens of Los Angeles but to people virtually everywhere: Germans in the Schwartzwald glancing (at 190 kph) from the autobahn the demise of at least a third of the trees written about by their great romantic poets, Japanese urbanites with their portable oxygen masks in downtown Tokyo, Latin American peasants who can no longer drink from their local streams and rivers, fishermen who are employed as scrubbers and beachcombers during high season, all televised nightly for those who are lucky enough not to experience those ghastly discomforts firsthand. Is the prevalence of environmentalism really such a political paradox?

Let me suggest at the same time that *environmentalism* has become one of those words that has already outlived its usefulness. Why should we think that there is one question or one set of interests at stake here? The environment is, by its very nature, all inclusive—everything around us, both natural and "unnatural." It includes the soil on the nation's farms, the air in New York, the garbage dumps in Paterson and Ann Arbor, the beer bottles on Route 10 out of Houston, and the petroleum products hitting the beaches and killing the fish in Galveston. Granted that everyone is concerned to some extent with the need to breathe (more or less) clean air and drink water that will not kill over time, why should we suppose that the concerns that face the farmer and those that face the urbanite are of all the same sort? Instead of "environmentalism versus," our questions ought to be more subtle and multiple; in different kinds of cases there are different kinds of risks, different kinds of costs, different kinds of gains and losses—not just in dollars but in quality of life. The urban environments of our great cities are as important to millions of people as the rustic environments of the great outdoors, and to ignore the one in celebration of the other—or to collapse the two into a single paradigm—is to undermine the meaning of environmental concern, which is ultimately a regard for nature and human beings wherever and however they live.

Environmentalism, as an ill-defined rallying slogan for a large family of humanitarian and aesthetic concerns, is undoubtedly a good idea whose time has come. My objection to Mark Sagoff's essay, which I hope will not be confused with my respect for his overall enterprise, is that it is divisive and reinforces just those divisions that any effective environmental movement(s) must overcome. The welcome popularity of environmental issues should not be reduced to populism, even as a corrective to the now-defunct thesis tat these issues are motivated by elitism. But like so many other philosophical essays on "applied" topics, Sagoff's essay is written from too far above the fray. It is yet another example of the moral superiority of the uninvolved. To be sure, there is ample room for a particularly moral and even reverential perspective on environmental issues, but there is no need for one more top-down social sermon filled with accusations about the ulterior motives of those who are newly involved. I share the view that we need laws with teeth to prevent many disasters and an environmental emergency fund to cope with those that will inevitably happen despite our best efforts. But the too-prevalent conception that such regulation should be based on purely moral considerations, opposed to utilitarian concerns, and forced down the throats of the corporations as well as the farmers and freeway drivers, is ill conceived and self-defeating. What we need is a shared sense of responsibility, not interminable courtroom battles.

Responsibility is all too often projected as the burden of the other, and our own responsibilities disappear from view. The greatest danger of the top-down view of morality is that one's own foibles escape our notice. In this context I want to remind us all of the contrast between the complex pressures and responsibilities of corporate leadership and the rather straightforward responsibilities we have as critics and commentators of corporate behavior. Our duties are rather simple— meeting a deadline, for example. And yet as I look over the arena of what one might with some irony call academic responsibility, I find that even the most conscientious scholars can be less than responsive and responsible. Of course, there are always reasons, such as "the paper isn't finished," but one might compare the exigency of such reasons with the pressures facing, say, the executives of a large corporation whose heads are on the boardroom block and whose faces are on the daily news. With this in mind, I urge that our high-minded criticism of others should always be coupled with a kind of ethical humility, with less blame and suspicion, a sense that meeting one's responsibilities is not always so easy and we are all in this together. I welcome the populism that Sagoff seems so suspicious of, but I see it as an opportunity for working together rather than an occasion for moral highmindedness.

NOTES

Not having received the version of Mark Sagoff's paper to be published before my own deadline, my comments here may or may not be fair to the final wording of his essay.

1. *Ecologist* 18(4–5) (1988).

2. William Tucker, *Progress and Privilege* (Garden City, N.Y.: Doubleday, 1982).

3. See Adrian M. S. Piper, "A Distinction without a Difference," *Midwest Studies in Philosophy* 7(1982).

4. The most recent but not the last self-absorbed and pathos-ridden book in this modern genre is Bill McGibben's "death of Bambi" attack on everything human coupled with an outrageously sentimentalized Disney version of nature. See his *The End of Nature* (New York: New Yorker Books, 1989).

5. Frederick Turner, *Harper's Magazine* (November 1989).

6. See Thomas Berry's most recent book: *Dream of the Earth* (San Francisco: Sierra Club Books, 1988).

7. I use "Big Brother" not just in deference to Orwell but to the volumes of literature now appearing that make it quite clear, in case anyone doubted it, that it is we males and our macho attitudes—no doubt exemplified by our passion for *Car and Driver*—who are solely responsible for the destruction of nature, the female of the species being much more "natural" in the requisite sense—such as Susan Griffin, *Woman and Nature* (New York: Harper & Row, 1978), Gerda Lerner, *The Creation of Patriarchy* (New York: Oxford University Press, 1958), and Carolyn Merchant, *The Death of Nature* (New York: Harper & Row, 1980).

8. On this, note the exchange between Alasdair MacIntyre and Rolf Sartorious in Norman Bowie and Tom Beauchamp, eds., *Ethical Theory and Business* (Englewood Cliffs, N.J.: Prentice-Hall, 1979).

9. Bernard Williams and Martha Nussbaum, *Risk and Culture* (Berkeley: University of California Press, 1982).

12

Comments on Sagoff's Environmentalism as Populism

JAMES S. HOYTE

Mark Sagoff has provided some interesting observations and a provocative analysis in his essay; however, in an apparent attempt to make his commentary lively and amusing, he impresses me as being a little too cute and facile. Sagoff's extensive quotations from *Car and Driver* and the *Farm Journal* are used in such a way as to make us wonder whether more than a little cultural and intellectual snobbery is being reflected in the effort to contrast "lower-middle-class Americans—the 'silent' or 'populist' majority" with "upper-middle-class suburban liberalism." Regardless of Sagoff's manner of characterizing these two groups, he seems correct in noting that public opinion polls currently reflect extraordinarily high public commitment to environmental protection regardless of cost on the part of large numbers of every socioeconomic segment of American society. It is useful to try to understand why this commitment is so prevalent.

Sagoff draws a distinction between prudential and ethical environmentalism, which he describes as a political one that can be roughly equated with a distinction between those who seek to protect nature for the sake of human welfare and those who wish to protect nature for its own sake. He notes that prudential environmentalism emphasizes a conservative approach on risk and scarcity issues and suggests that social decisions be based on sound economic and scientific analysis. The idea is that nature is to be viewed as a source of resources that should be allocated efficiently and equitably over the long run. He correctly notes that supporters of this view tend to see environmental problems as basically economic issues that should be analyzed in economic terms, including the economic and scientific analysis of risk.

Sagoff then contrasts this economic view of environmental protection with what he calls ethical or cultural environmentalism, which seeks conservation of natural resources out of a pure respect for or love of nature. He continues, "On this view [ethical environmentalism], protecting the environment is the morally right thing to do—the course that corresponds to our best values and aspirations—even when the economic benefits fail to equal the costs. Such an approach presents normative rather than positive arguments for preserving nature." He theorizes that the fact that environmentalism has become an overwhelming political force even though it runs counter to such American values and beliefs as laissez-faire government, materialism, faith in economic growth, and protection of property rights can be explained at least in part by this distinction between prudential environmentalism and ethical environmentalism.

The strong public support for environmental protection and natural resource conservation is difficult to explain. Surely Sagoff is correct when he suggests that this support reflects a more absolutist view of environmental protection. Risk assessment and risk management concepts are not palatable to the American public. To the extent that academics, not to mention public officials, express concern about environmental protection in terms of cost-benefit or even risk-benefit analysis, the public at large seems to have difficulty in relating to these expressions. Not only is the language of risk management difficult to understand, but the very process of weighing and balancing seems temporizing and lacking in commitment. Indeed the lack of confidence in government that seems to characterize public opinion now may be traceable, at least in part, to the apparent lack of an absolute commitment to environmental health that the government seems to reflect when government officials talk about public health and natural resource protection in terms of risk assessment and risk management.

Sagoff notes that the populist nature of environmentalism became apparent starting in about 1980, after Love Canal and other outrageous episodes of corporate irresponsibility. He further suggests that post-1980 statutes reflected a shift from a focus on command and control of industrial technological activity to strict liability for pollution regardless of individual degrees of fault. There is no question that this shift has in fact occurred. Furthermore, there is plausibility in the notion that this period also can be characterized by a shift from environmental protection based on risk assessment, risk management, and risk perception to one that reflects a societal view that condemns pollution and contamination as much on moral or cultural as on economic or risk benefit grounds.

One of the major difficulties with acceptance of the notion that environmental populism and environmental concern cuts across every socioeconomic category and every segment of the U.S. population is the clear absence of minorities among those individuals expressing concern about environmental issues. While it is clear that whites in virtually every socioeconomic category are among local and national advocates of environmental protection, there is almost never anyone of color speaking out on these issues. This seems to be true when we are looking at traditional environmental organizations at the national level, like the National Audubon Society, the National Wildlife Federation, the Sierra Club, or the Natural Resources Defense Council, or when we move to the state and local levels.

Under a theory of elitist and upper-middle-class suburban control of environmental organizations, it would not be surprising to observe an absence of minorities in such organizations; however, environmental populism, as Sagoff notes, has cut across every stratum of American society, including urban as well as rural and suburban groups. Furthermore, the 1980s brought a tremendous increase in political activism among African-Americans, including dramatic electoral victories for blacks in major cities. Thus, there would seem to be no lack of ability to mobilize urban minority populations around public issues of concern to them. Yet African-Americans and Hispanics have not expressed concern about the environment. One wonders how this seeming lack of interest in environmental issues on the part of politically active minority populations fits into Sagoff's analysis of environmental populism.

I question whether Sagoff's thesis that a study of moral values and aspirations, such as love of nature, respect for community, and reverence for the past, is at the heart of modern environmentalism can be reconciled with a noticeable lack of interest in environmentalism on the part of African-American and Hispanic communities in the United States. This is an especially interesting question when one considers that the prominence of environmental populism and the politicization of minority communities have been phenomena that have been proceeding side by side at a seemingly explosive pace throughout the 1980s. If, in fact, environmental populism is based on love of nature and moral values rather than perceived health risk, one wonders whether this populist movement is likely ever to have a great deal of appeal to African-American and Hispanic populations. This is not to suggest that these populations have any different moral values from any other citizen of the United States. However, it is probably true that these minority citizens feel that they have less of a stake in American society and more distrust of corporate and political leadership in this country.

There have been many efforts over the years to suggest a sense of identity between African-Americans and Africans, but there is very little evidence that African-Americans identify more closely with Africans than white Americans or that Africans feel a greater bond with African-Americans than with the white colonial powers that controlled their societies for so long. There is plenty of evidence, however, of African and Caribbean antecedents to food, dance, and certain cultural factors in black America. If there is any insight to be gained regarding likely future attitudes of Third World communities toward environmentalism through an examination of African-American involvement in American environmental populism, such an examination is very worthwhile. The global implications of environmental degradation are beginning to be documented. An extremely important issue to be determined is whether Third World populations will see the new industrial nation commitment to environmental protection as a commitment truly based on moral grounds or whether they will balk at attempts to limit their industrial development on the basis that it is a strategy of neocolonialism and Western cultural imperialism. The relative success of global environmental protection may depend on how the Third World peoples interpret the environmental populism of the United States and Western Europe.

___ 13 _____

Customers as Environmentalists

MICHAEL MCCLOSKEY

Businesses are the key forces in shaping our environment—in determining what natural resources get developed, what open space gets devoured, what production processes are used and how much pollution there will be, what amounts of toxics are used and released, how products are designed and which are produced, and what kind of waste we are left with. To the extent that businesses are responsive at all, they are most responsive (in a buyer's market) to customers and investors; they are least responsive to government and others outside the web of economic logic that they respond to. These fundamental facts should lead us to consider how customers and investors can elicit better performance from America's businesses in respecting the environment.

At the outset, though, we can well ask whether customers are even interested in exerting their power toward that end. Some recent public opinion polls shed light on that subject. Let us first look at their overall assessment of business performance. One poll in summer 1989 found that only 11 percent think business is doing a good job of protecting the environment (Peters Group, July 1989); 47 percent think business is willing to harm the environment to obtain greater profits (Harris, May 1989); and 42 percent think business would put its workers' health and safety at risk (Harris, May 1989).

What are they willing to do about this? Eighty-nine percent of Americans are concerned about the impact on the environment of the products they buy (Peters Group, July 1989). Over 90 percent of Americans are willing to make a special effort to buy products from companies trying to protect the environment, with people by the same margin willing to give up some level of convenience to get an environmentally safe product; some 88 percent are willing to pay more toward that end (Gallup, August 1989).

What further action would they take? Seventy-six percent would boycott a company's products to stop a company from doing something bad (Harris, May 1989); 56 percent would write protest letters to the company (Harris, May 1989); and 53 percent say they have already declined to buy products in the past year because of concern over effects on the environment (Peters Group, July 1989). And they have done this without any organized effort. Indeed, *Time* magazine recently said that "corporate misbehavior has sparked a fevered outburst of consumer protest and boycotts." Clearly the public is primed to act.

What tools are available to help the American public act on its convictions and concerns? What organized efforts are underway?

GREEN PRODUCTS

Companies are already competing in terms of special nutritional values for products and lack of preservatives. Now they are beginning to compete in terms of the environmental virtues of their products. Both Walmart and K-Mart—the second and third largest retailers—have announced that they are bringing out lines of green products that should be on the shelves soon. Recently I visited Loblaw's supermarkets in Canada and saw the shelves filled with products with bright green labels, each proclaiming a special feature—"no chlorine," "no dioxin" "tuna not caught 'on dolphin,'" and so forth. Huge green banners proclaimed, "You can make a difference." "Buy green, buy clean," others proclaim. Loblaw's sales mushroomed up by $5 million in its first few weeks after introducing this line, and others are joining in. A new catalog from Vermont, *Seventh Generation,* is putting out "Products for a Healthy Planet."

The green dimension gives businesses a new way to position their products to beat their competition, and suppliers will be pushed by retailers to compete in terms of more environmental features. Green products have made much more headway in Europe, but their time is now arriving in North America.

ECOLABELING

As businesses compete with each other in making claims of environmental benefits that are hard to verify, attention will turn to seal-of-approval programs to validate such claims. The most well-established program of this sort is in West Germany—the so-called Blue Angel program; over 3,000 products bear that seal there. A government-sponsored jury passes on the claims and evaluates the environmental acceptability of the production process too. Companies eagerly seek the seal on their products and pay processing fees. Other countries, including Japan, Norway, Sweden, France, and Canada, are also moving to set up ecolabeling programs. The European Economic Community is expected to launch such a program soon.

In the United States, the Council on Economic Priorities is spinning off a new nonprofit corporation, to be called the Alliance for Social Responsibility, to set up a similar program. It will have a wider scope to screen products in terms of many social responsibility criteria, but it will have a heavy emphasis on the environment. This is slated to be launched in spring 1990.

SHOPPING GUIDES

In the meantime, the Council on Economic Priorities is providing other tools to help shoppers. Its shopping guide—*Shopping for a Better World*—is already a best-seller and is now going into a mass market edition. It rates over 1,300 brand name products on ten social issue criteria, including the environment. Easy symbols tell whether the product passes muster. The guide is being supplemented by a *Shopping Pad,* which lists the top- and bottom-rated products on opposite sides of a tear-out sheet that can be taken to the market. The Consumer Federation of America also produces guides that contain information on energy conservation comparisons of products, and another guide rates the toxicity of over 1,200 brand name products (*Nontoxic and Natural*).

CODES OF CONDUCT

As consumers try to look beyond the formulation of each product, they need help in sizing up the company standing behind it. They may wish to encourage companies that are consistently responsible. They get some of that picture through the Council on Economic Priorities's work, but now an effort has been launched to provide it in depth. You may have read about the Valdez Principles, which the Social Investment Forum put forth recently under the heading of the CERES Project. These are code of conduct principles—ten guidelines for appropriate corporate performance in the environmental field. They deal with such subjects as minimizing pollution, sustainable use of natural resources, waste disposal, energy efficiency, safe products, risk reduction, disclosure of hazards, damage compensation, environmental management, and audits.

All corporations are being urged to subscribe to them. Strenuous efforts will be made to get as many corporations as possible aboard, and those signing up will be monitored to see whether they live up to their pledges. As the principles are market tested to get the first set of companies signed up, some initial interpretation of them will be provided, and then further elaboration will be developed over the course of time. Following this phase, attention will shift to pressing holdouts to sign up. Shareholder actions, including proxy battles, may be organized to press corporate boards of directors.

The CERES Project was kicked off recently with $140 billion in assets behind it—some $40 billion in portfolios managed by the companies in the Social Investment Forum, who report their customers are more concerned by far with environmental factors than any other set of social issues. Also standing behind it are the Interfaith Center for Corporate Responsibility with $5 billion church-related investments and the second and fourth largest pension funds (those from California and New York City). It is hoped that other institutional investors will place their assets behind the effort too, with the realization that the long-term health of the economy depends on a sound natural resource base and good public health.

Many of these same groups have worked together closely in the past over the South African antiapartheid issue and are now throwing their weight into the environmental cause. On antiapartheid, they have signed up hundreds of companies to subscribe to the Sullivan Principles, and now they expect to do the same with the Valdez Principles. Over a decade or more, campaigns will be waged to bring the hard cases in line.

PROTESTS

Where these efforts do not succeed, stronger medicine may be required. Environmental groups and others may want to employ direct action techniques—boycotts, picketing, leafletting, letter writing, and petition efforts—directed at getting companies to comply.

Environmental organizations have already begun to use boycotts successfully. Greenpeace has persuaded Iceland to comply with International Whaling Commission rules with respect to whaling through a boycott of Icelandish fish sold through fish and chip shops. Burger King gave into a boycott over using Central American beef raised on pasture cleared from rain forests. McDonalds gave into a campaign aimed at getting it to stop using Styrofoam packaging based on chlorofluorocarbons (CFCs). NRDC (National Resource Defense Council) got the supermarkets to drop selling apples treated with the dangerous chemical alar, and the Sierra Club got Citicorp to decouple its package of commercial loans for Brazil from plans to build dams in Brazilian rain forests that were to be funded by the World Bank. And now the National Audubon Society has launched a boycott of all shrimp to bring pressure on Gulf Coast shrimp fishermen who are needlessly decimating sea turtles. Cetacean International has begun a boycott of yellowfin tuna, which is caught in a way that destroys dolphins. The whole wildlife community is boycotting elephant ivory and is working to close down the international ivory trade.

The next step is to focus boycott efforts on the worst polluters in the country—on the companies, for instance, that are pumping out the greatest volume of toxics into the environment. Data are now coming into public hands through the community right-to-know provisions of the new Superfund law (SARA) to tell us who is doing this. Now lists are being developed of the "Dirtiest Dozen" companies in the toxics field. The means will soon be in hand to target the worst offenders. Customers should avoid them to teach them a lesson that cutting environmental corners is bad business; it is bad—even disastrous—for the bottom line.

The fundamental point is to plant the idea that spending or investing money is another way to vote—to put power in the hands of those in the economy who behave responsibly toward the environment and to take it away from those who do not. It has been said, "When we spend money, we vote for the products that reflect our values." It is a way to cast ballots for the things we want to see. It is a way to vote in this sector that will be understood because it uses economics as the medium of communication. If businesses do not always want to hear the messages sent through ordinary voting, they cannot miss this message.

Business interests have lobbied for years to stymie almost every environmental control program of the government. Effort after effort has been bogged down in endless wrangling. Now there is an opportunity to steer completely around the stalled government programs and carry the case directly to the polluters and others who shirk their environmental responsibilities. Once corporate behavior is reformed, the government control programs will no longer be the decisive battleground; these can be straightened out later, after most of the fight is over. The fight will be moved to a battleground that capitalizes on the advantage of the overwhelming levels of public support for environmentalism; it allows the crushing weight of that opinion to be brought to bear directly on individual firms and not be dissipated through the quagmire of government.

Many in industry already feel encircled by forces and circumstances on the issue of the environment. They are not only fending off governmental regulators; they face a critical press, critical public opinion, the threat of litigation that could bankrupt a company with tort suits, and now demands from their customers and investors. And they do so in a competitive environment that forces them to be concerned over issues that mean so much to their customers. Things may be near the tipping point where a reasonable amount of effort may move practice along by leaps and bounds.

With the ozone layer breaking down, the climate heating, and a toxics crisis on our hands, major new breakthroughs are needed. Ways are needed to bypass the stumbling points in government and to regain momentum. Customers as environmentalists may have the means to make breakthroughs if they use their money as a way to vote.

They must not dissipate their efforts on minor issues. So far consumer pressures in this field have mainly been marshaled over local landfill and solid waste issues and questions of paper versus plastic bags. These are part of the picture but are far from the whole picture. We need to appreciate a hierarchy of values in this field and focus our best efforts on the vital issues of the day:

Eliminating all uses of CFCs to save the ozone layer.

Reducing emissions of greenhouse gases.

Making it socially unacceptable to spray toxics into the air and environment.

Bringing trade in endangered species to an end.

Getting the tropical forests managed sustainably.

Turning the trends around on pollution.

The national environmental movement needs to take these new opportunities seriously and organize campaigns that will focus on the top issues of the day and the worst offenders and that can be buttressed by appropriate government action.

Moving the scene of the action from government to consumer behavior will represent a sea change for the environmental movement and a change of institutional culture, which has always been focused on public policy. It is a change that makes sense. What we are doing now is yielding diminishing returns, and new opportunities beckon. Our first forays into this arena have been tremendously encouraging. Public opinion is practically inviting us to pick up the baton and lead. We cannot hold back. Our greatest successes may be in store.

—— 14 ——

An Environmental Agenda
for the 1990s

LYNN A. GREENWALT

I am at home talking about and expressing the environmentalist's—the conservationist's—view as it relates to industry, commerce, and the business world and
our apparent conflicts. The environmental community is made up of a whole
spectrum of people. My organization, the National Wildlife Federation, is somewhere in the middle of that spectrum. It is a large organization, with 5.8 million
members and supporters. We have a large staff and are active on many fronts. We
are also a corporation.

We are also a corporation though our efforts are of a somewhat different cast,
but the principles frequently are the same. Let me hasten to disabuse you of what
may be some myths about the National Wildlife Federation. We do not take
umbrage if a tree is cut, nor do we go into a transport of remorse if natural
resources are used in some parts of the world. We do not object to the contemplation of poking holes in the ground to extract gas and oil. But we do take umbrage
and become testy if those decisions are made in the absence of concern for and
recognition of the probable consequences of those decisions. We are fairly simple
folks with fairly simple observations about life. We believe in the wise use—and
I emphasize *wise use*—of natural resources.

We do not look on the corporate community as the dark force, the evil spirits,
at odds with nature and all that nature represents. We are fairly pragmatic. The
idea of better living through chemistry, the ability to get from here to there in an
automobile, the production of steel, and all the other things that make our lives
enjoyable is appealing. Commerce and industry are not going to go away, nor
would we prefer that. Therefore, we have concluded that the best way to deal
with the issues that have arisen, that in the past ten or fifteen years created great
conflicts between our interests and those of business, ought to be dealt with
directly.

The president of the National Wildlife Federation, Jay Hair, took a personal and institutional risk about seven years ago when he created the Corporate Conservation Council. At present, about fifteen major organizations from the corporate world are involved in it. We brought these people together—they with some reservation and we with trepidation—with our associates in the conservation community standing on the sidelines wondering if we had, in fact, done one of two impermissible things: had lost our rationality or been co-opted by organizations willing to buy our interest. Neither was the case. We brought senior corporate people together in some early meetings to discuss a fairly simple idea: the worth of wetlands. We have since advanced our interests to more controversial ideas, including waste reduction and groundwater management, and have engaged in discussions on subjects about which all of us would have been uncomfortable several years ago.

Early on, the various representatives stood and looked at each other and at us, wondering whether this was the place they ought to be and whether they had any reason to talk to each other. Why would Weyerhaeuser talk with Monsanto but for the use of one another's products? Why would USX talk with Duke Power? They learned to communicate with each other and with us. They came to realize that the conservationist's concern about industry is not necessarily that it cease to exist, that the chemical industry be brought to its knees or the steel industry be relegated to some other offshore location, or the timber industry should no longer cut trees.

We discovered that there is a lot we have in common and very little about which we were at odds. And we all recognized, perhaps most fundamentally, that we could learn to trust one another by being honest. It was not unusual in some circumstances over the past seven years or so to be dealing rationally and in a friendly way with a company on one hand and filing suit against a federal agency for failure to enforce the law against that same company in another arena.

We exhibited our expectations toward the corporate community by indicating that the public is looking for environmental improvement. The polls say so. Polls may not tell that to the administration, but they tell the rest of us that the country is interested, concerned, and willing to pay the price.

Environmental regulation has been one consequence of this perception. Environmental regulation is odious in some ways, it is pervasive, and it is likely to grow stronger and more broadly based. Furthermore, business and industry have realized that it cannot afford to ignore environmental reality. More to the point, when one looks dispassionately and objectively at the circumstances facing all of us, the reality is rather frightening, and we conclude correctly that everybody has a responsibility to rectify the situation. We believe that during the next decade business and industry can and, indeed should, work with conservation and community interests, broaden its horizons, and embrace more and more people because those people are concerned.

The implications of Title III, the Emergency Right-to-Know section of the Superfund Amendent and Reauthorization Act of 1986 (SARA) is that industry has the responsibility to tell what hazardous substances are produced, used or stored in their facilities. On the other hand, those who are told have a responsibility to work constructively with their corporate industrial neighbors to do something about any problem in a way that is comforting to everybody and is practical.

The best advice one can give to industry is that it should improve its credibility, just as we in the conservation community have a responsibility to improve our credibility. There is no place on our side for idle rhetoric or unsupported overstatement. There is no time, no room, on industry's side for being defensive. We must come together to determine what the problems are and reach conclusions about how they will be solved. That solution should involve as many people as possible, including some of those to whom industry has rarely exposed itself before—neighbors and the private citizen generally. They make a difference to us, and they can make a difference to the corporate sector.

Alliances between corporations and organizations like ours can be useful. They are not difficult to make because the differences between the corporate world and the environmental world are not as broad as some may believe. We think it is important to promote environment in the educational sector. It is important that people who will be corporate leaders come to understand the issues and how they are likely to affect all of us over time.

The idea of environmental improvement and environmental responsibility has to permeate all levels of corporations from top to bottom. If the chief executive officer does not believe in it, the shipping clerk is unlikely to be a zealot. It is important that everybody understand the issues because industry, the business world, the academic world, and the financial world have skills and special talents that can be harnessed to the effort. This is as it should be, since it has been typical of this nation to marshal its collective efforts to solve collective problems.

Our most basic problems are not regional, nor are they problems of a national dimension. We face a serious confrontation with reality on a global scale. We are members of a species called *homo sapiens:* the thinking man. There are now almost 5 billion of us. When I was born—more years ago than I like to remember—there were about 100 million in the United States; there are now 240 million of us in this country. At the present rate of projected growth, by the early part of the next century, there will be as many as 11 billion people inhabiting the planet. Whether or not you believe this is a problem, it is an indicator of the kinds of difficulties we will encounter because not everybody then can enjoy or have the prospect of enjoying a life-style like we have. As we move into the future, with the prospect of what is called sustainable development, there are great expectations raised, great obligations imposed on us because things must be changed to bring about a balance in the total array of systems, natural and artificial, necessary to create a greater sense of stability, of reasonableness, around the globe. It is vital because the alternative is the opposite of Carl Sagan's *Cosmos.* It is chaos.

It does not matter whether we are wrong even to some significant degree in our predictions about global warming. If we are inaccurate in our prognosis, it may mean only that Battery Park is flooded later than we had thought, that the Maldives disappear altogether by 2075 instead of 2050, or that Bangladesh is awash with only half as much water as everybody expected. It does not matter how accurate these projections and ideas are; the facts are telling us something we cannot ignore: we have to work together. I find no better allies in the light of our experience than the industrial, commercial, corporate, and academic communities.

No matter what the makeup of the organization—whether it's Exxon (and Exxon was a charter member of our CCC) or Weyerhaeuser or the little store down the street—the individuals in those organizations are just like you and me. They like to fly-fish or boat on a whitewater stream, and they like places of relative solitude as surely as any conservationist does. They like to know there are deer in the forest, and they want assurance their children and their children's children can look forward to enjoying the same realities. When you bring that to the fore—whether in an aggressive conservation organization like mine, a progressive business, or the insightful, thoughtful academic community—only progress can ensue. Given the alternatives, progress simply must ensue. We have no choice.

___ 15

Worldwide Responses to the Environmental Crisis

NANCY W. ANDERSON

The Valdez Principles, produced by the Coalition for Environmentally Responsible Economics (CERES), were introduced to the public on September 7, 1989, in New York City. Representatives of the major environmental organizations in the country were present, as well as representatives of socially conscious investment firms that specialize in advising citizens on investments. The coalition includes investment advisers who are responsible for $4.5 billion in investments for individuals, pension funds, and other institutional investments; they are bankers, brokers, and mutual fund managers. According to Joan Bavaria, cochair of the CERES Project, the group includes institutional members and other major brokerage firms. The brokers manage funds for clients interested in social investments.

With these principles, the CERES Project of the Social Investment Forum has set forth the broad standards for the evaluation of activities by corporations that directly or indirectly affect the earth's biosphere. The CERES Project has created the Valdez Principles to help investors make informed decisions around environmental issues before they invest.

In 1977 Leon H. Sullivan, a member of the board of directors of General Motors and a minister, created the Sullivan Principles. These principles dealt with corporations doing business in South Africa. According to Bavaria, the Sullivan Principles are more than simply a symbol. They have dealt with such problems as integrated lunchrooms, equal pay, training programs, and career opportunities. More than $480 billion in pension funds, endowments, and other investment pools have become involved in socially responsible investing because of the Sullivan Principles. Bavaria states, "As citizens of the Earth's biotic community, we who do business on this planet hold the obligation to maintain it for generations to come. Yet so far, a deregulated economy and a throwaway culture have provided little positive incentive for corporate environmental responsibility."

The ten principles will commit the corporation to safeguard lakes, rivers, wetlands, coastal zones, and oceans; minimize pollutants; make sustainable use of renewable resources; reduce and safely dispose of waste; conserve energy; reduce health and safety risk to employees and communities; market environmentally safe products; compensate victims for damage; disclose potential environmental, health, and safety hazards posed by operations; and represent environmental interests in corporate boards, plan compliance procedures, and release an annual assessment and audit.

Signing the principles publicly affirms that corporations and their shareholders have a direct responsibility for the environment. Corporations must conduct their business as responsible stewards of the environment and seek profits only in a manner that leaves the earth healthy and safe. Corporations must not compromise the ability of future generations to sustain their needs.

The corporations that sign the principles recognize that they are participating in a long-term commitment to update their practices continually in the light of advances in technology and new understanding in health and environmental science. They intend to make consistent measurable progress in implementing these principles and to apply them wherever they operate throughout the world.

The CERES Project will cite corporations for policy and work that has a beneficial effect on the environment. An example of this might include 3M, manufacturer of Scotch Tape for its 3P program (Pollution Prevention Pays). This program began in 1975 and is responsible for annually eliminating 100,000 tons of air pollutants, 10,000 tons of water pollutants, 150,000 tons of sludge and solid waste, and 1.5 billion gallons of wastewater. This program has advanced technology, strengthened 3M's competitive position in world markets, and saved $235 million. The Minneapolis-based specialty chemical company H. B. Fuller has cut its underground waste storage from seventy-four to thirteen tanks since 1984 and has initiated the Worldwide Environmental and Safety Committee to monitor its activities throughout the world. These are just two examples of the companies that may receive special recognition. Safety-Kleen, an Illinois company, now recycles industrial solvents. In 1986 Safety-Kleen processed 3 million gallons of spent solvent; 93 percent was reclaimed as clean solvent.

According to Bavaria and the CERES Project participants, information on whether a company has signed the principles will be disseminated to shareholders, and eventually we will see widespread sharehold resolutions encouraging the companies to stop unnecessary waste and pollution. People are demanding that the earth be protected; resolutions are being passed everywhere. In the summer of 1988, I was in Scotland during the election for the European Common Market countries. The greens won an amazing number of votes and a remarkable increase in seats in the new parliament. The only goal of the greens is a livable world and a clean environment. According to Scottish newspapers, Margaret Thatcher was shaken by the results of the election in England and is beginning to think about the environment. And shortly after, President Bush spoke often of the environment at the economic summit. Politicians are beginning to get the word that people across the world know that we are about the business of destroying the earth for a profit. In 1987, Mikhail Gorbachev made a speech before the United Nations in which he called for the peoples of the world to work together to care for the environment. Europe, Asia, Africa, and South America are all facing environmental degradation that will ensure sadness, sickness, and death to future generations. We will kill ourselves and all those around us for a profit.

I have just returned from leading an environmental delegation to the city of Yerevan in Armenia. We were there for two weeks. I led this delegation for the city of Cambridge, Massachusetts, a sister city of Yerevan. I was accompanied by Norton H. Nickerson, chairman of the environmental studies program at Tufts University; Gregor I. McGregor, a well-known authority on environmental law; Nancy Wrenn from the Massachusetts Department of Environmental Protection; Ingeborg Hegemann, chairman of the Cambridge Conservation Commission and a land use consultant; Gerry Tolman, chairman of the Sierra Club, New England Region; Zareh Maserejian, an engineer with Charles T. Main corporation; Gary Alpert from Harvard University, an authority on pesticides; John A. Anderson, former chairman of the board of appeals in Reading, Massachusetts; and Joan Nickerson, chairman of a conservation commission and a member of the League of Women Voters.

Believe me when I tell you that there is freedom of speech in the Soviet Union. There were 350 persons attending the summit meeting. They were scientists, engineers, and academicians. At least half of them were women. They criticized their government and called for reform. The people of Yerevan have stopped operation of a rubber plant that emits chlorophrene. The people have also demanded and accomplished the closing of the nuclear power plant. In Minsk, there are huge marches of citizens demanding that the government do something about the half-million people who are sick and under medical attention because of the Chernobyl accident. The Chernobyl accident was caused by human error, not by a faulty plant, and the resultant effect on the public health and safety will not be known for at least thirty years. Already 500,000 are sick. Italy has voted by 80 percent in a referendum to get rid of its nuclear power, and many other countries are closing nuclear power plants. It horrifies me that our government is planning to open Seabrook in New Hampshire.

Margaret Catley Carlson, former president of the Canadian International Development Agency, has said that we have three great problems in our world today: war, environment, and poverty. And I add to this: how many people in the less developed nations are we going to kill in this foolish competition between two great nations just to increase the profits of the arms merchants who seem to control us all? Will we foul the environment to such an extent that it will reject us? How long are we in the United States going to endure the rape of the earth's surface too so that we can live? We are 6 percent of the world's population using 40 percent of the world's natural resources. How long are we going to keep the less developed nations of the world in debt just trying to pay the interest on the loans that our banks made to them during the Arab oil crisis? They borrowed the money at 5 or 6 percent, and the interest quickly went to 20 to 22 percent. We are practicing usury. When our president and the secretary of treasury tell these less developed nations to tighten their belts and be austere in order to pay the interest, this means "increase your poverty."

The environmental community is working hard with the World Bank to institute "debt for nature"—swaps with a little success—and also to institute environmental impact assessment before loans are granted. We are late and far behind. Something must be done to cancel these debts, or the tropical rain forests that produce oxygen for our earth will be gone. The United States recently sold 22,000 acres of forested land in Alaska to Japan for pulp for its chemical industry. And the United States pays for the roads to go in and cut these trees, roads that cost more than the government makes from the lease sales. We are destroying our western forests, cutting them ruthlessly, even our 2,000-year-old trees, and selling them to Japan as lumber and pulp. Thirty million acres of forests in Vermont, Maine, New Hampshire, and New York are in danger of the same fate.

We do not inherit the earth; we borrow it from our grandchildren and our great grandchildren. We have an obligation as business leaders and as citizens to protect this world. I do not want death to come to my great grandchildren from the waste that I buried. Even if it is clearly marked, it will be forgotten, and they will stumble over it. We cannot even find waterpipes that we put in the ground fifty years ago. How are future generations going to find nuclear waste in 1,500 years?

We have time, I hope, to overcome our greed before it destroys us all. The young people bring hope; however, they primarily learn by example. Remember saying, "Do what I say; not what I do" to your children? If so, you surely remember that they really do what you do and not what you say. That brings to us the burden of being an example to those who follow us. Many of us tried to escape this. We must reexamine our lives and how we live them. We cannot escape the responsibility for the future; we must begin now before it is too late. Regardless of whether we have a religion, taking care and doing unto others as we would have them do unto us is an extremely useful tool in evaluating our actions.

Community-Corporate Conflict and the New Environmentalism: Four Cases on the Use of Lime Lakes and Mine Cavities for Hazardous Waste Storage and Disposal

KAREN PAUL AND
FRANCES GOTCSIK

This is a comparative case study of four communities in which companies proposed to use existing industrial sites for waste disposal. Two cases involve the use of lime lakes (barren industrial waste sites) to treat sewage sludge, and the other two involve the use of existing mine cavities for storage of hazardous waste. The two former cases involve the potential rehabilitation of existing industrial waste sites, whereas the two latter involve the use of existing mine cavities that are not perceived by communities as environmentally damaged.

These four cases, all occurring in the 1980s, have given rise to expressions of an environmental ethic that has emerged through community-corporate conflict. In three cases the dominant reaction of the community tended to reflect a traditional environmental ethic, which emphasizes the prudent use of natural resources and is based on the rights of communities and considering the rights of future generations. However, a new environmental ethic is emerging that goes beyond traditional environmentalism and extends the idea of natural rights to nature itself (Nash 1989, p. 9). One case considered here illustrates the emergence of this new environmental ethic, which is based on the belief that nature itself is an important part of the universe of moral objects. Taking this premise as a starting point, then, communities and corporations may have obligations to safeguard the well-being of the environment, perhaps even to the point of remedying damages inflicted by previous generations (figure 16.1).

Community opposition to proposed usage of sites for toxic waste disposal or storage developed in three of these cases, based mainly on the pragmatic values of traditional environmentalism. In one case, however, widespread community support has been observed, rooted in certain ethical dimensions suggested by both the old and new environmental ethics. Community activists invoked ideals

Figure 16.1
A Comparison of the Traditional Environmental
Ethic with the New Environmental Ethic

Traditional Environmental Ethic

Nature seen as object; humans seen as moral beings. Moral obligation to conserve nature and use prudently, for human purposes.

Rights of existing individuals acknowledged; rights of communities probably acknowledged; rights of future generations may be acknowledged; rights of nature not acknowledged.

Moral imperative: Conserve and use prudently.

New Environmental Ethic

Nature and humans seen as part of one moral universe. Moral obligation to respect nature as an end in itself, not just as a means of serving human needs.

Rights of existing individuals acknowledged; rights of communities acknowledged; rights of future generations acknowledged; rights of nature acknowledged.

Moral imperative: Respect, conserve, and heal.

Source: Adapted from Nash (1989).

suggesting that a sensitivity to the new, more transcendent environmental ethic can enable support to be mobilized for certain types of waste disposal projects.

Paul Steidlmeier has suggested, "The primary object of business ethics is to change the rules of the game by which society is ordered . . . business ethics is really a process of social change" (1987, p. 108). In the case of environmental ethics, companies, governmental bodies, and communities are playing a part in the development, communication, and formalization of both old and new environmental ethics. In these four cases, conflict has mobilized public sentiment in support of environmental ethics both traditional and new, has provided definition for those ethics, and has indicated the likely dimensions for the formalization of new societal expectations in law. In one case this new environmental ethic has resulted in widespread community support being given to a new toxic waste disposal project because reclamation of an existing toxic waste site is associated with the project. The moral tradition suggested here is the idea of healing. It is quite likely that the obligation to remedy or to heal past environmental insults may be a central expectation in the emerging environmental ethic.

Two of the sites examined here are located in Ohio, and two are in New York (figure 16.2). All four have been the locus of previous industrial activities that have altered the environment. Two sites are existing mine cavities resulting from the excavation of salt in one case and limestone in the other. The other two sites

Figure 16.2
Four Cases

Case 1. Norton, Ohio: PPG proposed to use mine cavities to store toxic waste from a multistate area.

Current status: Proposal suspended

Case 2. Barberton, Ohio: PPG proposed to use barren lime lakes to dispose of sewage sludge from multistate area.

Current status: Proposal operational

Case 3. York, New York: Geostow, a single-purpose, new organization was formed to acquire mine cavities in order to store incinerator ash.

Current status: Project suspended pending court determination of ownership status

Case 4. Solvay, New York: The local government has proposed to use lime lakes left behind after the departure of Allied Chemical company to dispose of sewage sludge.

Current status: Project pending

---

are barren lime lakes created by past disposal of industrial wastes generated in the production of soda ash, used primarily in glassmaking. Two sites were proposed by a large multinational company (Pittsburgh Plate Glass, Inc., or PPG), one by an entrepreneurial shell corporation (Geostow, Inc.), and one by local government after the withdrawal of a large multinational (Allied Chemical) from the community.

CASE 1: NORTON, OHIO

Norton, a small city of about 12,500, is located on the outskirts of Akron, Ohio. PPG Industries, Inc., formerly Pittsburgh Plate Glass, has operated large limestone mines in Norton since 1941. Mine cavities now exist under about 450 acres of land. In 1981 PPG announced that it intended to use these mine cavities to store about 50,000 tons of hazardous waste a year from a multistate area. Included would be residues of chlorinated benzene and substances containing lead, mercury, asbestos, copper, chromium, and pesticide waste, packed in barrels sealed in cinderblock. The dry, deep, stable atmosphere of the mine cavities was presented as ideal to store this material.

Environmental Issues

Citizens of the community immediately expressed a number of concerns about the proposal: possible leaking from corroded barrels, subsurface water contamination through lateral migration, air contamination through access shafts, increased traffic, inadequate long-term monitoring, and a decline in property values. Ethical issues involving land use tended to emerge as the discussion process continued. In the first stage of discussion, there was a focus on pragmatic issues such as health risks and impact on property values. These issues clearly belong to the traditional environmental ethic, emphasizing the prudent use of natural resources so as to preserve the health and property values of the individuals and the communities affected (Henson and Chuparkoff 1981).

Over time, however, questions were raised about whether burying waste was the right thing to do. Why not recycle or reuse, detoxify, incinerate, solidify, or encapsulate it? One person observed that burying waste was what cave man practiced, the clear implication being that with the progress of civilization, society should have developed a more adequate means of waste disposal (Proctor 1982). This more transcendent orientation corresponds to the new environmental ethic in which the rights of nature itself are acknowledged.

Organizational Structure of the Norton Project

PPG met with city and county officials before publicly announcing the project and held two public meetings in the first three days after the announcement was made. Corporate officials from Pittsburgh were present to respond to community concerns. As community opposition was mobilized, however, PPG became more reactive and defensive in its response. Within a few months of the announcement, PPG was questioning the motives and the competence of local community leaders, charging those who opposed the project with not addressing the issues and lacking knowledge of toxic substances (Proctor 1982). However, in the years just prior to the proposal, PPG's own reputation as a company had been adversely affected by layoffs that had resulted from the scaling down of its mining operations. Furthermore, PPG's credibility was damaged by the fact that detailed engineering studies had not been completed at the time the project was announced, nor had the company completed studies detailing the anticipated economic impact of the project (Widing 1982).

Community Response

Community response to PPG's proposal was swift and negative. Within a week of the announcement of the project, 500 signatures of opposition had been collected at two public meetings. Within two weeks, a citizens' group named CODE (Citizens Opposed to the Destruction of Our Environment) had been formed. By the end of the first month, CODE's membership was five hundred, with ten committees at work on various aspects of the PPG proposal. This group sponsored a variety of informational and fund-raising events and lobbied local, state, and national officials to oppose the project. Among the founding members of CODE were several residents who had sufficient scientific background and technical expertise to be able to understand and to translate into nontechnical language information about toxic and hazardous waste issues. PPG's claim that citizens were ill informed lacked validity at this point and in fact contributed to the atmosphere of hostility and mistrust that had developed in the community.

Several members of CODE purchased single shares of PPG stock, giving them entry to the April 1982 stockholders' meeting in Pittsburgh. There they picketed and presented a statement to the shareholders detailing their opposition to the use of the Norton limestone mine for a toxic waste dump (Henson 1982).

By early March 1982 county officials responded to the concerns of their constituency, going on record as opposing the project. The county executive, who had previously declined to take a public stand, went on record as being opposed to the project. The executive director of the Hazardous Waste Facility Approval Board had initially stated that only legal and technical considerations were relevant and that public opposition mattered little but with the mobilization of community groups came to assert that arguments over health, safety, transportation of the waste, and possible decline of property values would be taken quite seriously ("County Executive," 1982). This acknowledgment was based on the recognition of the rights of the community. The rights of future generations were not stated by the officials at any stage to be a relevant consideration, nor was there any official recognition of the rights of nature itself.

Finally, in June 1982 Norton voters passed a special income tax of .025 percent designed to raise $375,000 over a three-year period to be used to fund legal and engineering costs involved in resisting the PPG proposal. In July 1982 PPG announced that it would postpone the proposed project until the general level of business improved. It continued to assert that the Norton mine was one of the best potential waste storage sites in the country and that the project was not dead, but no further attempts have since been made to secure the necessary approvals for the project to go forward (Wiegand 1982).

CASE 2: BARBERTON, OHIO

Barberton, with a population of approximately 30,000, is also located on the outskirts of Akron, Ohio, adjacent to Norton. PPG's operations extend across two townships where the company maintained a soda ash plant from 1899 to 1973. About 20 million tons of alkaline industrial waste by-products (calcium chloride, calcium carbonate, magnesium carbonate) were dumped into a 600-acre waste site. This area is now a series of 50-foot lagoons—white, highly alkaline, slightly mushy, and barren. A 1983 report of the Ohio Environmental Council singled out this site as the worst example of industrial water pollution in the Muskingum River basin (Khoury and Mohr 1983).

In 1984 a $1.7 million pilot project, funded by PPG, tested the outcome if sewage sludge, highly acidic, were mixed with the alkaline waste. A locust tree grew. Reclamation of the lime lakes seemed a theoretical possibility. In 1985 the PPG board of directors appropriated $1 million to fund a demonstration project whereby this land would be reclaimed through mixing sewage sludge, to be collected from municipalities, with the lime lake material, at a projected rate of 100 tons, or 20 semitrailers, per day, to create a synthetic soil.

Environmental Issues

Two environmental issues are involved in the Barberton case. Reclamation of an industrial wasteland is one issue. The lime lakes are aesthetically offensive, foul smelling, and a source of contamination of groundwater and the Tuscarawas River. Nearby residents complained to state officials of a high cancer rate in the area, but a survey conducted by the Ohio Department of Health and released in 1985 indicated no significant statistical abnormalities (Indian 1985).

The second issue is the disposal of sewage sludge. Sewage sludge is municipal waste, which is 20 to 35 percent solid material and is generally disposed of by incineration or by spreading on land. It may be reprocessed into fertilizer. Sewage sludge can contain toxic material such as heavy metals, human pathogens, and organic compounds, so its use must be carefully monitored. The corporate commitment to ongoing responsibility for the treatment site is of critical importance. The fact that PPG is a large multinational corporation with continuing operations in this community makes it at least possible that responsibility can be maintained.

Organizational Structure of the Barberton Project

In presenting its plans to the Barberton community, PPG relied heavily on local plant managers. This contrasts with its approach in Norton, where the announcements and negotiations were handled mainly by managers from corporate headquarters in Pittsburgh. PPG made extensive efforts to involve a wide range of community groups in the planning for the Barberton project; again, this contrasts with Norton, where PPG made little attempt to mobilize the support of local community leaders or community organizations. PPG stressed the long-term and experimental nature of its project. The company suggested that the reclamation project would take twenty to twenty-five years. The fact that no inflated claims were made of rapid results contributed to the company's perceived legitimacy in this project. Indeed, a positive moral judgment was forthcoming from the community because the orientation of the company appeared to be long range and hence grounded in values other than short-term profit maximization.

Expressions of concern with both traditional and new environmental values have come from within PPG itself. Indeed, the corporation has been a primary instrument for educating the community of Barberton about the technical and the philosophical aspects of the reclamation project. The rights of future generations, and the rights of nature itself, are suggested by one PPG manager's explanation of the company's program: "A lot of environmental problems were created by our ancestors—we got tired of it—we have legacies to live with" (Weber 1989).

Community Response

In Barberton there was an initial period of community uncertainty about the PPG project that revolved around several issues. Sewage sludge can contain toxic contaminants such as heavy metals and viruses that can accumulate in soil. Wildlife can suffer from exposure to these materials. In the past the lakes have been a source of offensive odor; the question arises as to whether adding sewage to them will aggravate this problem. There will be considerable traffic generated by the hauling of about twenty-one semitrailers of sewage sludge daily. Finally, there is no certainty that the lime lakes can be reclaimed from their present barren state. But the project is now operational, and small areas of the lime lakes have been reclaimed. The one issue that is a continuing source of community concern is odor.

The fact that the lime lakes were such a large and visible insult to the environment was a powerful incentive for local government, state environmental officials, and community action groups to cooperate with PPG. PPG encouraged a wide range of community groups to become involved in the planning of the project. The orientation of both company and community appears to go beyond the simple waste disposal issues involved and to emphasize the fact that this is a reclamation project. There is a frank acknowledgment by both company and community that past environmental damage has been done by the company and has been permitted by the community. The remediation intended to result from this project may be seen as an expression of the new environmentalism, which stresses the rights of nature itself and the obligation of communities and companies to remediate when possible.

CASE 3: YORK, NEW YORK

York, with a population of about 3,500, is located in the Finger Lakes region of upstate New York. It is a predominantly agricultural community on the outer fringe of the Rochester metropolitan area. The one large company operating in the area is the International Salt Company, which has been mining salt since 1882. In summer 1987 a number of property owners in York were approached by realtors and asked to sell purchase options on their land or on the cavities beneath their land left from past salt-mining activity. The prices offered were up to twice the previous market value. Rumors circulated about a large project of some undefined type being developed in the area, but realtors refused to reveal the usage they intended for the land. Only one large piece of land was transferred—a 900-acre tract whose new owner stated, "The land is emphatically not being obtained for waste disposal—not a burner, not a landfill, not a toxic waste dump" (Bickel 1987).

By September 16, 1987, the company making the purchases, Geostow, Inc., had begun procedures to obtain permission from the New York State Department of Environmental Conservation to use mine cavities to store 6,000 to 8,000 tons of ash per day, with the ash being shipped from a fourteen-state area. Geostow anticipated that over 5,000 acres of land would be involved, although only 900 had been acquired at that time and the legality of that purchase would be challenged in the courts. Geostow publicly announced its plans on November 12, 1987 (Department of Regulatory Affairs 1987).

Environmental Issues Emerge

Community suspicion had been aroused by the process through which land acquisitions had been made: inflated prices were being offered for properties; unidentified buyers were operating from outside the community; rumors were circulating that a large project was being proposed. Then Geostow filed its official proposal with the New York State Department of Environmental Conservation (DEC).

In addition to the general issue of the trustworthiness of Geostow, community concerns revolved around several environmental issues. First was the consideration of the increased traffic generated by an operation of this size. The traffic would consist of up to twenty trucks and one eighty-car train per day. The facility would operate 24 hours a day, 7 days a week.

Second was the issue of environmental damage. Geostow maintained that although this ash would contain lead and cadmium, it would be hazardous only if it got wet. While a salt mine might appear an unlikely place for this to be a danger, further investigation by the New York State Department of Environmental Conservation (DEC) revealed that one shaft required continuous pumping of 250 gallons of water a minute, and hence groundwater contamination was a danger.

Citizens also brought up health risks that could be associated with the issues of groundwater contamination and traffic in incinerator ash. This was the most prevalent concern expressed when the DEC held a public hearing on the proposal in February 1988.

Ethical issues involving land use tended to be expressed less frequently and later in the process than were ethical concerns relating to the methods by which Geostow appeared to do business. After the February hearing, however, four local churches made statements in opposition to the project, and one correspondent urged the DEC to consider the humanity of all persons affected, being mindful that those most vulnerable are those without political power (Department of Environmental Conservation 1988).

Yet another issue was the possibility of contaminating the salt mines themselves, a problem compounded by the adversarial relationship that quickly developed between Geostow and International Salt Company, which maintained that the mine cavities in question were not abandoned, that ownership had not reverted to the surface owners who had agreed to sell Geostow the right to usage, and that in fact Geostow's claims of ownership were fraudulent.

Organizational Structure of the York Project

Geostow was a corporate entity created specifically for this project. Its president, Brian Swartzenberg (since deceased), was associated with a number of other waste disposal corporations, one a subject of RICO (Racketeer-Influenced and Corrupt Organizations) prosecution by the state's attorney general, although the suit remains unsettled.

Geostow was loosely connected with a French company, Geostock, jointly owned by four major oil companies (British Petroleum, Elf, Shell, and Total). According to company publications, Geostock has underground storage facilities in France, Belgium, Great Britain, South Korea, and Morocco, although none of these facilities holds toxic ash. Swartzenberg represented that his company had approached Geostock in order to obtain its expertise in underground storage. The degree of active involvement by the French company was never clear, but on at least one occasion representatives of Geostock came from France to meet with the community and regulatory officials.

Community Response

A citizens' group was formed soon after Geostow initially approached landowners, prior to the actual public announcement of the project by Geostow in November 1987. The first meeting of town leaders, farmers, school officials, and local businessmen was held in August 1987. This group mobilized a community organization, PACE (Protect a Clean Environment), to oppose the project on the grounds that it represented a potential threat to the environment of York. This group identified a number of issues of concern to its members and to the community.

First was the issue of the trustworthiness of the company proposing the project. Apart from the history of the RICO investigation (which concerned the cleanup of the Love Canal by another company headed by the same entrepreneur), there were the current actions of the company with regard to the process by which land acquisitions had been attempted. The local individuals who had acquired land for the company had denied that any waste disposal project was involved. Landowners approached had been told that no such project was anticipated. Community residents perceived a pattern of lying on the part of company officials and individuals associated with the company's activities. One reinforcement to this image was the fact that the application to the DEC contained numerous misrepresentations and errors. For example, Geostow asserted that it owned 10,000 acres of land, when in fact only 2,000 could be substantiated.

Geostow's ownership of the mine cavities is disputed by the International Salt Company. Thus far the courts have upheld the salt company's claims (*International Salt Company v. Geostow et al.* 1988), although an appeal is pending. The combination of International Salt Company's resources and citizen activism has stalled the project. The heightened environmental consciousness generated in the community by the conflict has resulted in a number of community efforts to deal constructively with the solid waste issue. A Solid Waste Advisory Committee is active and has sponsored a number of community events, such as community recycling drives, informational meetings on composting and recycling, and lobbying of local stores to provide paper bags rather than plastic bags. Most significant, the community has negotiated with the local waste hauler to implement separated garbage pickups. This community has transcended the immediate, pragmatic issues of protecting property values and guarding against health danger and has moved to a level of environmental awareness and concern that approaches the new environmentalism.

Finally, the potential impact of the project on both property values and the health of York residents remains in question. In response to citizen concern, the local board of supervisors commissioned a study on the health effects of the type of waste that would be stored in the mine cavities.

CASE 4: SOLVAY, NEW YORK

Solvay is a town of 8,300 located in the metropolitan Syracuse area in upstate New York. Since 1881 Solvay has been the location of a soda ash plant operated by Allied Chemical Company. In February 1986, Allied announced that it was closing its facility in Solvay. As with the PPG facility in Barberton, barren lime lakes had been created by the disposal of waste on about 750 acres of land.

The New York State DEC entered into negotiations with Allied to force the company to do a study of the reclamation efforts that would be required to restore the lime lakes. Also involved in the negotiations was Onondaga County, since the county had used the lime lakes for dumping sewage sludge since 1980. The DEC would not permit this practice to continue after cessation of Allied operations, raising the annual cost to the county of disposing of sewage sludge to $4.3 million.

A need to reduce these high sludge disposal costs brought the government and some of the country's agriculturalists and other residents into conflict. In conjunction with their contracted sludge hauler, Bio Gro, Inc., of Maryland, Onondaga Country proposed that beginning in spring 1989, dewatered sewage sludge would be spread as fertilizer on fifteen private county farms, thereby cutting their disposal costs in half. Concerned with the long-term environmental effects of the application of sludge to land used for crops and dairying, opponents instead advocated using the Allied waste beds for sludge disposal following what they have termed "the Barberton process" (Gross 1988). Although the DEC has denied the county the necessary land-spreading permit because it is unable to meet regulations for killing pathogens in the sludge, Bio Gro, a company with experience in land spreading, still expects to institute this sludge disposal process. In addition, Bio Gro and the county have received approval from DEC for a one-year research project involving mixing of sludge with a 5-acre area and 25-acre area of the Allied beds.

Environmental Issues Emerge

There are three environmental issues in this case. First is Allied's responsibility to the community to address the waste beds in a matter that will not leave the two towns where the company has been located with future health risks and cleanup costs. Very real are the risks from chlorides leaching into Onondaga Lake and the possibility of eventual groundwater contamination by other as yet unknown chemicals from years of use of the beds for disposal of sewage sludge and other industrial waste.

The second issue is the safety of land spreading of sewage sludge. Possible dangers include the introduction of disease-carrying organisms, heavy metals, and carcinogens into the soil, food crops, and groundwater. Potential for contamination of sludge by human pathogens is already acknowledged; measures designed to eliminate this danger are of central importance to approval of the land-spreading project. Although ostensibly there are safeguards designed to make sewage safe before application, there is concern that equipment may malfunction, testing will not be rigid enough, and eradication procedures may not be sufficiently complete to eliminate all danger of contamination of soil, crops, and water supplies. Of special concern to Onondaga County agriculturalists is the application to land used for dairying because of the potential for contamination of milk through plant uptake, as well as through ingestion by cows of contaminated soil or the sludge itself as they pull up crops by their roots.

When it announced the closing of its Solvay facility in April 1985, Allied promised to do what was necessary to clean up the site (Wasserman 1987). Believing that Allied waste beds were adversely affecting Onondaga Lake, the DEC instituted an enforcement action against Allied. Allied signed a consent order with the DEC, comparable to an out-of-court settlement, agreeing to study groundwater contamination from its waste beds. Allied's study, not surprisingly, concluded that chloride pollution of Onondaga Lake from the beds was minimal; thus there was no justification for its cleaning up the waste beds. Allied and DEC are still negotiating the eventual disposition and reclamation of the waste beds. Although there is community concern about the environmental status of Onondaga Lake, thus far community activism has not developed to the point of forcing the DEC to become aggressive in dealing with Allied Chemical.

Community Response

Community response to the land-spreading aspect of the issue has primarily been expressed by local farmers, agricultural leaders, and town governments, motivated by their interest in preserving the county dairy industry. Local farmers know that fifteen farms in Pennsylvania have been declared useless after having been spread with sludge. Another consideration is that Del Monte will not accept crops grown on land spread with sludge. Furthermore, they feel that DEC has a poor record with respect to monitoring such projects. While not formally organized in opposition, they have used their political positions and associations to pressure the county and Allied to give greater consideration to expanding the Allied-county waste beds experiment.

Response to Allied's environmental legacy has primarily been directed by governmental rather than grass-roots citizen activist response. Environmentalists and county government praised Allied for its initial willingness to correct past environmental wrongs while acknowledging that some of what it offered to do was nothing more than legal requirements used as a proxy for ethics. The DEC is seeking to require that Allied internalize some of the external costs of its past operations.

In Onondaga County traditional environmentalism rather than new environmentalism seems to be the main source of community reaction. The cost of dealing with a problem (sludge disposal) is more salient to the community than is the ultimate state of the lime lakes. For the farmers who are seeking to block land spreading of the sewage sludge, the main concern appears to be continued viability of their land for agricultural productivity rather than the rights of nature. Yet there is a possibility that a more global community concern might develop about the state of the lime lakes and the environmental status of Lake Onondaga, which the lime lakes border. The county and Allied Company have a unique opportunity to combine efforts to solve their respective environmental problems. However, the community appears to be not yet sufficiently mobilized to force consideration of any issues beyond the most traditional environmental concerns expressed by the agricultural community.

Emerging Moral Issues

Three approaches for ethical action appear to emerge from these cases. These arise out of the rights of communities, the rights of future generations, and the rights of nature itself. The first is the moral obligation of corporations to do no harm to the environment, particularly no harm that will be irreversible or prohibitively costly to remedy. Associated with this is the obligation of relevant government units to permit no irreversible harm to be done to the environment. The second moral duty is to remedy wrongs done in the past, if possible within a corporate context that will maximize the likelihood of continuing commitment over an extended time. Associated with this second moral duty is the necessity for the government that has permitted abuse of the environment to remedy the wrongs done in the interest of both the existing community and future generations. Third, an emergent ethic is suggested that would take nature itself as an object of respect.

The Rights of Communities

Communities are made up of both the individuals and the institutions located in a particular geographic area. The rights of communities include the right to common enjoyment of public goods, such as clean air, clean water, roads, parks, and other commonly held community assets. These rights commonly form the first line of defense as communities attempt to mount their defenses against proposals that threaten the environment.

The Rights of Future Generations

A second set of rights tends to emerge later in the mobilization of public opinion regarding environmental issues. This set of rights concerns the rights of future generations. One moral philosopher has stated, "Justice, then requires that we hand over to our immediate successors a world that is not in worse condition than the one we received from our ancestors" (Velasquez 1982, p. 254). And yet some questions remain as to the ethical status of potential generations. The moral standing of as-yet-nonexistent humans is debatable. How can present generations know the preferences of future generations? What moral standing should future generations have if their interests conflict with the interests of already existing humans? This set of obligations appears to be somewhat more abstract and theoretical than the previous set and appears to emerge after the rights of existing communities have been discussed.

Corporations and the Rights of Nature

The suggestion that natural objects should or could have legal standing has been discussed theoretically (Nash 1989; Stone 1972, 1987, 1988). From a theoretical perspective this set of rights appears to be the most controversial of the ethical considerations discussed here; however, these cases illustrate that for many citizens, and indeed for at least some corporate spokespersons, nature itself may have rights and claims. The reaction of the community to the Barberton proposal illustrates that many citizens feel a moral imperative not only to preserve nature but also to restore nature when it has been damaged. Discussion of this obligation occurred when a proposal was made that might change the current environmental status of Barberton. Only after a certain amount of collective discussion was generated about the advisability of the new project did citizens express strong feelings about reclamation. However, restoration of the lime lakes came to be perceived as a morally righteous action by the community of Barberton and probably would also enjoy wide support in Solvay if sufficient commitment were made by government to ensure enduring and competent oversight of the project.

When a corporation proposes to exploit an existing resource, as in the two cases involving mine cavities, its moral grounding is much more uncertain than when it proposes to develop a project that has elements of remediation or healing. The communities of York, New York, and Norton, Ohio, reacted as if these proposed projects would deprive the community of a jointly held good. In each of these cases, the best argument the corporation could make was to assert that it would do as little harm as possible, would monitor for damage, would remedy problems if they should arise, and give other similar assurances. The extent of community protest in each case illustrates the moral outrage a substantial number of citizens feel intuitively when private interests attempt to encroach on public assets. The effectiveness of their protests is highly dependent on existing legal and regulatory mechanisms, as well as the pragmatic consideration of being able to command control over enough funds to defend environmental interests. In the case of York, the funds were supplied by a corporation whose interests happened to coincide with the community on this particular issue at this particular time; in the case of Norton the funds were raised by a special tax.

In the case of Barberton a corporation that is directly responsible for past environmental damage has accepted the responsibility for remedying that damage. The profit incentive is involved here because PPG expects to be able to realize a positive return in providing a repository for sewage sludge. This is a situation where both community and corporation have the possibility of benefiting. Here ethical action coincides with market mechanisms. Moreover, all three ethical issues coincide with the project proposal. The rights of the community are not perceived as being adversely affected by the project, partially because the extent of the existing environmental damage is so extensive. The rights of future generations are enhanced by the prospect of long-term reclamation. Finally, if nature itself has rights, these rights are being recognized by the attempt to remedy past harm and restore the area to an environmentally sound status.

In the case of Allied Chemical, the local government has been left holding the bag after the departure of the corporation. If Allied had proposed to follow PPG's example in restoring the lime lakes through the use of sewage sludge, it might have been able to generate some community support for its plans; however, the capacity of government to generate a significant level of support for this project is problematic. Local and state government do not have the access to the level of support for research and development that can be commanded by a large multinational corporation. A more effective legal mechanism for holding Allied Chemical responsible for its past actions is needed. Allied Chemical acknowledges its obligation to remedy past wrongs done to the environment but thus far denies that serious wrongs were done. The limited resources of the state have made the community as a whole dependent on the research and analysis supplied by Allied Chemical and DEC. For Allied Chemical it is certainly the case, and for DEC possibly the case, that their short-term interest lies in reporting that the extent of permanent environmental damage is not as great as it appears to be. Thus, short-term, pragmatic interests may directly conflict with long-term, ethical obligations. The DEC has insisted on a commitment from Allied to restore the lime lakes, but thus far the resources available to the government have limited the state in holding Allied accountable. With the company no longer maintaining operations in the area, the community is in a weak position to bargain.

This situation demonstrates the necessity of having effective environmental enforcement measures operative on the federal level. Currently large multinational corporations are able to escape responsibility for environmental damage, as Allied Chemical has done in Solvay, because environmental laws are not consistently enforced. In the York case, the fragmentation of this entrepreneur's various waste disposal enterprises precludes any substantial commitment to research and development on the scale required for environmentally sensitive projects, as well as providing a means for avoiding future liability for environmental damage. The Barberton case illustrates the advantages of having a large multinational such as PPG undertake the research and development, and future liability, of environmentally sensitive projects.

REFERENCES

Bickel, Bob. 1987. "Land-Buying Binge Leaves Residents of York Guessing." *Rochester* (New York) *Democrat and Chronicle*, September 9.

"County Executive Opposes PPG Waste Storage Plan." 1982. *Akron Beacon Journal*, March 5.

Department of Environmental Conservation. 1988. DEC Region 8. *Scoping Notebook*. Avon, N.Y., February.

Department of Regulatory Affairs. Department of Environmental Conservation Region 8. 1987. *Geostow Proposal*, vol. 1, attachment C: *Project Summary*. Avon, N.Y., November 12.

Gross, Esther. 1988. "State, County Clash on Allied Cleanup Plan." *Syracuse Herald Journal*, November 23.

Henson, Rich. 1982. "CODE Takes Mine Protest to Pittsburgh." *Akron Beacon Journal*, April 16.

Henson, Rich, and Karen Chuparkoff. 1981. "PPG Defends Dump . . . and the Public Responds." *Akron Beacon Journal*, December 11.

Indian, Robert. 1985. *Survey of Residents in Close Proximity to the Lime Lakes in Franklin Township*. Columbus, Ohio: Department of Health.

International Salt Company v. Geostow et al. 1988. Decision and Order, Civ. 87-1501L. U.S. District Court, Western District of New York, October 12.

Khoury, Chris, and Eileen Mohr. 1983. "Report on Sampling of Residential Well Water Supplies in the Vicinity of the Waste Dump Areas Utilized by the PPG Industries Installations at Barberton." Twinsburg, Ohio: Ohio Environmental Protection Agency.

Nash, Roderick Frazier. 1989. *The Rights of Nature: A History of Environmental Ethics*. Madison: University of Wisconsin Press.

Proctor, Glenn. 1982. "Norton Mine Target of Protest." *Akron Beacon Journal,* March 21.

Steidlmeier, Paul. 1987. "Business Ethics: Reconciling Economic Values with Human Values." In *Business and Society: Dimensions of Conflict and Cooperation,* pp. 101–20. Edited by S. Prakash Sethi and Cecilia M. Falbe. Lexington, Mass.: Lexington Books.

Stone, Christopher D. 1972. "Should Trees Have Standing? Toward Legal Rights for Natural Objects." *Southern California Law Review* 45: 461–87.

Stone, Christopher D. 1987. *Earth and Other Ethics.* New York: Harper & Row.

Stone, Christopher D. 1988. "Moral Pluralism and the Course of Environmental Ethics." *Environmental Ethics* 10: 139–54.

Velasquez, Manuel. 1982. *Business Ethics: Concepts and Cases.* Englewood Cliffs, N.J.: Prentice-Hall.

Wasserman, Elizabeth. 1987. "Allied to Study Pollution." *Syracuse Herald Journal,* January 8.

Weber, Steven. 1989. Telephone interview, February 9.

Widing, Robert E. 1982. "Is It Safe to Store Chemicals? Yes, Says PPG." *Akron Beacon Journal,* March 30.

Wiegand, Virginia. 1982. "PPG Will Delay Norton." *Akron Beacon Journal,* July 13.

III

ENVIRONMENTAL PROBLEMS AND SOLUTIONS

Not in Their Backyards, Either: A Proposal for a Foreign Environmental Practices Act

ALAN NEFF

This chapter proposes federal legislation designed to compel U.S. businesses to conform their foreign operations to U.S. environmental protection and natural resource conservation statutes and to related U.S. administrative rules and orders. Modeled on the U.S. Foreign Corrupt Practices Act (FCPA), the proposed statute would subject U.S. businesses operating overseas to criminal prosecutions and civil suits by public officials and private citizens in U.S. courts for violations of such statutes, rules, and orders.[1] The proposed statute also would provide a mechanism for resolving conflicts between the United States's and host countries' environmental protection and resource conservation laws, rules, and orders.

A JUSTIFICATION FOR THIS LAW

Recently the popular and technical press in the United States have given increasing coverage to the imperiled condition of the global biosphere.[2] Global environmental conditions probably have not received so much attention from the media since the second surge of the environmental protection movement in the 1960s and early 1970s, following the publication of Rachel Carson's *Silent Spring*.[3] *Scientific American,* for example, recently devoted an entire issue to global environmental protection.

Two related environmental issues that have received detailed coverage in the media are the greenhouse effect and the deterioration of the ozone layer.[4] Some meteorologists and ecologists believe that the earth is getting hotter and more vulnerable to ultraviolet radiation and at a rate faster than previously predicted because of fossil fuel use, deforestation, and chlorofluorocarbon (CFC) consumption.[5] If allowed to continue unchecked, these global environmental trends—if they are trends—might foster massive climatological shifts and threaten life on the planet. The prime ministers of Canada and Norway have called for an international atmosphere protection treaty to reduce the likelihood of irreparable global injury from the confluence of the greenhouse effect and high-altitude deterioration of the ozone layer.[6] President Bush and William K. Reilly, the head of the U.S. Environmental Protection Agency (EPA), have called recently for greater protection of the atmosphere from CFC and acid rain pollution.[7]

Similarly, hazardous industrial activity—both production and waste disposal—has received extensive coverage in the media in recent months.[8] Trends in hazardous industrial activity raise a question about whether the continuous accumulation of toxic by-products and wastes of human production and consumption is exceeding, or has exceeded, the capacity of the planet to neutralize or harmlessly absorb those pollutants.

As a direct and indirect result of all of these trends, international, regional, national, and local public agencies and governments are confronting the relationship of economic growth to environmental protection and natural resource conservation. Many governments are searching for the key to "sustainable development," a term for the optimal relationship of economic growth, environmental protection, and resource conservation.

One of the most troublesome variations of this perplexing relationship is faced by the rapidly industrializing countries (RICs) and the less developed countries (LDCs). Both are trying to grow out of their poverty, but because they lack foresight or regulatory resources, or both, they are polluting their air, water, land and endangering the health of their citizens.[9]

The United States and other developed countries have been exacerbating the problems of the RICs and LDCs, at least in the short run. Primarily to respond to the growth of foreign markets[10] and to avoid trade barriers and the impact of fluctuations in the dollar,[11] the United States and other developing countries have been exporting economic development by establishing factories and other business operations in RICs and LDCs.[12] Unfortunately, they also have been exporting the hazards associated with that development: hazardous production methods and management strategies[13] and hazardous products.[14]

Those exported hazardous operations combine to create pollution that threatens the health and safety of LDCs to a far greater extent than would be tolerated or permitted in the United States or in most other developed countries. Moreover, many of those hazardous operations may harm our national environment by returning to the United States along various paths through the biosphere.

These events underscore the developed nations' hypocrisy on the related issues of economic vitality and environmental protection. To support their economies, the developed nations have been promoting, condoning, or ignoring the production, use, and dumping in other people's backyards of products and wastes they no longer permit in their own backyard. The developed countries can do this because most other nations, especially the LDCs, have less stringent environmental protection and resource conservation laws than those of most of the developed countries or less vigorously enforce their laws, or both, but want the revenues, jobs, and resources that importation of foreign operations or products supports. Firms based in the United States and other developed countries compound this hypocrisy and increase the hazards associated with these activities by failing to manage their foreign production, sales, or waste disposal even as scrupulously as they must in their home countries.[15]

The relative stringency of environmental protection in the developed countries probably leads some business planners and managers to conclude that it is profitable to export hazardous production or products. The existing evidence on U.S. business siting decisions suggests, however, that most exportation of operations, products, and wastes occurs because other traditional economic factors favor export.[16] There is evidence, however, that certain mature U.S. industries, with high costs and low profit margins, are exporting their operations to avoid complying with U.S. environmental protection and resource conservation laws.[17]

Business planners in the developed countries make what seem to them to be rational decisions to export hazardous business activities—in the short run. It is certainly cheaper to produce and sell goods or dispose of wastes where markets' factors of production or sale favor those activities. In the long run, however, such conduct is dangerously shortsighted. The global environment may suffer irreversible damage so long as the developed countries export their hazardous operations. Moreover, individual firms can suffer substantial harm when a hazardous export strategy fails. Bhopal is a forceful exemplar of the cost of failure of a pollution export strategy. Union Carbide spent several years and millions of dollars in legal fees trying to settle the issue and amount of its liability for the fatalities and injuries that resulted from the release of methyl isocyanate into the surrounding environment by its Bhopal plant.[18] In 1988 it settled all claims related to the matter for $470 million.[19]

The firm now asserts also that it was a victim of sabotage, but that is beside the point.[20] Union Carbide of the United States, Union Carbide of India Ltd., and the Indian government tolerated the uncontrolled growth of shantytown communities right outside the walls of the plant,[21] with no emergency planning or notice to the community of the risks associated with the operation of that plant.[22] Union Carbide's oversight of the operation and Union Carbide of India's management of the plant were by several measures far riskier than Union Carbide's management of its own facility in Institute, West Virginia, which produces and stores methyl isocyanate.[23] Finally, the Indian government's regulatory oversight of the plant was deficient to nonexistent.[24] It seems unlikely that either environmental protection laws or political conditions in the United States would permit Bhopal-like circumstances to arise here.

Many commentators have asserted that the nature and magnitude of the world's environmental problems mandate that governments collectively and comprehensively attack hazardous and wasteful business operations.[25] Certainly the world's governments should multilaterally agree to strengthen environmental protection laws and enforcement. Complex international problems require coordinated international solutions—and achieving sustainable development is as difficult a problem as the world faces.

International politics, however, will keep comprehensive, treaty-based, environmentally sensitive behavior elusive for many years. The time and effort required to enact the CFC Montreal Protocol bears witness to that. The deterioration of the ozone layer has been under observation for many years, and the likely chemical causes of that deterioration have been suspected for years. Yet the treaty took years to write and sign, and it permits developing nations to rely on these chemicals in a phaseout program for some years to come.[26] Reacting to recent reports that the stratospheric ozone layer is deteriorating even more rapidly than had been predicted, many of the nations that support the Montreal Protocol now favor accelerating the timetable for ending the use of CFCs by 2000. Enacting these changes in the protocol's timetable will nevertheless take until at least 1990 at the earliest.[27] Moreover, this timetable does not include establishing effective enforcement machinery and achieving compliance with the protocol in the nations that have signed it. Many more nations have not even agreed to be bound by the protocol.

Until a comprehensive and enforceable multilateral treaty exists, individual nations should act vigorously to minimize the pollution and resource depletion their corporations' activities inflict on their ecospheres and on those of more vulnerable nations. The United States could take a leading role in national initiatives by declaring its intention to compel its domestically owned or controlled businesses to comply with U.S. environmental protection and resource conservation laws wherever they operate. It can do that by enacting and enforcing a foreign environmental practices act.

Patterned on the FCPA, this law might dissuade U.S.-owned, -supported, or -controlled firms or their agents from engaging in environmentally dangerous conduct in host countries. It should authorize civil suits, fines, supervision, and, if necessary, criminal prosecution and imprisonment, to sanction firms whose activities and agents willfully or negligently harm other countries' environments. The law should recognize that U.S. firms also operate in countries whose environmental protection laws are more stringent or more vigorously enforced than comparable U.S. laws; consequently, it should provide a mechanism for resolving conflicts caused by differing national legal standards.

This proposed law concentrates on environmentally hazardous production, service, and waste management processes. It does not address the separate problem of export of hazardous products; solving that problem would require comprehensive amendment of several statutes that govern exports of products whose sale or use in the United States is banned or restricted.[28] Moreover, the problem of hazardous product exports almost certainly requires an all-or-nothing remedy:

either U.S. firms must prohibit foreign sales of their goods banned for U.S. domestic consumption or must permit such foreign sales. Except by banning outright foreign sales, they probably cannot control negligent or reckless repackaging or end use overseas of any products produced in the United States or overseas by U.S. firms.

In contrast, U.S. firms can control their production, service, and disposal processes by several methods: careful choice, training, and supervision of personnel for foreign facilities; capital investment in state-of-the-art pollution control and resource conservation equipment in foreign facilities; and scrupulous use and maintenance of foreign facilities. These kinds of control are not cost free, but they are well within the traditional span of control that management can exercise over corporate activities; the developed countries mandate such controls on operations in their countries, although with varying stringency. Most significant, the absence of such controls represents some of the deficiencies that contributed to the Bhopal disaster.[29] Domestically these same kinds of deficiencies appear almost certainly to have contributed more recently to the *Exxon Valdez* oil spill.[30]

It is noteworthy that Congress has begun to grapple with the problem of regulating U.S. firms' foreign operations. In May 1989 Congressman Mike Synar of Oklahoma and three other sponsors introduced in the House of Representatives H.R. 2525, which would require U.S. hazardous waste exporters to conform their processes and practices in host countries to legal requirements that govern their treatment and handling of such waste in the United States.

H.R. 2525 is a useful starting point for discussion and regulation of foreign environmental protection and resource conservation practices of U.S. firms, but it attacks only one part of the problem—hazardous waste disposal—and therefore would not regulate all of the hazardous operations of U.S. firms abroad. Moreover, piecemeal legislation of this sort would not advance comprehensive review and coordination of all U.S. environmental protection and resource conservation laws for domestic and overseas application—a valuable complement to discussion and implementation of the statute proposed here.

If respected, the law I propose would have readily discernible virtues. It would reduce the global risk of environmentally hazardous and wasteful conduct. It would reduce the risk that U.S. firms would suffer catastrophic economic damage from a foreign environmental disaster. It would encourage cost-driven innovation in environmental protection processes and technology. It would improve the performance and image of the United States as a responsible international actor. It might enable the LDCs and RICs, with support from the United States in such venues as trade negotiations, to pressure other developed countries to oversee more vigorously their exports of hazardous operations. Finally, legislative consideration of this proposed law could promote national debate and careful examination of how United States environmental protection and resource conservation laws might most efficiently operate domestically and internationally.

POSSIBLE OBJECTIONS TO THIS LAW AND RESPONSES

This proposed law will evoke certain objections to it. First, the law arguably would be a form of cultural imperialism in which the United States would attempt to impose its social values on cultures that do not share them. Second, the proposed law arguably might discourage U.S. investment abroad and might retard development of RICs and LDCs that require that investment to advance socially and economically. Third, it could be argued that social cost-benefit analysis would not justify it. Fourth, it is arguable that the costs of compliance and enforcement might force U.S. firms to raise prices of their goods and services to recover those costs, putting the firms at a competitive disadvantage with firms from less environmentally scrupulous countries. Fifth, this proposed law arguably might contravene principles of international law. Finally, some critics might argue that the free market can regulate pollution more efficiently than government intervention and that any regulation of the market renders it clumsy and inefficient. Each of these objections can be rebutted.

First, this law is a form of moral imperialism, but it may be useful moral imperialism. It is one thing to assert—as have cultural-relativist critics of the Foreign Corrupt Practices Act—that the United States has no right to tell other nations how to run their marketplaces. Moreover (the critics of the FCPA have argued), U.S. firms harm their chances to compete in those marketplaces by ethnocentrically refusing to give the gifts, kickbacks, and bribes that lubricate many foreign markets. Those observations may offend moral absolutists, but they may be accurate. In some countries, U.S. firms probably must respect markets' customs and laws to earn local market shares; however, there is evidence that the analogous FCPA has had no adverse effects on U.S. firms' market shares abroad.[31]

The comparable social consequences of market rules on the one hand and of pollution on the other, moreover, are easily distinguishable. Market values usually are local in reach and effect; they typically stop at national borders. One market's rules can and will vary from another's. Pollution, in contrast, is wholly indifferent to political, cultural, economic, and religious boundaries. As our experiences with DDT, stratospheric ozone depletion, and acid rain suggest, and as Chernobyl reminded us, hazardous pollution can transcend national borders. Pollution elsewhere can and does injure us.

Furthermore, evidence is accumulating that LDCs may be more supportive of such legislation than they were in the early 1970s and 1980s. For example, the recently negotiated international treaty to regulate hazardous waste transport was partly the product of pressure from the LDC recipients of such wastes.[32]

The argument that this proposed law would discourage U.S. firms' direct investment abroad and consequently impede development of less developed nations also is rebuttable. First, U.S. business managers and planners have concluded that the dominant trend in market organization is global. Advancing communication and transportation technology enable U.S. firms and other nations' firms to compete internationally. Second, U.S. firms' planners and managers clearly believe that they must invest overseas to gain access to foreign markets and to compete with firms from other nations that compete for access to those markets.

Thus, to gain shares in many foreign markets, U.S. firms must and will continue to internationalize their operations. In short, market structure for many industries will impel foreign investment, even in the face of regulatory constraints. The FCPA—the nearest regulatory analogue to this law—has shown no evidence of retarding foreign investments; during most of the period in which the FCPA has been in force, and specifically, since 1985, U.S. foreign investments have increased.[33]

Also, even if the statute I propose increases the costs of foreign operations, the increased costs might only reduce the comparative value of those foreign markets as sites for investment. The advantages of foreign operations might persist because foreign operations enable access to foreign markets.

Of course, U.S. foreign investment might have grown more without the FCPA or might increase more rapidly without the legislation I propose, but that is undeterminable. Foreign investment patterns change with relative cost advantages: advantages vary from time to time, place to place, and industry to industry. They also fluctuate in relation to currency exchange rates.

International markets are certainly ruled by more than merely legal issues. For example, Japanese investment in the United States recently has grown substantially, despite comparatively tough U.S. laws about business practices. Obviously the Japanese see advantages in so investing: desirable products and services abound in the United States, currency rates have favored it, labor markets desire it, and political relations all but compel it.

More stringent pollution and conservation requirements abroad might increase U.S. foreign investment—in pollution control and resource conservation equipment and processes, in education of foreign personnel, and in posting of American personnel overseas for supervising and training foreign personnel to use them. The possibility of increased local investment might make U.S. firms more attractive to host countries; they might be willing to offer compensating benefits or concessions for the increased costs of investment. And these investments in environmental protection capital and personnel should enlarge the U.S. share of the environmental protection processes and services markets, which almost certainly will be growth markets for the foreseeable future.

Critics who would use social cost-benefit analysis to attack this legislation probably would identify three kinds of costs associated with it: direct costs of equipment, personnel, and training that business pays to comply with the law; regulatory costs that taxpayers pay to enforce the law; and consequent opportunity costs that society will suffer because the capital it would spend to comply and regulate would become unavailable for other socially valuable purposes.

The costs of compliance and enforcement might increase social opportunity costs but only if all other compliance and regulatory costs remain the same or increase and no social savings compensate for these additional costs. This is a complex issue, but it is possible that the social benefits and savings resulting from compliance with this proposed statute might offset or exceed social opportunity costs.

Social cost-benefit analysis is at best imprecise. It is relatively easy to quantify the costs of improved environmental protection and resource conservation. It is far more difficult to quantify the costs of relatively weaker environmental protection and resource conservation. It is similarly difficult to quantify the benefit of more stringent environmental protection. For example, what dollar value should we attach to protecting hosts' citizens from hazardous operations? What are the short-term or long-term costs of allowing hazardous wastes to accumulate in a nation unable to manage them safely? What are the near-term or long-term costs of allowing the stratospheric ozone layer to continue to deteriorate?

Moreover, U.S. industry has found and can continue to find ways to improve its cost structure. During the years the FCPA and environmental and conservation laws have been on the books, many U.S. firms have reduced their costs of domestic production and become more competitive internationally.[34] U.S. firms in various industries have innovated and restructured to reduce or eliminate their competitive cost disadvantages in production.[35] It is noteworthy that some U.S. businesses have become more cost-effective and profitable specifically by employing innovative waste minimization techniques, which reduce operating costs, increase margins of profit, and even generate new businesses.[36] In short, compliance with environmental protection mandates can be profitable.

Moreover, net regulatory costs need not increase. This proposed law would not require the creation of new regulatory machinery; the administrative and judicial processes necessary to compel compliance with the statute already exist. The only additional expense necessary might be an increase in law enforcement personnel necessary to monitor or compel compliance. Since it is probable that most firms would comply, or attempt to comply, in good faith with this proposed law, the enforcement machinery might have to focus only on outlaws, and fines of those outlaws could be set high enough to offset additional costs of enforcement. In any event, this proposed statute would direct the EPA administrator to review relevant U.S. laws to establish comprehensive guidelines for compliance, which should help to minimize any inefficiencies or duplication of regulation or compliance.

Even if gross regulatory costs increase, offsetting social savings might flow from improved environmental protection and resource conservation inside and outside the foreign workplace. For example, improved environmental protection might increase the productivity of U.S. firms' foreign operations by reducing turnover and absenteeism resulting from sickness and injury caused by environmental pollution of the hosts' environments. Improved environmental protection in hosts might also produce savings for U.S. firms by reducing their costs associated with cleaning up pollution in hosts. Improved environmental protection and resource conservation, through innovative waste minimization techniques, could reduce U.S. foreign operations' costs, increase foreign operations' profits, and preserve an adequate resource base for longer-term, more profitable operation in host countries.

Taken together, potential social savings could more than offset any increased direct costs of regulation and compliance. The social savings thus could reduce net social opportunity costs rather than increase them.

As to price-related competitive disadvantages that increased foreign environmental protection might induce, it should be remembered that products can win markets without simple price advantages. Except for fungible commodities, combined perceptions of quality-price-brand-feature relationships may be more significant than price alone to potential buyers of many kinds of products and services.[37] Many consumers continue to buy expensive brand-named products rather than cheaper generic alternatives because of brand loyalty or reputation. For example, IBM lost some of its personal computer (PC) market share to manufacturers of much cheaper PC clones only as buyers convinced themselves that the clones were of at least equal quality and that the clone manufacturers would survive to service them.

Moreover, studies of the actual impact of the FCPA on market shares of U.S. firms abroad suggest that that law has had no adverse impact on those shares.[38] These studies suggest that other geopolitical and economic influences have far more impact on foreign market shares than could a statute designed to affect environmental practices abroad.

The United States can use its trade policy and trade negotiations to encourage less environmentally scrupulous nations to increase their expenditures on environmental protection and resource conservation. The United States remains the largest and most lucrative national market for goods and services; as part of its trade policy, it could declare that firms from other nations that want access to the U.S. domestic market must behave as prudently in hosts as the United States would under this proposed law. For example, we already require foreign cars manufactured for U.S. sale to satisfy U.S. emission regulations, even though they may be stricter than those of the exporting country.

Some critics would assert that this proposed statute would violate principles of international law, primarily by interfering with the sovereignty of host governments. This is not the place for a lengthy discourse on international law, but it is important to remember that this statute would authorize only administrative actions and civil and criminal suits in U.S. courts against U.S. nationals and businesses. Relevant principles of U.S. foreign relations law clearly authorize the United States to prescribe or proscribe actions by U.S. nationals and firms within U.S. borders; this lawful regulation clearly would encompass civil litigation and criminal prosecution to proscribe or sanction decisions of U.S. firms on

U.S. soil that would promote hazardous business operations abroad. Moreover, principles of its foreign relations law clearly oblige the United States to proscribe conduct that injures the property or resources of other nations.

The only possible situation in which this statute might contravene accepted principles of international law would arise if a host were to insist that a U.S. operation on host soil be allowed to engage in hazardous operations. Given the changing view of hosts to hazardous operations within their borders, this situation seems decreasingly probable.

Finally, it is possible to rebut the arguments of free-market adherents who would assert that this proposal would tighten unnecessarily the grip of the dead hand of regulation on business. Pollution and resource waste by U.S. firms in hosts have occurred in what probably are essentially unfettered markets: many hosts—and probably all LDC hosts—lack regulatory systems to control the conduct of foreign businesses within their borders. Pollution and resource waste in hosts thus probably result from free markets in those hosts and in choices among potential hosts. In short, free markets have created these pollution and conservation problems and show no signs of solving them without intervention.

The opponents to such legislation will threaten a speculative series of adverse consequences. There are equally valid counterarguments. There is evidence that action to protect and preserve the global environment becomes more critically necessary each day. For these reasons, the United States should take the initiative and enact a foreign environmental practices act.

NOTES

1. 15 U.S.C. 78dd-1, et seq.

2. See, e.g., P. Shabecoff, "As Ozone Is Depleted, Much of Life Could Go with It," *New York Times,* April 17, 1988, sec. 4, p. 28; P. Shabecoff, "Global Warming Has Begun, Expert Tells Senate," *New York Times,* June 24, 1988, pp. 1, 10; W. Want, "Hazardous Waste: A Business Primer," *Business and Economic Review* 34 (July–September 1988): 3–8; S. Begley, "The Endless Summer?" *Newsweek,* July 11, 1988, pp. 18–20; R. Kerr, "Report Urges Greenhouse Action Now," *Science,* July 1, 1988, pp. 23–24; J. Main, "Here Comes the Big Cleanup," *Fortune,* November 21, 1988, pp. 102–18; R. Kerr, "Evidence of Arctic Ozone Destruction," *Science,* May 27, 1988, pp. 1144–45; G. Taylor, "Water, Water Everywhere—No Place Else to Dump?" *National Law Journal,* November 28, 1988, p. 8; C. Knox, "What's Going on Down There?" *Science News,* December 3, 1988, pp. 362–65; P. O'Leary et al., "Managing Solid Waste," *Scientific American* (December 1988): 36–42; B. Hilleman, "Global Warming," *Chemical and Engineering News,* March 13, 1989, pp. 25–44; R. Houghton and G. Woodwell, "Global Climatic Change," *Scientific American* (April 1989): 36–44.

3. Historians of the environmental movement might argue that the first wave of environmentalism in the United States actually occurred during the late nineteenth and early twentieth centuries as a result of the coincidence of the progressive political movement under Theodore Roosevelt and the environmental preservation movement, led by, among others, John Muir, founder of the Sierra Club, and Gifford Pinchot.

4. See, e.g., Shabecoff, "As Ozone Is Depleted," and "Global Warming Has Begun"; Begley, "The Endless Summer?"; Kerr, "Report Urges Greenhouse Action Now," and "Evidence of Arctic Ozone Destruction"; Hilleman, "Global Warming"; Houghton and Woodwell, "Global Climatic Change"; National Research Council, *Ozone Depletion, Greenhouse Gases, and Climate Change* (Washington, D.C.: National Academy Press, 1989).

5. See for example, the views of James Hansen, director of the Goddard Institute for Space Studies, discussed in Shabecoff, "Global Warming Has Begun", supra note 4; and the views of Richard Houghton and George Woodwell of the Woods Hole Research Center, "Global Climatic Change."

6. P. Shabecoff, "Norway and Canada Call for Pact to Protect Atmosphere," *New York Times,* June 28, 1988, p. 24.

7. P. Shabecoff, "Bush Backs Halt in Use of Pollutant in Ozone," *New York Times,* March 4, 1989, p. 9, and "E.P.A. Nominee Says He Will Urge Law to Cut Acid Rain," *New York Times,* February 1, 1989, pp. 1, 10.

8. See, e.g., H. French, "Toxic Wastes Crossing Borders," *Worldwatch* (January–February 1988): 9–10; P. Shabecoff, "Irate and Afraid, Poor Nations Fight Efforts to Use Them as Toxic Dumps," *New York Times,* July 5, 1988, p. 22; S. Greenhouse, "Toxic Waste Boomerang: Ciao Italy!" *New York Times,* September 3, 1988, p. 4; A. Vir, "Toxic Trade with Africa," *Environmental Science and Technology,* November 1, 1989, pp. 23–25; Want, "Hazardous Waste: A Business Primer"; P. Shabecoff, "E.P.A. Sets Strategy to End 'Staggering' Garbage Crisis," *New York Times,* September 23, 1988, p. 10; Main, "Here Comes the Big Cleanup"; Taylor, "Water, Water Everywhere"; Knox, "What's Going on Down There?" P. O'Leary et al., "Managing Solid Waste."

9. See generally J. Ives, ed., *The Export of Hazard* (Boston: Routledge and Kegan Paul, 1985); C. Pearson, ed., *Multinational Corporations, Environment, and the Third World: Business Matters* (Durham: Duke University Press, 1987); David Weir, *The Bhopal Syndrome* (San Francisco: Sierra Club Books, 1987); and H. Jeffrey Leonard, *Pollution and the Struggle for World Product* (New York: Cambridge University Press, 1988). See also recent articles on the export of toxic wastes: French, "Toxic Wastes Crossing Borders"; Shabecoff, "Irate and Afraid"; Greenhouse, "Toxic Waste Boomerang: Ciao Italy!" Vir, "Toxic Trade."

10. See, e.g., L. Uchitelle, "Trade Barriers and Dollar Swings Raise Appeal of Factories Abroad," *New York Times* March 26, 1989, pp. 1, 13, and "U.S. Businesses Loosen Link to Mother Country," *New York Times* May 21, 1989, pp. 1, 12.

11. Ibid.

12. Ibid.

13. See Ives, *Export;* Pearson, *Multinational Corporations;* Weir, *Bhopal Syndrome;* and Leonard, *Pollution.*

14. See, e.g., in Ives, *Export:* S. King, "Hazardous Exports: A Consumer Perspective"; A. Waldo, "A Review of US and International Restrictions on Exports of Hazardous Substances"; R. Ruttenberg, "Hazard Export: Ethical Problems, Policy Proposals and Prospects for Implementation"; Rashid A. Shaikh, "Export of Hazardous Products from the United States: A Bibliography." See, e.g., in Pearson, *Multinational Corporations:* L. Goodman, "Foreign Toxins, Multinational Corporations and Pesticides in Mexican Agriculture," and S. Scherr, "Hazardous Exports: U.S. and International Policy Developments." For a recent review of the legal literature and prominent examples of

export of hazardous products, see Cross and Winslett, "Export Death: Ethical Issues And The International Trade In Hazardous Products." *American Business Law Journal* 25 (1987): 487, 488–498.

15. See, generally, J. Ives, *Export;* C. Pearson, *Multinational Corporations;* D. Weir, *Bhopal Syndrome;* and H. J. Leonard, *Pollution Export.*

16. See L. Uchitelle, "Trade Barriers," and "U.S. Businesses."

17. See, for example, H. J. Leonard, *Pollution Export.*

18. L. Hays and R. Koenig, "How Union Carbide Fleshed Out Its Theory of Sabotage at Bhopal," *Wall Street Journal,* July 7, 1988, pp. 1, 12 (Union Carbide's legal fees to that date exceeded $24 million).

19. S. Hazarika, "Bhopal Payments Set at $470 Million for Union Carbide," *New York Times,* February 15, 1988, pp. 1, 27.

20. See, e.g., Union Carbide, "Setting the Record Straight on Employee Sabotage and Efforts to Provide Relief" (public relations release, n.d.); Hays and Koenig, "How Union Carbide"; and A. Kallelkar, "Investigation of Large Magnitude Incidents" (paper prepared for presentation at the Institution of Chemical Engineers Conference on Preventing Major Chemical Accidents, London, May 1988).

21. See, e.g., Weir, *Bhopal Syndrome,* p. 36; Pearson, *Multinational Corporations,* p. 227; and Ives, *Export,* p. 218.

22. See, e.g., Pearson, *Multinational Corporations,* p. 231, and Ives, *Export,* p. 218.

23. See, e.g., in Ives, *Export,* B. Castleman and P. Purkavastha, "Appendix: The Bhopal Disaster as a Case Study in Double Standards," pp. 213–18 (citing deficiencies in plant design, operation, executive management, staffing, community relations, and government regulation); in Pearson, *Multinational Corporations,* T. Gladwin, "A Case Study of the Bhopal Tragedy," pp. 227–34 (citing failures to anticipate the risks, to equip the plant, to inform workers, surrounding communities, and the government, to control the plant, and to comply with Union Carbide's internal operational standards).

24. See, e.g., B. Castleman and P. Purkavastha, "Appendix," p. 218, and T. Gladwin, "Case Study," pp. 234–38.

25. See, for example, the following articles in law reviews: G. Galli, "Hazardous Exports to the Third World: The Need to Abolish the Double Standard," *Columbia Journal of International Law* 12 (1987): 71, 90; Judy, "Hazardous Substances in Developing Countries: Who Should Regulate Foreign Corporations?" *Virginia Journal of Natural Resource Law"* 143, 169–177 (1986): 143, 169–77; Johnston, *Systemic Environmental Damage: The Challenge to International Law and Organization, Syracuse Journal of International Law and Commerce* 12 (1985): 255, 281–82; Joyner, "Towards Transnational Management of Desertification: The Eco-Politics of Global Concern," *International Law* 16 (1982): 67, 87, 92–93; N. Robinson, "Introduction: Emerging International Law," *Stanford Journal of International Law* 17 (1981): 229, 259; G. Head, "The Challenge of International Environmental Management: A Critique of the United Nations Environment Programme," *Virginia Journal of International Law* 18 (1978): 269, 277–88; R. Falk, "The Global Environment and International Law: Challenge and Response," *Kansas Law Review* 23 (1975): 385, 390–92, 420; Z. Nanda, "The Establishment of International Standards for Transnational Environmental Injury," *Iowa Law Review* 60 (1974): 1089, 1127; and Busterud, "International Environmental Relations," *Natural Resource Law* 7 (1974): 325. But see G. Smith, "The United Nations and the Environment: Sometimes a Great Notion?" *Texas International Law Journal* 19 (1981): 335 (asserting that the United States should withdraw from the United Nations Environment Programme and that nation-to-nation agreements based on national

perceptions of self-interest will reflect more effectively the interplay of economic market forces and international environmental protection and produce more useful international environmental protection).

26. See National Research Council, *Ozone Depletion,* pp. 15–16.

27. C. Whitney, "80 Nations Favor Ban to Help Ozone," *New York Times,* May 3, 1989, p. 13.

28. Including, among other statutes, the Export Administration Act, 50 U.S.C. sec. 2401, et seq; the Federal Insecticide, Fungicide, and Rodenticide Act, 7 U.S.C. sec. 136, et seq.; and the Federal Food, Drug, and Cosmetic Act, 21 U.S.C. sec. 301, et seq.

29. See the discussion of managerial problems at Bhopal in Castleman and Pur-kavastha, "Appendix," and Gladwin, "Case Study."

30. See, e.g., R. Witkin et al., "How the Oil Spilled and Spread: Delay and Confusion off Alaska," *New York Times,* April 16, 1989, pp. 1, 16; J. Holusha, "Chairman Defends Exxon's Efforts to Clean Up Oil," *New York Times,* April 19, 1989, p. 13; M. Wald, "Exxon Is Still in Early Stage of Training a Cleanup Staff," *New York Times,* April 23, 1989, p. 12.

31. B. Richman, "Can We Prevent Questionable Foreign Payments?" *Business Horizons* (June 1979): 14–19 (reporting that firms that had made large amounts of questionable payments in the past and had ceased making such payments reported high or record profits, revenues, and backlogs); J. Graham, "The Foreign Corrupt Practices Act: A New Perspective," *Journal of International Business Studies* (Winter 1984): 107–21 (the FCPA was found to have no negative effect on the export performance of American industry; market shares of U.S. firms in countries where the FCPA was reported to be an important trade consideration were no different from U.S. firms' market shares in other countries).

32. See the articles on hazardous waste exports cited in note 9.

33. See L. Uchitelle, "Trade Barriers," and "U.S. Businesses."

34. See, e.g., S. Nasar, "America's Competitive Revival," *Fortune,* January 4, 1988, pp. 44–52, and T. Schellhart and C. Hymowitz, "U.S. Manufacturers Gird for Competition," *Wall Street Journal,* May 2, 1969, pp. A2, A8.

35. Ibid.

36. For example, ARCO, Ciba-Geigy, and Dow have undertaken waste minimization programs in the United States that have reduced their costs and generated additional streams of revenue. For a discussion of these firms' profitable waste minimization techniques, see R. A. Frosch and N. F. Gallopoulos, "Strategies for Manufacturing," *Scientific American* (September 1989): 144–52.

37. See, e.g., Kotler, *Marketing Management* (Englewood Cliffs, N.J.: Prentice-Hall, 1988), pp. 191–93 (asserting that buying behavior varies with the type of buying decision, which turns on the complexity of the decision, the cost of the product under consideration, the fungibility of the product under consideration, habit, and desire for variety); B. Sternquist and T. Ogawa, "Japanese Consider U.S. Products Inferior," *Marketing News,* September 26, 1988, p. 4 (noting that tastes of Japanese consumers, differences in Japanese and U.S. markets, and the power and role of the consumer-buyer in Japan make it difficult to persuade Japanese consumers of the comparable quality of U.S. products); C. Han, "The Role of Consumer Patriotism in the Choice of Domestic vs. Foreign Products," *Journal of Advertising Research* (June–July 1988): 25–31 (research showing that national patriotism appeared to affect consumer buying behavior significantly).

38. See Richman, "Can We Prevent," and Graham, "Foreign Corrupt Practices Act."

The Ethics of Development and the Dilemmas of Global Environmentalism

DAVID P. HANSON

Environmentalism is a pledge to preserve the possibilities of our world for future generations. It is based on an acceptance of interdependence and the need for self-restraint in the interests of those yet to come. The environmental ethic forces us to confront the economists' truth: resources are limited, and not all interests can be satisfied. Whose interests shall we defend? What resources are we willing to sacrifice?

Environmental problems are increasingly matters of international concern. They are the result in large part of well-established patterns of economic development. In considering what to do, we should evaluate environmental issues in the broadest possible context by looking at the impact of historical patterns of global economic and social change to determine if the present rate of economic development can be sustained.

A strong argument can be made that the poorer countries have a moral right to economic development. The technological and economic developments of the last century have led to a moral revolution in Western societies. From the perspective of those who are accustomed to developed standards of living, the lives of most people in traditional societies are nasty, brutish, and short. Economic and technological development has produced enormous advances in basic human values: nutrition, sanitation, health, longevity, education, and overall security.

Economic development has also brought a moral resolution in social relations. In traditional agricultural societies, the control of land has been a major basis for social power. The pace of technological change has generally been very slow. In the short term, potential production has been constant. As a result, peasant and master have generally fought over a fixed quantity, where the gains of one come at the expense of the other. In this struggle, landlords had the superior position as long as there were too many peasants and a scarcity of arable land. As a result, class relations in traditional societies have often been characterized by violence and exploitation by the few, who are very rich, against the many, who are very poor.

Resources in the developed societies are produced by larger groups of people acting in cooperation. Competition in the market economies occurs as much among these competing corporate bureaucracies as between individual producers. The competitive position of companies in the market economies is increasingly determined by the judgment and skill employees bring to the production process. Even in the traditional manufacturing industries, quality and design have become as important as the more traditional criteria of cost and volume.

The increasing dependence of managerial elites on the commitment and skill of subordinates has led to increased demands for highly qualified personnel. Over the last fifty years, these processes have led to the development of a large middle class made up of managers, professionals, technicians, and skilled workers. With this has also come the development of a social ethic based on the acceptance of interdependency, consensus, professionalism, and the need for self-restraint.[1]

The reality of rapid and sustained economic growth in the Western societies has also transformed social conflicts. With economic growth, all can benefit in the long run. Social conflict becomes a barrier to the welfare of all rather than a tool for the prosperity of a few. The results of this transformation can be seen in the institutionalization of the welfare state and a general acceptance of environmental ideals.

The existing patterns of economic and technological development are historically unique. With few exceptions, the conditions of life for most people, in, for example, Mesopotamia in 2000 B.C. were not significantly different from the living standards of the average French citizen in the year 1500 A.D.

The pace of economic and technological development has accelerated dramatically in the last fifty years. Per capita energy consumption, a reasonable measure of technological and economic development, has risen thirty-fold in North America between 1870 and the present.[2]

If population growth can be curtailed, the availability of raw materials need not pose an obstacle to continued economic development. If we take care of the land, fertility can be sustained indefinitely. Few materials are ever lost from human use; they are only transformed and transported into different forms. The transformation of ore into iron, for example, does not make the metal any less available.

The major barriers to continued development are environmental. The traces of carbon dioxide (CO_2) and related gases in the atmosphere block the radiation of energy from the earth into space. Any significant increases in the atmospheric concentration of these gases will result in rising temperatures on earth.[3]

Unfortunately, the major energy source for economic development has been based on the conversion of mineral carbon into gaseous CO_2. Every year, we are dumping between 6 billion and 10 billion tons of CO_2 into the air. The amount of

CO_2 in the atmosphere is increasing by almost 1 percent per year. If this rate of CO_2 dumping continues, we can expect an increase of 6 to 9 degrees Fahrenheit in the mean temperature of the earth over the next fifty years.[4]

The consequences for the human community are generally unfavorable. Climate zones should shift toward the poles. Both precipitation and the length of the growing season at high latitudes should increase. The increases should be most pronounced at higher latitudes. Arable lands located around 30 degrees north-south latitude are likely to become increasingly arid. A most serious consequence is likely to be the melting of the polar icecaps and the rising level of the ocean. A 3-foot rise in the water level would make many cities uninhabitable and, in many parts of the world, could significantly reduce the amount of arable land.[5]

The processes of climactic change will lead to environmental stress quite apart from the increase in final equilibrium temperatures. There will inevitably be a lag between the death of existing plant, animal, and human communities and the reestablishment of new species and technologies for life.

Unless we are willing to discount the welfare of future generations against our own, there is a compelling case for reducing the emission of carbon-based gases down to the level at which these gases are being removed from the atmosphere. Dumping at any higher level than zero net emission will slow the pace of change but may not change the result.[6]

Energy utilization in the developed economies can be reduced by at least half through conservation without significantly altering standards of living. Roughly equal amounts of energy are used for manufacturing, transportation, and heating and cooling. Major cuts in the amount of energy required for transportation and heating and cooling can be achieved through increased utilization of existing technology and through changes in the criteria and processes of public planning.[7]

There are limits to what can be achieved toward energy conservation in manufacturing. The amount of energy required to produce the steel, aluminum, and cement for building new houses, roads, and cars is fixed by the laws of chemistry and physics. There do not seem to be any viable low-energy substitutes for these materials in the construction of the public and private goods we associate with economic development.

To an extent, we can shift over to less polluting energy sources. Solar power might be able to supply up to one-quarter of all electric energy needs.[8] Biomass could also provide a closed-cycle, carbon-based fuel source. Geothermal, wind, and ocean thermal energy conversion processes may replace carbon fuels.

A changeover from carbon-based fuels is not likely to be easy or cheap. Many of these technologies are best suited for the production of electricity, which has the problem of high capital costs and low conversion efficiencies. The initially promising option of nuclear power has already been derailed by a record of high costs, high risks, and high opposition. Solar power will not be feasible in many parts of the world or for many industrial applications. Raising crops, such as sugar cane, for conversion to fuels will take abundant supplies of land, capital, and labor.

A failure to restrict carbon utilization while promoting worldwide economic development will severely complicate the problems of the greenhouse effect. Raising worldwide per capita consumption of carbon-based energy to just one-fourth of current U.S. levels would increase aggregate CO_2 production by almost 90 percent. Even if the developed countries then reduced their per capita carbon consumption to the "one-quarter U.S." level, the aggregate result would still be a 26 percent increase in global CO_2 emissions.[9]

Maintaining a balance between economic development and energy conservation will be far more difficult for the poorer countries. Among the developed countries of the Organization for Economic Cooperation and Development, there is no relation between per capita income and per capita energy consumption. The correlation between per capita income and energy consumption for all nations though is 0.88.[10]

In effect, the demand for material- and energy-intensive goods in the developed countries is becoming satiated. Much of the growth in the developed economies is in the design, manufacture, and distribution of intellect-intensive goods, such as computers and aircraft.[11] The relation between energy consumption and economic development is much stronger for poorer nations. The demand for energy-intensive basic construction materials and manufactured goods, such as houses, roads, telephone systems, airports, and cars, has not yet been met.

In the developed world, a transition to a low-pollution economy for a given level of economic development could be implemented relatively easily. The resources of capital and technology are readily available. Rising costs of energy production could be offset through the adoption of conservation technologies in housing and transportation. The problems posed by changing energy sources will be far more severe in the developing countries. The poorer countries have tended to specialize in the production of basic minerals and agricultural goods, surprisingly energy-intensive processes. World markets in most of these goods are highly price competitive. Poorer countries that unilaterally restrict their rate of carbon utilization are likely to face increasingly severe competitive disadvantages.

Population size is another long-term limit to environmental protection and economic development. For a given level of technology and per capita income, the level of CO_2 production will be directly related to population size. Thus, we may be able to maintain a smaller population at a higher standard of living, subject to the constraints of carbon utilization.

Population growth tends to be quite high in the poorer countries and almost zero in the developed countries. In the poorest countries, the rate of increase may be as high as 3.5 to 4 percent per year, and the population will double every seventeen to twenty-two years. Thus, the social dislocations caused by population growth are far greater in the poorer countries, which have the fewest resources, and far less in countries with abundant resources. The imposition of pollution restraints on developing countries, leading to an increased demand for scarce intellectual and capital resources, is likely to accentuate these difficulties.

Rapid population growth in the poorer countries compounds the social problems of economic development. The work force is usually divided between a large traditional agricultural sector and a small, relatively modernized urban sector. Population growth in the traditional sector generally outpaces economic growth in the modern sector. At the same time, the modernization of agriculture often leads to the displacement of inefficient, labor-intensive sharecropping systems for more productive plantations using seasonal wage labor. The results of these two trends are seen in rising unemployment levels, the explosive growth of the urban population, and widening gaps between rich and poor.[12]

Population growth in poorer countries often leads to greater pressures on land utilization. In parts of Africa and Latin America, overpopulation and population growth have led to overcultivation, erosion, and an actual drop in per capita agricultural production. In Latin America, Africa, and Southeast Asia, this has led to a search for new agricultural land through the widespread destruction of the rain forests. Between 15 and 30 percent of total CO_2 production is caused by this deforestation.[13]

The moral importance of encouraging development in the Third World must therefore be balanced against the practical imperative of limiting atmospheric pollution. Progress on either goal will require effective action on population growth. Can any of these goals be achieved?[14]

An honest answer is not a comforting one. The problems of population control, economic growth, and atmospheric pollution require effective responses that must be based on what will be possible, which is not necessarily what will be fair or equitable.

The priorities for action can be evaluated according to the consequences of failure. A failure to stabilize atmospheric CO_2 levels will lead to a progressive deterioration in the conditions of life for all—rich and poor alike. Partial solutions that only slow the rate of CO_2 buildup will merely postpone the greenhouse effects; they will not avoid them.

This is not true for the problem of population growth. To an extent, the problems of rapid population growth can potentially be offset by rapid economic and technological development. While a failure to control population growth is likely to result in a progressive immiseration of life, the effects will generally be confined to the poorer countries, where the population growth is outstripping resource development.

From a global perspective, the problems of economic development are less pressing. Like the issue of population growth, the consequences of a failure to develop are largely local. If we can solve the population problem, then a failure to promote economic development results in the persistence of the status quo rather than in a progressive reduction of human welfare. Furthermore, economic development is not an all-or-nothing proposition; any increase in income will potentially increase social welfare.

There are also differences in the capacities of government for effective action on these three issues. Our capacity for effective action on the tasks of economic development, population control, and pollution abatement is significantly limited by our reliance on the independent nation-state as the fundamental political unit. The division of the world into many small administrative units has created an incentive for governments to emphasize local over global issues. In both the developed and underdeveloped world, governments generally respond to local interests over international concerns. We cannot expect governments to act where the local costs significantly outweigh local benefits.

The division of the world into rich and poor states also poses problems. The invention of guns, large sailing ships, the factory system, and the corporation gave the European powers a vast military and economic advantage over the traditional societies. The result was the global expansion of Europe through colonialism and empire. The benefits to the home countries came in the forms of cheap resources and guaranteed markets. Colonialism broke down because the costs of occupation outstripped the benefits of market domination. It became easier to turn local administration over to local elites while maintaining ties of trade and investment.

The moral results of decolonization have been mixed. Independence is consistent with the strong ethical claim of all people for autonomy and self-determination. Forceful intervention by a stronger country into the affairs of a weaker one, even if the motives were to be good and results beneficial, is morally unacceptable. However, the colonial powers often turned authority over to local elites, who were likely to safeguard the interests of the colonial government in trade and investment ties. The end of colonialism has too often resulted in the emergence of ineffective or corrupt institutions of governance. Political control over trade ties with the outside world has often become a new source of power rivaling the traditional control over land. The results have often added a barrier to development: a tendency for Third World governments to emphasize short-term political and class interests over long-term popular development interests.

The end of colonialism has also put a new perspective on the roles of the Western powers. It is now the responsibility of the newly independent governments, not the colonial powers, to promote the interests of the developing societies. It is true, though, that lip service has been paid to international development efforts. Poor people can neither produce nor buy very much. Poor countries tend to be unstable and politically troubled. However, the desire of foreign governments to maintain existing military alliances, trade ties, and investment security guarantees encourages an accommodation with elites who may have little concrete interest in development.

The social and political interests of the upper classes in many developing countries also constitute major barriers to economic growth. Raising the income of the poor usually implies a radical shift in the positions and interests of the rich. If so, then development assistance programs will not be effective unless they are accompanied by substantial political changes in both the developing and the developed countries.[15]

What is to be done? How do we achieve the antithetical goals of restraining atmospheric pollution and promoting economic development? How can we encourage progress on population control, which may be a precondition for progress on either goal?

It is unrealistic to expect strong action by the poorer countries on problems of global pollution. On one hand, their contribution to both the magnitude of the problem and the effectiveness of the response are likely to be low. On the other hand, the costs to the poorer countries of limiting carbon-gas emissions, relative to available resources, are likely to be high. Countries that do not impose these costs on their local economies potentially enjoy cost advantages in international markets.

It is unlikely that the developed countries will be able to promote economic development effectively in the Third World. To the extent that the social structure and government policies of the developing countries constitute major impediments to development, the role of the developed countries is limited to encouragement and support. To the extent that these changes would upset existing political and economic ties, the developed countries are unlikely to support development efforts.

It is even more difficult for foreign governments to promote population control in the developing world. Economic development has a major effect on reducing family size. Where they are effective, family planning programs also reduce population growth. The effectiveness of these programs, however, depends heavily on an involved commitment by government and other social institutions. Neither economic development nor the necessary commitment to population control can be mandated from the outside.

It will be up to the developed countries to take effective leadership on the issue of carbon buildup in the atmosphere while essentially leaving the problems of population control and economic development to the poorer states.

The effectiveness of the response from the developed countries on the issue of pollution control will depend on their capacity for concerted action. Only by applying uniform rules for all developed countries can we avoid the conflict between economic advantage and environmental progress. Therefore, the desirability of program alternatives must be matched against the reasonable availability of international institutions through which they will be administered.

Fortunately, a major consolidation of political units at the supranational level has taken place among the developed nations over the last fifty years. World governance in the post–World War II period has been characterized by the development of specialized institutions such as the General Agreement on Tariffs and Trade, the International Monetary Fund (IMF), and the International Maritime Organization (IMO), which have been surprisingly effective. It is possible that institutions will develop to regulate global environmental conditions similar to the effective role played by the IMO in regulating oceanic pollution.

This does not answer the question of how the developed countries can encourage the less developed nations to follow suit. One possible tool is through influence over international energy markets and prices. Historically the consumption rate of carbon-based fuel in the developing world has declined when energy prices on international markets increased. The generally cooperative relation between the developed countries and the Organization of Petroleum Exporting Countries provides an example of how these market prices could be managed.

Unfortunately our ability to block the utilization of domestic coal or oil resources in countries such as China or to prevent deforestation in countries such as Brazil is limited given our lack of political control and their need for additional land and cheap energy. Other tools may be needed to encourage developing countries to pursue a domestic policy of environmental restraint.

The incentive might be based on a conditional acceptance of programs for capital subsidy and commodity price stabilization that many developing countries have been advocating in the United Nations and elsewhere. The penalty for noncompliance could come through conditional restrictions imposed by the developed countries on international credits and market access. The model for these programs could be taken from the role played by the IMF in encouraging domestic fiscal restraint.

Another key might be through technology transfer. Western countries could encourage the utilization of energy-efficient production techniques by reducing restrictions on the diffusion of the relevant technologies and by subsidizing the capital costs of energy-efficient equipment. A similar program of technology transfer has already been incorporated into the Law of the Sea treaty.

Another strategy might be to encourage developing countries to break away from the production of basic agricultural and industrial materials. Countries such as Mexico and Hong Kong have based development programs in large part on low-energy, labor-intensive manufacturing and assembly operations. Tourism and banking services are becoming increasingly important in many developing countries. Industries such as programming and software development are both highly labor intensive and potentially portable across national boundaries.

These programs are likely to be, at best, only partially effective. The experience of the IMF has shown that short-term considerations of domestic politics often override long-term incentives for reform from international agencies. Countries such as the People's Republic of China and the Soviet Union that have traditionally pursued policies of autarky are less likely to be swayed by incentives and penalties imposed by international institutions.

Even if the developing countries concentrated on low-pollution industries and adopted the best available technologies, development is likely to increase pollution levels. Development implies the acquisition of manufactured goods and a dramatic expansion of civil construction. The production of these goods is still energy intensive. In short, there are no easy solutions.

NOTES

1. Rheinhard Bendix, *Work and Authority in Industry* (New York: Wiley, 1956); Amatai Etzioni, *The Comparative Analysis of Complex Organizations* (New York: Free Press, 1961).

2. Chauncey Starr, "Energy and Power," *Scientific American* (September 1971): 37–50.

3. C. Genthon et al., "Vostok Ice Core: Climate Response to CO_2 and Orbital Forcing Changes Over the Last Climactic Cycle," *Nature,* October 1, 1987, pp. 414–18. Other gases besides CO_2, such as methane and Freon, contribute significantly to the greenhouse effect. The concentrations of these gases have also been rising steadily in recent years, largely as a result of human activity. The distinctions among the sources and effects of these gases are not particularly relevant for this argument and will be ignored in the balance of this chapter. V. Ramanathan et al., "Trace Gas Trends and Their Potential Role in Climate Change," *Journal of Geophysical Research,* June 20, 1985, pp. 5547–56.

4. Stephen H. Schneider, "The Changing Climate," *Scientific American* (September 1989): 70–79.

5. Michael Malik, "Fear of Flooding: Global Warming Could Threaten Low Lying Asia-Pacific Countries," *Far Eastern Economic Review,* December 22, 1988, pp. 20–21.

6. It is not clear how much CO_2, if any, we can safely release into the atmosphere. There are 740 million tons of CO_2 in the atmosphere. Each year natural processes release and absorb roughly 400 million tons of CO_2. The contribution from human activity is therefore a very small percentage of the total interchange. Schneider, "Changing Climate," p. 73.

Other factors complicate predictions about climate changes. The earth has been unusually warm for the last few thousand years. It is possible that any temperature rise induced by human activities will be offset by a naturally occurring shift toward a colder climate. Finally, mathematical models are still too imprecise to allow for confident predictions about the long-term results of atmospheric changes. Particularly troublesome are the effects of cloud cover and estimates on the rate at which CO_2 will be taken up by the oceans. The analysis in this chapter reflects the predominant view. See James E. Hansen, director, Goddard Institute for Space Studies, "The Greenhouse Effect: Impacts on Global Temperatures and Regional Heat Waves," testimony before U.S. Senate, Committee on Energy and Natural Resources, June 23, 1988.

7. Earl Cook, "The Flow of Energy in an Industrial Society," *Scientific American* (September 1971): 135–44; Arthur Rosenfeld and David Hafemeister, "Energy Efficient Buildings," *Scientific American* (April 1988): 78–85.

8. Yoshihiro Hamakawa, "Photovoltaic Power," *Scientific American* (April 1987): 92.

9. Calculations based on data in John H. Gibbons, Peter D. Blair, and Holly L. Gwin, "Strategies for Energy Use," *Scientific American* (September 1989): 136–43.

10. Between 1980 and 1986, the U.S. gross national product grew by 16 percent. During this period, steel consumption dropped by 7 percent, and energy consumption declined by 3 percent. Data from *Statistical Abstract of the United States, 1988* (Washington, D.C.: U.S. Government Printing Office, 1989), pp. 422, 681, 741.

11. Calculations based on data from ibid., pp. 805, 816.

12. James Clad and Margot Cohen, "Genesis of Dispair," *Far Eastern Economic Review,* October 20, 1988, pp. 24–30; "Development and Income Inequality Revisited," *Applied Economics* (April 1988): 509–31.

13. Schneider, "Changing Climate," p. 73; Lester A. Brown, Christopher Flavin, and Sandra Postel, "A World at Risk," in Lester A. Brown et al., *State of the World: 1989* (New York: Norton, 1989), pp. 1–20.

14. Several representatives from developing countries argued vigorously at a 1971 international conference in Founex, Switzerland, that the pollution and exhaustion of resources caused by economic activity in the developed countries are major barriers to the growth of the undeveloped economies. See "The Founex Report on Development and the Environment," *International Conciliation*, no. 586 (January 1972): 7–36; Miguel A. Ozorio de Almieda "The Confrontation between Problems of Development and the Environment," *International Conciliation*, no. 586 (January 1972): 37–56.

15. For a discussion of this point from the Alliance for Progress, see Walter LaFeber, "The Alliance in Retrospect," in Andrew MacGuire and Janet Welsh, eds., *Bordering on Trouble: Resources and Politics in Latin America* (Bethesda: Adler and Adler, 1986), pp. 337–88.

The Improbability of Third World Government Consent in the Coming North-South International Toxic Waste Trade

THOMAS F. SLAUGHTER, JR.

Can there be propriety in a North-South international trade in toxic waste? I think not. In this chapter, I make the assumption that progress in international thinking about the practice of shipping dangerous waste to less developed countries is marked by the results of U.N.-sponsored deliberations. Current doctrine provides for a distinction between illegal dumping and permissible trade. Key in the distinction is the provision of consent by the governments in less developed countries, which are to receive the waste in virtue of the proposed trade. I argue against identifying a government's possible act of signing a contract with an act of consent, given the historical context. As consent in the context involves speaking for others and involves ongoing state relations of international economic exploitation, I take the position that bona-fide consent would entail (1) the furtherance of justice as an equitable distribution of social benefits and liabilities, (2) reciprocal recognition and respect for persons, and (3) the government's authority to make the agreement, especially with regard to the government's antecedent, financial capacity to carry the domestic burden(s) forthcoming from the contract. I claim that none of these conditions is fulfillable today. With regard to industrialized countries' motives for promoting the trade, I take the position that it has less to do with the expediency of lowering costs and assuaging public discontent than it has to do with the absence of technological solutions for the safe disposal of toxic wastes.

If we take the recently resolved Basel Convention on the Control of Transboundary Movements of Hazardous Waste and Their Disposal (Basel, Switzerland, March 1989) as our high-water mark of global moral sensibility about the North-to-South transport of toxic waste, then there seems to be international consensus now that illegal dumping is wrong.[1] In its 1985 publication, "Environmental Aspects of the Activities of Transnational Corporations: A Survey," the United Nations Centre on Transnational Corporations set forth conditions that define "unregulated waste tourism":

Concern arises . . . when the international movement of hazardous waste is conducted in an uncontrolled or environmentally unsafe manner such as when details of the shipment are kept secret (the Seveso case . . .); when there is inadequate notification of regulatory authorities in the originating, transit and recipient countries; when the recipient country does not possess the institutional infrastructure, laws and knowledge necessary to deal wisely with the wastes (. . . the Nedlog affair [U.S. and Sierra Leone for radioactive waste; aborted] . . .); when the shipment is falsely or improperly labeled with regard to nature, composition, quantity, place of origin, and security instructions; when an adequate waste disposal facility ready to accept the shipment does not exist in the recipient country (Mexican authorities in March 1981 arrested a United States citizen for importing wastes such as polychlorinated biphenyls [PCB] and mercury cinders into Mexico from a number of American companies and then improperly disposing their wastes in a dry river bed and selling the empty waste barrels to local people for use as water containers); and when the producer of the toxic waste is able to absolve himself from responsibility or liability by means of subcontracting.[2]

Perhaps the most mentioned recent case of international waste dumping is the scandal in KoKo, Nigeria.[3] Sometime in or before 1987, a Nigerian concern, the Iruekpen Construction Company, entered the European waste trade. Gianfranco Raffaelli, an Italian businessman and long-time resident of Nigeria, headed the operation. In August 1987, Iruekpen Construction began receiving waste-filled drums from a sender somewhere in Italy. Raffaelli and his associates carried on business for ten months. During the period from August 1987 to May 1988, five shipments amounting to 3,800 tons of highly toxic and volatile waste entered Nigeria by way of the Iruekpen Construction Company.

The Nigerian government had no official knowledge of the operation, and this was the case even as the Italian public read about the trade in their daily newspapers. The government received its first indication of the goings-on in KoKo by virtue of a letter. The alert came from some concerned Nigerian students who were in Pisa, Italy, and were abreast of the local news there. The eight students surely knew too that their government was prominent in African resistance to European waste dumping. President Babangida is outspoken on the issue. That the government could take the posture it takes and at the same time there be in the country private interests actively engaged in the denounced trade must have seemed peculiar. The government acted upon the information. Authorities located the dumping site on June 2, 1988.

The owner of the land was found to be Sunday Nana. For one of his sources of income, he ran a business renting out lots on his land to importers for storage needs. From his perspective this particular cargo was no different from any other, and he denied knowledge about the contents of the drums in question. Crisis experts from various nations and agencies arrived in KoKo. They found many of the drums to be in advanced states of deterioration. Arti K. Vir, the writer for

Environmental Science and Technology from whose article this information is taken, reports that 4,000 of the drums were specified as being variously damaged, leaking, rusting, malodorous, and swelling from heat. Outside markings on the containers included skulls and crossbones; the letters, "R," "D," "X"; and the names, "polychlorodifenile" (PCBs), "fluorosilicate," "erocitus," and "rheoe 53" [*sic*]. Among the agencies on the scene was the Japanese Atomic Energy Research Agency. From this source it was learned that highly radioactive material was present in three of the drums. Vir conveys the pan-European genesis of the wastes as follows: "It has been reported that among the waste at the KoKo site, methyl melamine waste originated from Dyno-Cyanamid of Norway, dimethyl and ethylacetate formaldehyde came from Italian chemical manufacturers, and PCBs came from Elma, a Turin-based electromechanical plant."[4]

To manage his trade, Raffaelli and his associates had falsified or forged import documents and permits. Raffaelli himself managed to flee the country on June 2 as reports of the government raid on the dump came over the Nigerian news media. Others were not so quick. Another Italian, Desiderio Perazzi, and fifteen unnamed Nigerians were arrested. A special tribunal may be enacted to hear the case, and those convicted could receive the death sentence, according to news accounts. Nigeria recalled its ambassador to Rome and announced its intent to make Italy take back the waste. On June 10, the authorities commandeered the Italian ship, the *M. V. Piave*.

By July 6, the cleanup began with a work force of about 150 acting to prepare the waste for reshipment. During the process the crew on site suffered casualties. One individual suffered partial paralysis, three incurred severe chemical burns, and an unspecified number were hospitalized for vomiting blood. The waste left Nigeria for Italy in two shipments. The first, a load of 2,270 tons, left on July 30 aboard the *M. V. Karin B;* the second, leaving the site clean of containers, went out on the *M. V. Deep Sea Carrier* on August 15.

Although the surface has been cleaned, the ground is unsafe, and the area is off-limits. A watch is to be kept for groundwater contamination. The world scientific community will use the site to study the effects of the dumping on the environment and the people of KoKo.

Benin, on Nigeria's border, is under contract to take 5 million tons of waste a year from abroad. This agreement is with Gibraltar-based Sesco Ltd. for $2.50 a ton. (As of 1987, handlers on the U.S. end of the trade were getting between $60 and $140 a ton.)[5] Under a new $18 million deal with France (elsewhere described as *"30 years'* special financial and economic assistance";[6] while on the U.S. end of the trade, the giant multinational, Waste Management, Inc. showed a $180 million profit in one year alone, 1985).[7] "Three cargo vessels are on their way from France to Benin carrying the first consignment of waste, including cyanide, asbestos, and high-level radioactive material."[8]

One purpose of the Basel Convention is to improve the chances of stopping the illegal North-South movement of toxic waste. The dynamics of the agreement are complex. For the South to get support from the North to police exports of waste from the North to unconscionable designations in the South, the South has had to yield to the same trade but this time by consent. Hence in this instance, rather than regulation leading to the cessation of this activity, "global regulation" means only that innocent people in less developed countries stand a better chance of being informed about what poison they are being made to take, when, and where. The legal, supposedly amoral gambit being played by the international hazardous waste merchants is that a country that consents should not be viewed as being forced to take the waste.

"U.N. Conference Unanimously Backs Treaty Curbing Export of Hazardous Wastes," is the way the *New York Times* worded its header for the inside-page continuation of its front-page story on the Basel Convention.[9] But as one reads the story, one also learns that no African country signed the agreement and that African officials present complained about the successful efforts of the American and West German delegations to water down the treaty. The resulting document legitimizes the trade and gives countries targeted as importers of waste no leverage over the exporters in the matters of derelictions and failures. Two knowledgeable observers make telling remarks. A representative from the Natural Resources Defense Council is reported as saying, "This treaty takes a half step forward, at a time when the increased pressures to export waste are taking us 100 yards back." And a representative from Greenpeace declared, "This treaty puts an international stamp of approval on a horrible business." The *Times* reporter conveyed the sentiments of the treaty's defenders by writing that they believe the agreement is "a needed first step to regulate a complex area and that that step will be built on by other conferences."[10]

Coming out of the Basel meeting, we have what passes for due process in the opening of an until now uncharted area of activity. But not surprisingly the resulting compact is skewed: a new, intuitively reprehensible activity is sanctioned, and no new protections are rendered to the unshielded parties who, going into the meeting, stand to lose and in whose behalf for that reason the meeting was presumably called. The real tragedy is that less developed countries, in their case-by-case victimization by industrialized countries, must turn for hearings to existing international tribunal-like provisions—in this instance, the United Nations system of agencies. But the authority (which is not to diminish the several vital services performed) of an international tribunal like the U.N. extends just about as far as it reached in the Basel Convention on the international movements of hazardous and toxic waste. The gathering and its inherently formal proceedings (the process) perform the legitimation of what powerful interests intend to see done at any rate, while those who come with desperate hope that this time the proceedings will incorporate remedies in their behalf leave frustrated, doing a typical public fast-step where one both "unanimously backs" the good-faith gesture embodied by the fact of the meeting and announces the betrayal of one's real interests in the negotiations.[11] "It's a beginning," we say time after time.

Although the North-South waste trade is a very recent development, still in its nascency as historical watersheds of this magnitude go, our mentality is such that we all act as if the traffic is already an accomplished, full-blown fact, and so efforts to stem it should be cautious, measured, and incremental as though a long-established tradition were being handled judiciously. The only thing venerable about the traffic in question is its fit in the legacy of colonialism.

It is no accident that in the contemporary rush, when an impoverished country is targeted as a dump site, the setup in certain instances is overseen by the former colonizing mother country from the earlier period in which the targeted country originally underwent its undevelopment. Hence France opens up Benin, and Portugal, Guinea-Bissau.[12]

Again, the upshot of the Basel Convention is that progress in the debate over the propriety of the North's intent to shift the burden of its undisposable waste onto the South has reached the point where all eyes are turned now to the prospect of consent to the "trade" on the parts of governments of less developed nations—especially those in the most dire economic straits or those in which unaccountable power elites seek hard currency for the purchase of arms to strengthen their domestic hand. To my mind, while there probably will be legal deals made, no agreement that will be reached will meet the requirements of consent in this peculiar circumstance. (In the case of governments that actively solicit trade wastes, the issue of consent becomes a problem of legitimation and shifts back to the internal relation between that government and its disfranchised populations.)

There exists no possibility that meets the requirements of justice when it comes to arrangements for depositing industrial and consumer wastes in the South at this time. My position consists of contingencies. It is the way things sit among nations today and the way they have come to be the way they are that makes all real (as opposed to all conceivable) arrangements illicit. When I speak of justice, I have in mind the equitable distribution of social benefits and liabilities. Given the alignment of our thinking that follows upon our recourse to terms like *North* and *South* to designate the principal lines of stratification of the world today, no one wonders where to look to find general prosperity and where to look to find pervasive poverty. Disagreement starts only over how to account for the contemporary lay of poverty and prosperity.

The better accounts to my mind are those that place past European imperialism, colonialism, and slavery at the heart of present-day world wealth distribution. I include the economies of North America and Japan as variants in that same economic path, begun in Western Europe in the sixteenth century A.D. Hence for me, North and South are historical phenomena. And the affluence of the one and the destitution of the other are but two sides, as Walter Rodney would have it, of the same historical process.[13] Moreover, *North* and *South* for me are not value-neutral, descriptive terms. They are immediately moral terms. Their referents inextricably interpenetrate. What the word *North* designates to the detail would not be what it is were it not for the past and present superexploitation of the South; and, to the detail, the wretchedness of the South in its full inventory today is attributable to the legacy of imperialism, colonialism, and slavery. Justice is not even on the horizon.

In the age of well-being as material possession, the North has abundant know-how on the extraction and centralization of wealth. This is the realm of instrumentation, that is, instrumental judgment and invention: I-It relatedness. Where the Northern mind suffers endemic befuddlement, though, is in the moral evaluation of actions leading to clear and apparent advantage, where "advantage" is discriminable in terms other than moral. Profit, efficiency, and expediency are the obvious countervalences to bear in mind here. Morality is superfluous, I/Thou-ness ephemeral.[14]

The North-South toxic waste shift should be seen for the I-Thou problem that it is. But the North, with its comparatively overdeveloped I-It sensibility, is unable to risk and hold to the requisite humanity for very long. What spurs the impending poisoning of humanity in the South—redundant though it be, given the long-standing abuses of primary resource extraction and the callous marketing of hazardous commodities that already exist—is the fact that I-It sensibility has reached its nadir (perhaps its essence) around the problem of waste. There is nothing more you can do with waste. But the anterior processes of which it is the material residue render it something more than mere, sterile, inert refuse; it is positively lethal for most life-forms on earth. And in the concrete, almost as if to close a circle of errant conceit and futility, waste disposal poses a problem for which there appears to be no technical solution. Still, something must be done with it.

I view today's waste management problem as an endemic outcome of the historically evolved valuing consciousness and present-day design of production and consumption in the North. The quantity and kinds of waste whose disposal creates the world crisis we talk of today are the North's peculiar problem. But although the North has made its capacity for production and consumption its point of pride and prejudice in comparison with the South, it wants to share the waste, especially the most deadly, with the South as a joint obligation in the interest of common humanity. The very project, however, denies the humanity of Third World peoples. The blatant absence of reciprocal recognition is consistent with the history and present-day maintenance (with entities like the World Bank and the International Monetary Fund being integral in apparatus) of North over South superexploitation. To me, consent not only implies the furtherance of justice; it also implies mutual respect and well-being (positive, not relative) going into and coming out of the agreement.

Respect for persons (Kantian) is especially crucial in the application in question because the Third World government officials who fight to get dangerous waste for their people are speaking for unsuspecting contemporaries and unborn generations. Consider this:

Scientists still don't agree on exactly how long the [radioactive] wastes should be isolated from the environment, but the DOE [U.S. Department of Energy] advocates 10,000 years—enough time for almost all of the isotopes to decay. But critics point out that iodine 129 and plutonium, major constituents of spent fuel rods, will remain dangerously radioactive for millions of years.[15]

Take another note from the public debate in America:

> They [the federal government and industrial cohorts] had another reason to keep quiet. The government itself produces large quantities of nuclear waste and wanted to minimize its disposal problems. Much of that waste is high-level and extremely dangerous. Plutonium, a by-product of nuclear weapons fabrication, is one of the deadliest substances produced by man. It loses only half of its radioactivity in 24,000 years, and a microscopic speck can cause cancer and death. Yet, the government didn't classify it as high-level waste, which made disposal a lot simpler.[16]

As one gains historical perspective on the toxic waste debate, one discovers that North-South dumping made the headlines and became a refrain in 1988. But the problem of waste disposal had been in the public eye in America for at least ten years, going back to the Love Canal scandal in 1978. Public awareness of the problem of waste disposal can be set in the broader context of concern over environmental pollution, which in America may be reconstructed as beginning with the publication of *Silent Spring* by Rachel Carson in 1962. Coming forward over those years, it is the slowly dawning realization in industrialized countries of the magnitude of the problem of waste poisoning that leads to the seemingly natural and irreversible interest in the international waste trade—which benefits the people in less developed countries because now their hard-pressed governments gain access to previously inaccessible hard currency. They get a chance to join the future because "for once they have something to sell."

In a business transaction money changes hands for the delivery of goods or services. Clearly taking hazardous waste for payment falls under the heading of performing a service. From the point of view of inhabitants of industrialized countries who want the poison out of their midst, I see the picture clearly. What I have difficulty understanding is what happens on the other end.

Under today's conditions, I do not see how receiving dangerous waste into an underdeveloped country is just another business operation: "Recent events . . . suggest the continent is about to acquire the dubious status of being the global dustbin for substances too lethal for those producing them to want them disposed of in, or [even] near their territories."[17] Mustn't the assumption be that the Third World government in question can do a better job with the "too lethal" stuff than the society that sends it? Doesn't one of the promises have to be that the receiver government is going to be more careful with the waste than was the sender government? But if a head of state in an impoverished country even cared to voice such guarantees, how could that leader back them up? If one cuts through all the numbers and the claims and counterclaims that fill today's debate over toxic waste, one sees there are no solutions. And I take the expression "too lethal" in the quotation literally. I do not read it to mean too lethal relative to the preference and available options of the producer society. Literally, the waste in question cannot be lived with. It is too lethal. The idea of better handling is gratuitous.

Under one count published by the United Nations, industry in America generates 300 million tons of toxic waste each year.[18] And yet no new hazardous waste facility has been opened anywhere in the United States since 1980.[19] What can that mean? Of course, it could be due to costs. According to figures quoted by the National Solid Wastes Management Association (U.S.) in 1988, it cost $16 million to build a 40-acre landfill.[20] And high-temperature incinerators can cost $30 million. What about radioactive waste? No new site for nuclear waste has been opened in America since 1971. In fact, due to complications (trenches leaking, plutonium on the move across perimeters, and surrounding nature becoming radioactive), what were six privately owned low-level radioactive waste burial facilities in the United States became three as of 1978. And those remaining three are faring hazardously. Radioactive tritium is on the move (migrating off the site) at the Barnwell, South Carolina, site; improperly stabilized uranium caused a fire and exposed workers to radiation at the Beatty, Nevada, site; and at the Nevada and Hanford, Washington, sites, improper shipping and handling resulted in split-open containers, found empty of their contents by the time of their arrival at the dumps.[21] The United States, though, is planning a permanent burial site for nuclear waste:

As now envisioned, the repository will be a four-mile-square chamber mined out of rock or salt 1,000 to 4,000 feet underground. The waste will be converted into relatively inert pellets and encased in 160,000 heavily shielded canisters. Total cost for two repositories: $25 to $30 *billion,* which will be paid for by consumers in the form of higher electric bills.[22]

Going back to the hypothetical waste dump in the less developed country and assuming that the project represented a geologically sound gamble— "There isn't a radioactive landfill in any area with 30 to 40 inches of rainfall a year that hasn't leaked. Landfills act a lot like teabags: The water goes in, the flavor goes out"[23]—wouldn't the Third World government, soon to be caretaker of "too lethal" waste, have to command financial resources superior to those just described in order even to come up to speed on facilities to handle the trade into which it is being inducted?

Where is that much capital to be found? Perhaps the question is immaterial. I am sure there is someone who entertains the thought that adequate facilities can be had cheaper in the South. In the first place, "adequate" is a grossly irresponsible license of thought in the present context. In the second place, let us let go of the myth that things are cheaper in the South. The only things cheaper in the South (after resources outflow, of course) are human labor and the dollar value of human lives. Union Carbide's legal fortune in the Bhopal settlement is the latest testimony to that fact. But when it comes to material flows inbound to a Third World country, like the equipment, the supplies, and the information that will be required to start up waste dumps in target countries, all such items cost dearly. All things being routine, the cost of opening and maintaining a dump in the South should be considerably higher than the cost in the North.

The other possibility is that the lethal waste–expelling countries will make it easy for the dump targets to go into operation. Although the following example does not begin to approach the size of the "technology transfer" I envision, already it has happened that as Guinea-Bissau was being wooed into the traffic, "Intercontract [Switzerland] offered the government . . . a fleet of trucks to handle the waste, while Bis Import-Export [a London-based firm with a Portuguese CEO] and Habday [Isle of Man] proposed the construction of new port facilities on the Cacheu River near the Senegal border, presumably to receive toxic materials."[24] Such gifts are particularly odious since Senegal has been unable to put up enough collateral to go forward with schools, medical facilities, gutters and sewers, and other necessities since independence.

While we are on the subject of costs, there is another point to consider. The waste disposal crisis in the North today is a combination of pressure to manage the quantity of waste presently produced and pressure to clean up the mess from past mismanagement. There is a lesson to be learned from America's struggle to deal with the cleanup. This is a problem less developed countries that enter the trade today are surely going to have to face, probably in a shorter time than America came to its crisis. There will be another difference too. When the moment comes, less developed countries are going to have to call in outside experts to deal with their (and by that time, it will surely be their) problem. Accidents, failures, and the cleanup are surely waiting down the line. The experts called upon are going to be the same trade waste transnationals pushing the waste onto the unprepared countries now. And when the disaster specialists are called on to solve a problem, they are going to charge dearly for their lifesaving equipment and technological know-how.

Less developed countries lack the financial resources, the technology, and the elaborate store of information that will be required to handle the clear and certain eventuality whose clock they start by coming into agreement with the North to take its waste. Such an agreement is nothing less than an assent to take over the North's hand at precisely the dénouement of a Faustian deal. From a historical point of view, a Third World government's act of coming into the trade is a false step of the first magnitude. The table stakes, were they to be conscientiously declared, should be astronomical. Using America as the case in point, the lesson to be learned is that just the cleanup alone is a trillion-dollar proposition. To guarantee that adequate funds are available when they are needed, governments that consent to have toxic waste put into their countries should post in advance multibillion dollar cash bonds against future occurrences. When it comes to being on the receiving end of international toxic waste shipments, contrary to the government's being destitute and in need of hard currency, that government, as an antecedent condition, should command positively indeterminate social-financial backing if the nation in question is going to have the assets, the capability, and the government the authority to make and carry out a deal of the species in question.

To focus on the aspect of costs speaks to the point about a less developed country's capacity to carry (apart from the ceremony of signing to take on) the burden of service as the North's global dustbin. But that focus has the discursive drawback of permitting the notions to creep in that there are solutions to the waste disposal problem but that the cost in the North is so much as to make export to the South merely the option of choice to cut costs and avoid public discontent.[25] But that is not my position. I maintain that the coming practice of sifting waste southward (I have the image of shaking cinders and clinkers down from the upper to the lower chamber in a coal-burning home furnace in order to clear the upper chamber for fresh fire) happens in the wake of the realization that the weight plus range plus time frame of risks makes the problem of waste disposal insoluble.

All you can do with waste is move it around; you cannot dispose of it. This is what one writer refers to as a "bleak game of chemical leapfrog."[26] Let me insert the following description of the state of the art in dump site construction in America. It would seem that having something like this in place would be the minimum required of a consenting Third World government before the first shipment of waste (scheduled for this sort of disposal) were taken into the country:

A prime example of a modern disposal facility is the one operated by Waste Management, Inc., at its C.I.D. Hazardous Waste landfill in Chicago. A giant excavation 35 ft. deep covers two acres. A floor of compacted clay approximately 40 ft. thick has been laid below the bottom of the hole. On top of this virtually impermeable bed, workmen are placing a plastic liner to be topped by a plastic-grid system that will collect and direct any seepage into a series of sump pumps. Above the grid will be another plastic liner, another layer of clay and yet more plastic. A plumbing system will pump rainwater out of the area. Nearby, the company is spending $1.6 million to improve its large surface collection tanks, made of concrete lined with epoxy, that receive waste from steel-processing plants. New fiber-glass liners are being placed inside the cylinders. In the past, such wastes were merely poured into noxious surface lagoons. . . . Such techniques are, of course, expensive. [The author appends a note directed to the fact that while the dump design is commendable, in other areas of its operations Waste Management is not innocent of gross misconduct in its disposal practices.][27]

To take up the matter of the absence of solutions for waste disposal, let us listen carefully to the debate again, beginning with the prospects for high-level radioactive waste:

No satisfactory solution to permanent nuclear waste storage has yet been found. As more nuclear plants come on the line and more waste accumulates, the problem will continue to grow. This ever-growing pile of almost inconceivably deadly material, with a life span measured in hundreds of thousands of years, is a threat to the future of the planet.[28]

With regard to low-level radioactive waste,

While the Barnwell [South Carolina] dump is considered a shining star in the waste-management business, significant levels of tritium, a suspected carcinogen, have been detected 200 feet southwest of its trenches.

This story is played out hundreds of times a year. The names and places change, but the problems of low-level radioactive waste stay the same. No one knows how to define it, who should be responsible for it, or how and where it should be discarded.[29]

The following are some points that have been made in relation to "the bleak game of chemical leapfrog":

Superfund so far has been more sound than fury. . . . All too often, as the OTA [U.S. Office of Technological Assessment] study points out, Superfund money has been devoted to moving wastes from one problem site to another. . . . And even the sites to which the waste is moved may not be secure. "The requirement that no unit be leaking would probably rule out all the operating landfills in the country," states William Myers, a former EPA [Environmental Protection Agency] scientist.[30]

Most experts consider any landfill only a temporary solution to the chemical-waste problem. Eventually, all will develop cracks or gradually give way to the corrosive action of the potent chemicals. . . . Six California environmental groups recently surveyed seven landfills in that state. . . . "Every one of the sites examined is leaking, without exception; and every one is out of compliance with currently applicable regulations." Wastes placed in them from other failed sites may soon have to be picked up and moved once again. The result is a bleak game of chemical leapfrog. . . . Daggett [Christopher Daggett, EPA administrator for New York and New Jersey] and his boss, EPA Director Thomas, contend that *there is no ready technology that can promptly solve the disposal problem*.[31]

The dimensions of the problem explode even as the means of solving it dwindle. Last year Congress limited or barred use of land disposal for certain substances and decreed that all forms of land disposal should be barred within 66 months. But good intentions are no substitute for hard thought. . . . If not land disposal what? . . . Law enforcement people worry that as more and more landfills close down, toxic wastes like PCBs and dioxins will end up in the high-temperature waste recovery plants that are springing up all over the country, where they may or may not be incinerated properly. Such concerns are by no means academic. Hazardous waste in the garbage stream has already destroyed a waste recovery plant in Akron, Ohio.[32]

Hence we come to incineration:

Many environmentalists object to incinerators as well as to landfills. The opposition stems mainly from one word: dioxin. In the late 1970s, studies in the United States, Japan, Switzerland, the Netherlands, Germany, and Canada found that incinerators emit dioxin gases, believed by many scientists to be carcinogenic.[33]

Despite their known toxicity, dioxin and furan are not regulated by the federal government. "These are two of the most toxic substances made by man," says Dr. Paul Connett, a chemist at St. Lawrence University in Canton, N.Y. "They can damage the lymphatic system, cause birth defects, and promote cancer." When burned, chlorine compounds in waste products such as plastic, bleached paper, and table salt regroup and form these toxic molecules.[34]

The issue of incinerator ash—in particular, how to dispose of it—has drifted to the forefront of the burn-plant debate. In EPA tests, every sample of fly ash, the fine particulate matter trapped in the plants' air-pollution control devices, showed unacceptable levels of toxic metals such as lead and cadmium. Tests of bottom ash, the unburnt residue that collects on an incinerator's grate, showed unacceptable levels of these elements in 10 to 30 percent of the test cases. Concentrations of the potent carcinogens dioxin and furan are also present in fly ash. . . . In short, incinerators turn bulky garbage into compact, toxic waste.[35]

The technique of incineration comes down to the question of how to dispose of the residue, especially the fly ash:

Major U.S. cities, as well as Federal agencies, have joined the waste export bandwagon, sometimes with the approval of the State Department. Among them is Philadelphia, which has faced a rise in waste disposal costs from $20 to $90 a ton since 1980. The city intends to transport as much as 600,000 tons of ash residue a year from its municipal incinerator to Panama . . .[36]

Guinea has received 15,000 tons of toxic U.S. waste, according to *Africa Analysis,* Nigeria's *African Guardian* and *African Concord* and *Lettre Afrique Energies.* The hazardous material—probably incinerator ash—was falsely labeled "raw materials" and buried on Kasa, an offshore island near Guinea's capital, Conakry. A Guinea-based firm owned by Guinean and Norwegian businessmen, *Société Internationale Aluko Guinea,* reportedly accepted the shipment from a company in Philadelphia. . . . [A House subcommittee] is investigating reports that two Philadelphia-based ships, the *Khain* and the *Bark,* transported the ash to Guinea. And while the EPA confirms that a company based in New Jersey applied to send dangerous waste to Guinea—and that Guinea refused the shipment—an EPA official declined to name the company. . . . The waste was dug up and packaged for reshipment, but not before Kasa's vegetation was decimated by the toxic substances.[37]

Our remembrance of the scandal on Kasa lands us back with illegal dumping. That was before the Basel Convention. The Basel accord instructs us that the idea of a North-to-South toxic waste redistribution is not to be categorically condemned and the forthcoming practice pronounced unconscionable in all of its forms. After Basel, we have the problem of consent.

When we talk about a government's consenting to take in toxic waste, we understand right away that whether or not the country's people are apprised of the terms of agreement, it is they who assume the liabilities of the deal. Moreover, the list of those who lose extends to neighboring countries and, further, to wide regions of the earth under possibilities like explosions and toxic clouds or the migrations of contaminated fish. Mathieu Kerekou, the president of Benin, allegedly selected the mouth of the Oueme River as the dump site for the nuclear waste he is getting from France.[38] With regard to the clear and apparent liability-culpability of transporting "too lethal" waste into an underdeveloped country and dumping it there, I can see the possibility of the exporters' arguing that the poisoning of the repositor's country is not one of their intentions. That would be moronic duplicity, but the exporters are not moral while they are exporting. Let us not spend a lot of time with that. The more interesting questions become: To whom and for what are heads of state in the South accountable in the moment of consent to the North-South waste trade?

NOTES

This chapter is a slightly modified version of a paper originally delivered, *Colloque Du 11–13 Mai* 1989, *Ethique Et Entreprise Au Maghreb,* Casablanca, Morocco.

1. "U.N. Conference Supports Curb on Exporting of Hazardous Waste," *New York Times,* March 23, 1989, pp. A1, B11.

2. United Nations Publication Sales No. E.85.IIA.11, p. 60.

3. Arii K. Vir, "Toxic Trade with Africa," *Environmental Science and Technology* 23(1) (January 1989): 23–25.

4. Ibid., p. 23.

5. Andrew Porterfield and David Weir, "The Export of U.S. Toxic Wastes," *Nation,* October 3, 1987, reprinted in Robert E. Long, ed., *The Problem of Waste Disposal* (New York: H. W. Wilson Company, 1989), pp. 132–40 (hereafter cited as *PWD*).

6. "The West's Wastebasket," *Africa News,* June 13, 1988, p. 6 (emphasis added).

7. Kenneth Dreyfack and Richard Hoppe, "Waste Management's Image Is Still Less Than Pristine," *Business Week,* September 9, 1985, pp. 58, 60.

8. "The West's Wastebasket," p. 24.

9. *New York Times,* p. B11.

10. Ibid. All quotations are taken from p. B11. The reporter is Steven Greenhouse.

11. I am alluding here to the performative use of language as first clarified by J. L. Austin in *How to Do Things with Words* (Cambridge, MA: Harvard University Press, 1975). Under this capacity, our very utterance of the words *is* the performance of an act, as in "I now pronounce you . . ." or "I promise . . ."

12. "The West's Wastebasket," *Africa News,* June 13, 1988, pp. 6–7.

13. Walter Rodney, *How Europe Underdeveloped Africa.* (Washington DC: Howard University Press, 1982).

14. During the week of April 17, 1989, a woman who was jogging in New York City's Central Park was assaulted, beaten about the head, raped, and left for dead by a gang of youths. At the time, the eight black teen-agers were on a rampage just for thrills, they said. After they were arrested and interviewed some days later, the boys still showed no remorse.

15. Tom Yulsman, "Burying Nuclear Waste," in *PWD,* p. 180.

16. Susan Q. Stranahan, "The Deadliest Garbage of All," in *PWD,* pp. 190–91.

17. "Africa: A Global Dumping Ground?" *Africa,* no. 174 (February 1986): 54.

18. Environmental Events Record, *UNEP News* (January–February 1986): supp. 4. The original text quotes the figure as 3,000 million tons, but that is probably a misprint.

19. R. C. Mitchell and R. T. Carson, "Property Rights, Protest, and the Siting of Hazardous Waste Facilities," *American Economic Review* 76(2) (May 1986) 285–90.

20. Antonio Fins, "Meet the Kings of the Garbage Heap," *Business Week,* September 12, 1988, pp. 112–16.

21. Stranahan, "Deadliest Garbage," p. 191.

22. Yulsman, "Burying Nuclear Waste," p. 181 (emphasis added).

23. Marvin Resnikoff, codirector of the Sierra Club Radioactive Waste Campaign, quoted in Gale Warner, "Low-level Lowdown," in *PWD*, p. 184.

24. *Africa News*, (June 13, 1988): p. 6.

25. Most of the literature on the North-South traffic, including the U.N.'s material, takes this line. For a curious call on transnational corporations to be the moral conscience of the new expediency, see John F. Mahon and Patricia C. Kelly, "The Politics of Toxic Wastes: Multinational Corporations as Facilitators of Transnational Public Policy," *Research in Corporate Social Performance and Policy*, vol. 10, ed. Lee E. Preston (Greenwich, Conn.: JAI Press, 1988), pp. 59–86.

26. Ed Magnuson, "A Problem That Cannot Be Buried," in *PWD*, p. 107.

27. Ibid., pp. 109–10.

28. Robert Emmet Long, "Editor's Introduction," in *PWD*, p. 153.

29. Warner, "Low-level Lowdown," in *PWD*, p. 183.

30. Cook, "Risky Business," in *PWD*, p. 129.

31. Magnuson "Problem That Cannot Be Buried," p. 107 (emphasis added).

32. Cook, "Risky Business," p. 130.

33. Tony Davis, "Garbage: To Burn or Not to Burn?" in *PWD*, p. 18.

34. Mann, "Garbage In, Garbage Out," in *PWD*, p. 22.

35. Ibid., p. 21.

36. Porterfield and Weir, "Export of U.S. Toxic Wastes," p. 136.

37. "The West's Wastebasket," p. 7.

38. *Africa News*, (June 13, 1988): p. 6.

Water Resources, Economic Development, and Species Extinction: A Case Study

JACK L. WEIR

West Texas is embroiled in a dispute centering around a snake and a lake. The snake is the Concho water snake, and the lake is Stacy Reservoir. The conflict is that the lake probably will destroy the snake. Water is a scarce economic resource in the semidesert climate, and allegedly several cities will run short by the early 1990s unless the reservoir is finished. Since the fall in oil prices, the local economy has been severely depressed, and relief from any source is badly needed. Reports of a global greenhouse effect and recent dry years have compounded local fears. According to the regional water authority and the local chambers of commerce, the water is needed for population growth, industrial and business development, agriculture, and recreation.

Resolving such disputes between environment and economy depends on numerous empirical and conceptual factors. The relevant empirical aspects include plentiful and complex questions from biology, ecology, geology, climatology, agriculture, population demographics, macroeconomics, and microeconomics. The conceptual factors also include multiple and complicated issues ranging from economic and sociopolitical beliefs about private property, ownership rights, general welfare, free enterprise, and democracy to metaethical beliefs about ultimate meaning and value.

Because of the multifaceted nature of the problem, its resolution requires interdisciplinary cooperation and expertise. As a philosopher and ethicist, I specialize in logical and conceptual analysis. In this chapter I use the Concho water snake as an actual case to analyze and evaluate four currently debated metaethical theories of value and their consequent normative implications for the broad question of our human interrelationships with the environment: respect for life, sentience, self-conscious rationality, and environmental wholism.

THE CASE

Also called Harter's snake, the species is a wildlife resource unique to Texas. It is Texas's only endemic snake. Although some biologists consider them to be distinct species, the current taxonomy lists two subspecies: *Nerodia harteri harteri,* or the Brazos water snake, which occurs along 180 miles of the upper Brazos River drainage; and *Nerodia harteri paucimaculata,* or the Concho water snake, which is found 135 miles southwest along 200 miles of the Concho and Colorado River drainage, which is tributary to the Brazos. Compared to the grayer Brazos snake, the Concho snake is paler brown in color and has inconspicuous or missing spots on the tips of its ventral scales (hence the name *paucimaculata,* "fewer spotted"). Both snakes are nonvenomous, average 2 feet in length, and feed during the daytime on small fish that are stymied by rapidly moving water. The snakes require rocky riffles with an unshaded shoreline littered with flat rocks. This habitat is used by the adults as a birthing ground and by the juveniles as a feeding and hiding area. No other snake indigenous to the United States swims as rapidly; its usual defensive behavior is to swim rapidly diagonally downstream to the opposite bank.

Due to the construction of water impoundments that flood the rocky riffles, the Concho snake is endangered. The construction of Robert Lee dam in Coke County in 1968 flooded over half of the snake's habitat, leaving only 69 miles of riverbed with only 41 riffles on the Concho and Colorado rivers in Concho, Coleman, Tom Green, and McCulloch counties. Prior to 1985, the Concho snake had never been found more than 200 feet from shallow rapids. In 1985 estimates, the snake population was between 330 and 660 snakes. The young are live-born during September, with as many as 22 siblings from one mother. Consequently snake populations and locations vary dramatically depending on season, disturbance, weather, and predation.

Currently under construction, Stacy Reservoir will inundate at least 24.8 additional miles of the Concho water snake's habitat. Dry weather will reduce the number of riffles and confine the snake to 22 miles of riverbed. In addition, the few remaining riffles may be destroyed by siltation or further development, especially by ranchers constructing low water crossings and private dams for irrigation and livestock. According to Alan Tennant, a Texas herpetologist, the remnant environment is probably too small and too vulnerable to preserve the snake from extinction.[1]

In October 1977 the Colorado River Municipal Water District (CRMWD) applied to the Texas Water Commission for a permit to use water from the Colorado River for Stacy Reservoir to be constructed at the confluence of the Concho and Colorado rivers south of the cities of Ballinger and Coleman. A less expensive alternative proposal was that a pipeline be constructed from an oversupplied existing reservoir, Lake Buchanan, but this proposal was rejected since Lake Buchanan's water was controlled by a rival water authority. Projections by the Texas Water Development Board were that several cities in West Texas would run short of water by 1990. The reservoir would provide water for the cities of Big Spring, Snyder, Odessa, Midland, San Angelo, Stanton, Robert Lee, and Pyote.

A water rights dispute erupted, the longest and most expensive in Texas history. In June 1979 the Texas Water Commission issued a permit that was immediately challenged in court. The Lower Colorado River Authority, the city of Austin, and several irrigation companies claimed that the reservoir would deprive them of downstream water. But before the litigation was resolved, in January 1980, the CRMWD applied to the Army Corps of Engineers for a construction permit. In March 1980 the plans for a power station at the reservoir were dropped, making the excess water available to the city of Abilene, which in August 1985 in a general election approved a contract for the water.

Meanwhile, in February 1984 the New Mexico Herpetological Society petitioned the U.S. Fish and Wildlife Service to declare the Concho water snake a threatened species because the proposed reservoir would inundate the habitat of the snake and thereby annihilate the species. According to the Endangered Species Act (1973), such a listing would prohibit the Corps of Engineers from issuing a permit for construction. The Fish and Wildlife Service had already conducted a study in 1981 that concluded that existing dams already threatened the survival of the snake.

In November 1984 the Texas Supreme Court ruled against the CRMWD that the water had already been allocated to the downstream plaintiffs and that the Texas Water Commission should not have issued the permit for Stacy Reservoir. Immediately the CRMWD petitioned for a rehearing, and subsequently the court reversed its ruling, upholding the state's right to issue the permit but ordering the Texas Water Commission to rehear the case. In January 1985, after threats of retaliation from West Texas state legislators and extensive political pressure from Governor Mark White, Lieutenant Governor Bill Hobby, and House Speaker Gib Lewis, the Lower Colorado River Authority reached an agreement with the CRMWD. The Texas Water Commission issued a new permit in May 1985.

A year later, in May 1986, the Fish and Wildlife Service announced that it was going to issue a biological opinion that the Concho water snake was threatened. Plans had been proposed by the Municipal Water Authority to find natural and to build artificial alternative habitats for the snake, which the report found to be unacceptable for the survival of the species. The first draft of the report was officially issued in July 1986, and the report recommended that the Corps of Engineers deny a construction permit.

In August 1986, extensive political pressure from U.S. Senator Phil Gramm, U.S. Senator Lloyd Bentson, and U.S. Congressman Charles Stenholm convinced the Fish and Wildlife Service to withdraw its opinion. Promises were made that the CRMWD would hire a herpetologist to monitor the alternative habitats of the snake.

In February 1987 the Corps of Engineers issued its final environmental impact statement in which it stated that the alternative habitats would offer "reasonable and prudent" means for preserving the snake. The permit requires that 30 miles of the Colorado River shoreline be bulldozed to provide an alternative habitat, that sufficient water be released from Stacy Reservoir to maintain the snake's downstream habitat, and that an extensive study of the snake's life history be funded. Estimates are that the reservoir will cost $70 million and the snake habitat an additional $3.7 million. In April 1987 the Corps of Engineers issued the construction permit, and groundbreaking was in May 1987. The reservoir is under construction and is scheduled for completion in 1990.

Early results of the life history study resulted in increased population estimates and the identification of previously overlooked populations, most notably in both Lake Moonen and E. V. Spence Reservoir. In contrast to the Brazos snake, which was known to occur in Possum Kingdom Lake and Lake Granbury, the Concho snake had never previously been found in a large reservoir. Such discoveries do not mean that the snake will survive after the construction of Stacy Reservoir. The construction activities may account for some of the population displacements. Dams fragment populations, leading to genetic isolation and perhaps breeding populations too small to maintain essential genetic diversity. High dams prevent movement of the snake into areas where catastrophe has eliminated a population, and controlled water flow causes siltation in the riffles, which encourages the invasion of woody vegetation. In the very long term, impoundments will change significantly due to siltation, probably eventually leading to the extinction of the subspecies, unless funds are continuously appropriated for long-term dredging and environmental maintenance.

RESPECT FOR LIFE

Popularly identified with Albert Schweitzer, respect (or reverence) for life is the view that value is life based.[2] Similar approaches are respect to conation (William James, George Santayana, Ralph Barton Perry, and Joel Feinberg), respect for "nature" (that is, natural teleological centers of life) (Paul Taylor), and "being alive" (Kenneth E. Goodpaster).[3] These approaches are all similar in that value is located in living entities. Allegedly living entities have intrinsic value and interests (or a good of their own) that can be benefited or harmed.

Both conation and reverence for life assume that natural urges are good, which they may not be. These urges resulted from natural selection, and probably not until rationality and language are achieved by a species can we meaningfully talk of any type of self-conscious valuing. Although life and conation are necessary for full moral status, they are not sufficient. Without cognitive awareness, life involves no beliefs, desires, or aims. Conative demands are not of equal value, and conflicts must be resolved if injustice is to be avoided. Feinberg suggests that we have duties to those near and dear to us and duties to our own species that override other duties.[4] Human claims are more valuable than animal claims because of human properties not found in lower animals—properties such as rationality, morality, aesthetics, and culture.

All life-based approaches encounter the same problem: they produce overwhelming conflicts and incoherence and thereby reduce to absurdity. If every individual living thing is equally valuable, then all ought to be preserved, including every individual Concho water snake and every blade of grass. If this were so, humans would have to depend on artificially and chemically synthesized foods for nutrition or else starve to death since no killing could be normative. Moreover, humans perhaps ought to police the planet, preventing all species from killing and preying on each other. Surely this is absurd. Resolution of these conflicts can come only by appeal to some factor(s) other than being alive.

SENTIENCE

Sentience is the capacity to experience pleasure and pain, and the value of sentience is the alleged intrinsic goodness and badness of the respective mental states. All beings capable of pleasure and suffering, because of this capacity, can be treated rightly and wrongly. A widely used distinction introduced by G. J. Warnock is that between moral agents and moral patients, the former referring to rationally reflective moral beings but the latter referring to merely sentient beings.[5]

Perhaps the fullest treatment of animals based on the sentience criterion is Peter Singer's. In *Animal Liberation* (1975), Singer argues on classical utilitarian grounds that we ought to be vegetarians because animals are sentient and using them for food produces an imbalance of pain over pleasure.[6] This argument has been thoroughly criticized, especially by R. G. Frey,[7] as entailing only that animals be humanely raised and mercifully slaughtered, not that we ought to be vegetarians.

Moreover, unless self-conscious, sentient experiences would not seem to be a moral concern since no individual who endures through time would be having the experiences. Without an enduring self-consciousness, sentient experiences are little more than intermittent isolated packages of pleasure and pain belonging to no distinguishable individual. Sentience-based approaches are reductionistic: complex living organisms are reduced to mere packages of mental states. The intrinsic value of the individuals would seem to be little more than the sum total of their intrinsically valuable packages, and there would be no reason for not trading off the packages and for not trading off the individuals, including killing them. Regrettably, conflicts may often force both kinds of trades. To make matters worse, the packages of sentience also can differ qualitatively; surely a human being's aesthetic pleasure at hearing *Don Giovanni* is beyond any sentient animal's hedonistic pleasure.

More recently Singer has argued for preference utilitarianism. Classical hedonistic utilitarianism, he concedes, treats moral agents and patients as "mere receptacles" of pleasures and pain—as having no value of their own. In contrast, preference utilitarianism considers the ends to be achieved to be preferences (including interests and desires), and instead of weighing pleasures and pains, preferences are weighed.[8]

Despite requiring a more complicated utility calculus, Singer's preference utilitarianism fails to answer the criticisms. Since even future preferences can be outweighed and replaced by other preferences, including the preferences of other individuals, killing is not prohibited. Killing is more difficult to justify but certainly not impossible, not even killing self-conscious beings. Both of Singer's versions locate moral value in sentient mental states such that the (moral) beings possessing these states are treated as receptacles—as means to achieve the valuable mental states, including those of others. Actions remain justifiably right or wrong based on overall utility.

How does the sentience criterion apply to the Concho water snake? Whether the snake actually experiences mental states of pleasure and pain is highly questionable given its rudimentary brain. Its behavior seems to be controlled by instinct and environmental stimulus. Even if its sentience is conceded, it does not follow that the species as a species has rights but only that individual snakes have rights. The species as a species does not experience pleasure and pain. Based on the sentience criterion, to determine the morality of destroying the snake, a utility calculus of the total aggregate of pleasures and pains needs to be made. Every individual snake's pleasure and pain needs to be counted, as would all the pleasures and pains of all other relevant sentient individuals. Although the individual snakes probably would die painfully when their habitat is flooded, the pleasures of the millions of future fish, reptiles, birds, and other animals— including the humans who will play at the lake and use its water in their cities— would surely exceed even an exaggerated amount of snake suffering. Sentience does not give the individual snakes any added advantage over any other sentient individual, and since many sentient beings are more sentient than the snake, the snake likely would lose in the trade-off. More pointedly, a strictly hedonistic and sentient calculus might require building the dam and killing the snake in order to maximize the total aggregate of sentient pleasure.

To this utilitarian concern with sentience should also be added broader, long-term utilitarian factors, such as the need for ecological diversity (which includes species pluralism), preserving the snake's gene pool as an unrecoverable resource for unforeseen future needs and emergencies, and the potential long-term contribution the snake might make to evolutionary generation. Extinction irreparably shuts down the generative process. However, since the snake's habitat is quite confined and local, the snake's demise probably would have negligible impact on other species and the future potential of the planet. The snake also has no apparent or foreseeable commercial or domestic value for food, clothing, entertainment, medicine, or decoration. In contrast, Stacy Reservoir has immediate regional commercial and domestic value for municipal water, recreation, agriculture, population growth, attraction of new industry, and growth of existing industry. Although West Texas might be better off in the long run by adopting a policy of strict water conservation, the easy immediate solution is constructing the dam. The citizens seem to prefer green lawns and swimming pools, and the business management evidently prefers not to relocate businesses to a less arid region where ample water and labor already exist. Regrettably, if population trends and ecological destruction continue, West Texas at some future time, perhaps by the end of the century, will be forced to adopt strict policies of conservation. The multidimensional aspects of sentience and the empirical difficulty of making long-term estimates of consequences emphasize why it is difficult to resolve most moral issues with a sentience-utilitarian standard.

SELF-CONSCIOUS RATIONALITY

Derived from a critical reading of Immanuel Kant's *Groundwork of the Metaphysic of Morals* (1785), critical Kantianism holds that the only absolute, unconditional (categorical), and nonarbitrary value is rationally self-conscious and autonomous persons. Because they are capable of formulating universally necessary moral duties (or laws) regarding values, ends, instruments, motives, attitudes, intentions, conduct, and character traits, rationally autonomous persons have unconditional, categorical value. By virtue of their rational autonomy, such beings have the ability to choose their own ends; they are their own lawgivers. Although one might selfishly and prudentially want to be egoistic, egoism is logically self-contradictory since conceivably one's own egoistic actions and desires eventually will conflict with others' egoistic actions and desires. By nonegoistically treating all rationally autonomous beings as ends in themselves, one can consistently maintain one's own status as a rationally autonomous moral being and that of all like beings. Such moral beings ought not to be treated merely as a means to others' ends since to do so would result in self-contradiction; in other words, upon pain of self-contradiction, all rationally autonomous persons should treat all other rationally autonomous persons as free moral agents who can rationally deliberate and choose their values, formulate goals, and act to achieve those goals. To treat someone as a mere means is to treat them as a thing, as something lacking in rational autonomy. Metaethically, a "moral being" is a "rationally self-conscious autonomous person."

Normative implications result when such beings act and value in an actual sociocultural context. Since morality is grounded in rational autonomy, actions and character traits are morally obligatory to the extent that they tend to enhance or develop one's own or others' rational autonomy, and actions and character traits are morally prohibited to the extent that they tend to limit or defeat one's own or others' rational autonomy. Such actions and traits are thus "objectively" obligatory (or prohibited). Precisely what actions and traits are objectively and morally obligatory (or prohibited) will in principle vary from person to person and from one sociocultural situation to another, although certain virtues and abilities, such as respect for others' autonomy and development of one's own rational abilities, are universally required.

Based on this Kantian-type metaethical and normative position, it follows that nature and merely sentient beings are not intrinsically valuable. Their moral value is solely located in the extent to which they promote (or inhibit) rationally autonomous beings and in the extent to which they are nonmorally valued by rationally autonomous beings. If there were no rationally autonomous valuers, there would be no value. The pleasures and pains of lower animals are not morally valuable in themselves, and no natural wonder—whether forest, lake, canyon, or animal species—is morally valuable. These nonmoral things become objects of moral concern only to the extent that they are valued by rationally autonomous persons and to the extent that they objectively contribute to the self-enhancement and self-destruction of rationally autonomous persons.

This Kantian-type position would not prohibit exterminating the Concho water snake unless the snake were an object of significant subjective or instrumental value to persons, which it is not. As Texas's only endemic snake species, Texans perhaps should preserve the snake for the sense of wonder and pride it brings, as the nation does with whooping cranes and bald eagles. Such nonmoral, subjective (and aesthetic) valuing requires respect from other persons, but the respect is directly toward the persons doing the valuing, not toward the snakes, cranes, and eagles.

ENVIRONMENTAL HOLISM

For environmental holism, value is not the individual but the collective whole, the biosphere, the totality of things and systems in the natural order. Everything is in some sense morally relevant, not just indirectly as it relates to human persons but directly. To use Aldo Leopold's term, "the land" is of ultimate value, and the land is the collective total composed of soil, water, plants, animals, rocks, air, and humans. Normatively, acts are right if they tend to promote the integrity, beauty, diversity, and harmony of the whole; otherwise they are wrong.[9]

Holism is nonanthropocentric, if not antianthropocentric. In contrast anthropocentric-humanistic approaches treat ecosystems as resource values to be exploited for human ends. A scientifically enlightened humanist would have no reason not to use the planet as a mere resource according to long-term ecological science and according to the highest humanistic values.

Perhaps the best defender of collective holism is Holmes Rolston III. By metaethically denying the is-ought fallacy, Rolston argues for a resurgent naturalistic ethic in which morality is derivative from the holistic character of the ecosystem. Like it or not, all values are objectively grounded and supported by the empirical possibilities and limitations within the earth's ecosystem. All values are a product of the interrelationship and interaction of human persons with an objective environment. What counts as beauty, stability, and integrity emerges from the interaction of world and concept. Rather than being located solely in human persons, values are collectively relocated in human persons in the environment.

Rolston rejects the anthropocentric view that ecology is merely enlightened and expanded human self-interest. We preserve the environment not because it is in our best long-term economic, aesthetic, and spiritual self-interest but because there is no firm boundary between what is essentially human and what is essentially ecosystem. A scientific ecological fact is that complex life-forms evolve and survive only in complex and diversified ecosystems. If "human" as we know it is to survive, we must maintain the oceans, forests, and grasslands. To convert the planet into cultivated fields and cities would destroy human life. We also ought to preserve the diversified ecosystem to enable the future evolution of the planet, including that of human mental and cultural life.

Normatively, Rolston maintains, right actions are those that preserve ecosystemic beauty, stability, and integrity. Preserving the ecosystemic status quo, however, may not be entailed because humans can improve the environment. Biosystemic welfare allows alteration, management, and use, but a comparable benefit must result.

Regarding species, Rolston contends that our duties are to the species as forms of life rather than to the individual members of the species. The species is the form, whereas the individual merely re-presents and passes on the form. The locus of dignity is the form. Biologically and ecologically, the individual is subordinate to the species. Although extinctions do occur in nature, natural ones are open-ended, usually producing diversification, new species, and ecological trade-offs. In contrast, human extinctions are dead ends, destroying diversity and leading to monocultures. Duties toward species begin when human conduct endangers species. Unless preserved in their ecosystems, species will not be preserved, and evolution will halt.[10]

According to a holistic ethic, the Concho water snake ought to be preserved by not building the reservoir. Even without considering the snake, the reservoir should not be built. Building the reservoir will alter the natural beauty, integrity, and diversity of the West Texas ecosystem without any substantial comparable ecological or humanistic benefit. The instrumental human benefits resulting from the lake are questionably justifiable for the semiarid environment. Industries needing more water should go to where the water already naturally exists, and farmers and ranchers should raise crops and livestock ecologically fitted to the environment. Wanting to be able to be more competitive, greedy business leaders should move to where the resources already exist, and the human population should be restricted to what the environment can qualitatively maintain. The two major causes of ecological disaster are overpopulation and economic exploitation. Stacy Reservoir threatens the snake only because other water impoundments have already reduced its habitat to minimal survival limits. The limit has been reached; population growth and economic development must now be stopped, or the ecosystem will suffer irreparable harm. Unless West Texans learn from others' mistakes, further ecological damage will result.

Holistic approaches are often criticized as implying a subtle egoism of the whole or as being pantheistic, panentheistic, or fascist. In some approaches, the whole is a sentient, conscious, or living "mind." None of these objections applies to Rolston.

However, three significant objections have been raised by William K. Frankena. First, if only sentient and rational beings are morally considerable, there is no moral grounds to consider the whole unless the whole is sentient or conscious. Moreover, the value concepts of beauty, integrity, balance, and so on are values possessed as objects of contemplation by minds like ours, and the values are not intrinsically in the whole but only in relation to us. This type of value was referred to by C. I. Lewis as "inherent" value.[11] That is, an entity may have the capacity to contribute something of value, but another being's experience or contemplation of the entity is what is intrinsically valuable—not the entity in itself. Even if ecosystemic beauty and integrity are not dependent on the observer, morally we ought to do something about them only if and insofar as they affect minds like ours, present or future. Finally, holism is based on two much-debated claims: (1) that the value of the whole is not reducible to the value of its component entities, but the value of the whole at the same time depends on those entities and their distribution, and (2) that the value of the whole ought to be maximized even if it lessens the value of the component entities or individuals. Although these two claims have not been shown to be false, they have also not been shown to be true.[12]

Rolston's insistence that human individuals, concepts, and values emerge together naturalistically out of the environment addresses the alleged conflicts between individual and environment, between nonnaturally based (human) concepts of value and environmentally based (natural) values. Rolston's claim that what is good for the environment is generally good for human individuals is explicitly a mixed empirical and metaethical claim. As a general principle, it is probably true, and Rolston recognizes that it has exceptions—humans can improve the environment. But given the overpopulation, industrial exploitation, and environmental abuses of today, conflicts are occurring and sacrifices must be made. If we do not make the sacrifices, future generations will inherit an exponentially worse situation. Since we are closer to the abuses and have benefited more from them, should we not make the sacrifices?

Even if only sentient and rational beings are intrinsically valuable and morally considerable and even if the ecosystem is only inherently and instrumentally valuable, an ecological ethic still results. Morally responsible persons ought not wantonly to destroy or waste anything of value—especially inherently and instrumentally valuable environments that contribute to the essential being and identity of the persons within them.

CONCLUSION

From my analysis of these four theories of value, I obtain a synthesis of the last two. Two values have emerged: rationally self-conscious persons and collective holistic ecosystems. Both values are "absolute" in the Kantian sense of being categorical and unconditional; the denial of either produces rational self-contradiction. All rational beings must ascribe to both on pain of self-contradiction. Both values are also "naturalistic" in Rolston's sense of emerging nonreductionistically and complementarily out of the natural holistic environment. Because we are our environment, to harm the environment is to harm ourselves, and rationally autonomous persons cannot consistently will to harm themselves. To harm the environment is to destroy the basis and sustenance of our own rationality, identity, and being. The resulting ethic could be labeled "eco-humanism" or "Kantian holism."

From these two values, all rationally autonomous persons have two duties: the deontological duty to treat all rationally autonomous persons as ends and never merely as means and the teleological duty to maximize ecological beauty, diversity, stability, and integrity. Rationally autonomous persons are incommensurable deontological values, whereas holistic ecosystems are commensurable teleological values. This mixture of deontological and teleological elements makes this proposal at most a "Kantian-type" normative solution—a mixed deontological theory.

When these two values conflict, as they currently are due to overpopulation and economic exploitation, deontological considerations should have priority over teleological ones because persons ought never to be used as mere means to ends, even to achieve the survival of other persons and of ecosystems. Although ecosystems may be inherently valuable apart from human experiences, the values become actual only when conceptualized and experienced by rationally autonomous persons.

Although not incommensurably valuable due to their nonrationality, lower species are still significantly valuable due to their importance for ecological beauty, diversity, stability, and integrity, including continued evolutionary generation. Individuals of lower, nonrational abilities are instantiations of their species-form such that one individual is as valuable as another, except when human social attachments (such as pets) and instrumental factors (such as draft animals) apply. Our duty, therefore, is to preserve species populations in ecosystems; this duty does not prohibit domesticating and using individual plants and animals for human or ecological ends, such as food, clothing, labor, and medicine, provided the integrity of the ecosystem and species populations is maintained. Regardless of its level of existence, no individual life ought to be wantonly and unnecessarily destroyed since such acts are ecologically harmful and wasteful. Because they can suffer, merely sentient animals ought not to be needlessly allowed to suffer or be inflicted with pain. They ought always to be treated humanely and, when necessary, killed mercifully.

Although it may not be conducive to human welfare or survival, some type of environment will always obtain. Ecological balance is necessary for human life. Our environment is so diversely multifaceted and our environmental sciences so primitive that we can neither control nor even predict the consequences of many of our actions. Since we are animals evolved within ecosystems, we must preserve these environments or else we will destroy ourselves. Our values are at least to this extent objectively natural. But we are both in and outside nature; we can adapt to an amazing variety of environments. We can also act to improve or destroy nature. We can live in a technological maze or a natural wilderness. We can surround ourselves with concrete and steel or with living plants and animals. Morally, our acts ought to enhance our own rational autonomy by enhancing holistic eco-human values. It is irrationally self-destructive for rationally autonomous selves to act so as to destroy the eco-human basis of their rational self-identities.

Given political realities, the Concho water snake is doomed. Compared to acid rain, ozone depletion, deforestation, and the greenhouse effect, the Concho snake may seem unimportant. Nevertheless, all these cases have a similar underlying unity: we are unwilling to curtail either population growth or economic development. The tragedy is that we are fully informed: we know our actions are destroying the environment that sustains the kind of lives we find worth living. Yet very few individuals or businesses are willing to take the immediate losses that are needed to avert the long-term disaster. At the personal, individual level, we should immediately in our life-styles and homes begin to consume less— using less energy, recycling waste, and living lower in the ecological pyramid. At the management level, in corporations and in the government, we should adopt policies and practices that reward environmental preservation, that minimally use resources, and that so severely penalize waste and abuse that these become unprofitable. However, until cataclysm strikes, I do not expect these changes to occur. Based on what is happening in West Texas—the ecological ignorance and greedy consumerism of Texans and the absence of enlightened and courageous political and business leadership—I am not optimistic.

NOTES

1. Alan Tennant, *A Field Guide to Texas Snakes* (Austin: Texas Monthly Press, 1985), pp. 198–99.

2. Albert Schweitzer, *The Philosophy of Civilization* (New York: Macmillan, 1953), p. 309.

3. See Joel Feinberg, *Rights, Justice, and the Bounds of Liberty* (Princeton: Princeton University Press, 1980), pp. 201–2; Paul Taylor, *Respect for Nature* (Princeton: Princeton University Press, 1986); and Kenneth E. Goodpaster, "On Being Morally Considerable," *Journal of Philosophy* 75 (1978): 308–25.

4. Feinberg, *Rights*, p. 202.

5. G. J. Warnock, *The Object of Morality* (London: Methuen, 1971).

6. Peter Singer, *Animal Liberation* (New York: Avon Books, 1975), pp. 1–26, 92–191.

7. R. G. Frey, *Rights, Killing, and Suffering* (Oxford: Basil Blackwell, 1983), pp. 159–73, 190–217.

8. Peter Singer, "Animals and the Value of Life," in *Matters of Life and Death*, 2d ed., ed. Tom Regan (New York: Random House, 1986), pp. 338–80.

9. Aldo Leopold, *A Sand County Almanac* (New York: Oxford University Press, 1949; New York: Ballantine Books, 1970), pp. 239, 262.

10. Holmes Rolston III, *Philosophy Gone Wild* (Buffalo: Prometheus Books, 1986),

pp. 19–20, 25, 206–20, and *Environmental Ethics* (Philadelphia: Temple University Press, 1988), pp. 126–59.

11. C. I. Lewis, *The Ground and the Nature of the Right* (New York: Columbia University Press, 1955), p. 69.

12. William K. Frankena, "Ethics and the Environment," in *Ethics and Problems in the 21st Century*, ed. K[enneth] E. Goodpaster and K. M. Sayre (Nortre Dame: University of Notre Dame Press, 1979), pp. 15–17.

Defending the Use of Animals by Business: Animal Liberation and Environmental Ethics

ERIC KATZ

In recent years much attention has been focused on the proper treatment of animals by business. Among those who care about animals, two concerns seem paramount: that animals are being used for the wrong purposes and that animals are being mistreated or abused, whether or not the purposes are justifiable. Thus, arguments are made against the use of animals for fur, food, or experimentation in the cosmetic industry; additionally, arguments are made against the treatment of animals in laboratories, on factory farms, and in zoological parks. In part, the role of business in the misuse and mistreatment of animals has received attention as a spillover from the organized protests against the use of animals in scientific and medical research.[1] Also in part, business has been scrutinized because of environmental concerns; the annual Canadian baby seal hunt and, more recently, the Exxon oil spill in Alaska draw attention to the killing and abuse of wild animals. But more directly, business has come under increasing attack from those who advocate the general principle that animals deserve moral consideration, that animals have both legal and moral rights, that animals should be "liberated" from the oppression and domination of humanity.

The animal liberation movement descends from the animal welfare or humane movement of the late nineteenth and early twentieth centuries, but its purposes and tactics clearly differ. The goals of animal liberation go far beyond urging the benevolent care of pets and animals used for labor. Animal liberation seeks to end all unnecessary cruelty and suffering that humans perpetrate on animal life, especially the use of animals in scientific experimentation, in industrial product testing, and in food production. Animal liberation thus advocates vegetarianism and alternative methods of research and experimentation. Most animal liberationists use traditional tactics for effecting social change: lobbying, boycotts, and philosophical and political arguments. But some elements of the movement have resorted to acts of violence, coercion, and terrorism. In 1989 demonstrators at Saks Fifth Avenue in New York protested the sale of furs and harassed wearers of fur coats who passed by the store. One splinter group, the Animal Liberation Front, is considered a terrorist organization by the FBI. Recently national attention was focused on this group because of the alleged bombing attempt of a surgical supply company that practiced vivisection in the sales demonstrations of its surgical tools.[2]

And so business is faced with the task of defending its treatment of animals from the moral arguments and political tactics of the animal liberation movement. In this chapter I present a method—or at least, several arguments—that business can employ to blunt these attacks. I suggest that the adoption by business of a more conscious environmentalism can serve as a defense against the animal liberation movement. This strategy may seem paradoxical: how can business defend its use of animals by advocating the protection of the environment? But the paradox disappears once we see that animal liberation and environmentalism are incompatible practical moral doctrines.

Arguments in favor of the direct moral consideration of animals follow two major lines of thought.[3] First, it is argued that no morally relevant criterion can be applied to all human beings to differentiate them from nonhuman animals. Traditional criteria such as rationality, autonomy, or linguistic capability are not possessed by all humans. Other criteria, such as the possession of an immortal soul, are problematic at best. Thus, the animal liberationist argues that a moral preference for humans over animals, insofar as it is based on mere species membership, is an irrational prejudice analogous to racial or sexual bias. Animal liberationists often label such arguments "speciesist."[4] Like racism or sexism, speciesism is a groundless bias in favor of one's own kind.

This first argument is essentially negative. It demonstrates the absence of a significant difference between humans and other animals in the establishment of moral consideration. The second argument for the moral consideration of animals is positive. It claims that moral standing is derived from the ability to feel pleasure and pain or, as it is commonly termed in the literature, sentience. As Peter Singer writes, "If a being suffers there can be no moral justification for refusing to take that suffering into consideration. . . . If a being is not capable of suffering, or of experiencing enjoyment or happiness, there is nothing to be taken into account."[5] Any moral agent must consider the pain and pleasure that result from his or her actions. This is the minimum requirement of morality. Since most animals experience pain and pleasure, a moral agent must take these experiences into account. Animals must be given moral standing, moral consideration. The capacity to suffer, to undergo experiences of pain and pleasure, is the primary moral similarity between human and nonhuman animals. Sentience, then, is the nonarbitrary, nonspeciesist basis of moral value.

These two lines of argument are generally combined to form the strongest case for the moral consideration of animals. Yet the two arguments are actually quite different; they derive from totally different philosophical roots. The second argument, with its focus on pain and pleasure, is an outgrowth of classical Benthamite utilitarianism. It is a consequentialist doctrine, in which pain and pleasure are the only two determinants of moral value.[6] The first argument, with its focus on rights, uses a deontological model of thought. Within this model, the central problem in normative ethics becomes the search for a moral criterion that is not directly connected to the results of an action. The possession of rights is not determined by the consequences of action but by the inherent qualities of the possessor. The differing supports for the moral consideration of animals suggest the possibility of differing critical attacks. Each line of thought can be subjected to a unique criticism that weakens the case for animal liberation and points in the direction of a more comprehensive doctrine of environmentalism.

The utilitarian criterion of sentience is problematic for at least two reasons. First, how far down the scale of animal life can one safely assume the experience of pain and pleasure? Is the kind of experience required for animal suffering (and hence for the moral consideration of animals) limited to the so-called higher animals—mammals, birds, and so on? One author suggests that insects have the requisite nervous system for the possible experience of pain.[7] Insects then would be serious candidates for moral consideration. Does this possibility suggest that the utilitarian basis of an animal liberation ethic can be pushed too far, offering a reductio ad absurdum of the position? Or does it place limits on the operational application of the concept of sentience, rendering only higher animals morally considerable? Both alternatives are problematic. The first case includes too many animals under the purview of moral consideration. The second presents a new, more subtle form of speciesism: only animals that resemble humans, who experience pain and pleasure in ways recognizable to us, gain entry into the moral kingdom.[8]

To a certain extent, this criticism is a theoretical quibble. Except for insects killed by pesticides, almost all animals used in business meet the minimum standards of sentient experience. Animals that are used in scientific research, that are hunted, or that are raised for food clearly do feel pain. Nevertheless, this mere theoretical criticism tends to demonstrate that the arguments in favor of the moral consideration of animals are not consistent. There are implications, weak points, and even holes in the arguments that are not addressed by advocates of animal liberation.

The second problem with the criterion of sentience is the contextual significance of pain. The utilitarian advocate of animal consideration contends that pain is an intrinsic evil, but the argument focuses on an abstract concept of pain separated from natural reality. In its concrete natural existence pain has an instrumental function in organisms: a warning of internal stress or external danger. Understood in context, pain is not an evil at all; it is an essential part of a successful organic life. An organism that does not feel pain cannot survive. It cannot reproduce itself, condemning its species to extinction. Once one adopts a more contextual environmental perspective, one can understand the role of pain in organic life. In the natural world pain serves a crucial positive function. But the hallmark of utilitarian animal liberation—the absolute, abstract denial of pain—ignores this context. It proscribes the infliction of any and all pain. Such a denial is both practically impossible and conceptually meaningless.[9]

The deontological concern for animal rights fares no better as a moral argument. The advocates of animal moral consideration claim that the denial of animal rights without a specific moral criterion shows a preference for human beings that is analogous to racism or sexism. The absence of a nonarbitrary moral criterion that distinguishes all humans from all nonhuman animals leaves no justifiable defense of preferential treatment for human beings. This animal rights argument rests on the claim that "marginal" cases of humanity—the severely retarded, the insane, comatose humans, newborns with severe birth defects, fetuses—are treated as normal or typical humans from the moral point of view. The crucial point is that even though marginal humans do not meet standards of moral consideration such as rationality or linguistic capability, they are given a full moral standing that is denied to animals—even when the animals are not inferior to the marginal humans. The moral consideration of marginal humans thus shows the speciesist bias in our treatment of animals.

This argument is empirically false. No observer of the contemporary world, or the history of humanity, could possibly believe that marginal humans are given full moral consideration. The cases obviously differ, but all in all, these humans are clearly deemed to have less moral value because of their reduced capacities. It is true, as animal rightists claim, that we do not eat retarded humans or babies. But we do perform scientific and medical experiments on marginal humans, and we generally find it easier to sacrifice their lives. The factual moral truth, however depressing as it might be, is that the hierarchy of moral value exemplified in the human treatment of animals is echoed and repe :ed in the human treatment of other humans. The animal rightist claim about human speciesism is hollow, for it assumes the equal treatment of all humans, a treatment that is superior to all animals.[10] There is not an arbitrary speciesist preference for humans. There is the imperfect application of ambiguous criteria such as rationality, autonomy, and linguistic capability. These criteria are used, not altogether consistently, to determine the moral considerability of various classes of humans and nonhumans alike. A recognition of this picture of moral thinking softens the sharpest attack of the animal rights advocates.

Defenders of the use of animals by business and industry thus can raise several problems for questioning the moral consideration of animals. These criticisms are supplemented by the adoption of an "environmental ethic," that is, a direct concern for the moral consideration of nature and natural processes.

The term *environmental ethic* has been used extensively since the mid-1970s to denote a more benign relationship between humanity and the natural world. Within academic philosophy the term has developed in several overlapping, but often contradictory, directions.[11] This is not the proper place for a review of these various formulations. Instead I will merely suggest that the most useful environmental ethic for business to adopt as a countermeasure to animal liberation is ecological holism. This ethic uses the normal functioning of natural ecological systems as the baseline for human decisions that affect the environment. The primary and direct ethical focus is on the continuation of environments, natural ecological systems, not the lives or experiences of individual natural entities. As Aldo Leopold wrote over forty years ago, "A thing is right when it tends to preserve the integrity, stability, and beauty of the biotic community. It is wrong when it tends otherwise."[12] Consequently the way animals live in and through natural ecological systems would be the model for their treatment by humans. Business, or any other human institution, would look to the operations of natural ecological systems as a guide to the proper behavior regarding animals and other natural beings.[13]

As a countermeasure to animal liberation, ecological holism reinforces the proper role of pain in organic life. Since pain is as necessary as pleasure in a successful organic life, it cannot, and should not, be considered a moral evil. Pain, and even death, are crucial aspects in the operation of natural systems. Pain is a warning to individual natural organisms. It is an instrumental good for the preservation of individual life. The death of individuals in nature is a means for reusing and redirecting the energy in the system. In being eaten by a predator, an organism "donates" its energy to another individual in the system. Its corpse decays into basic organic elements, donating its energy to the rest of the system. From an ecological point of view, it is thus a mistake to consider pain and death as merely intrinsic evils that must be eliminated.

Indeed, advocates of animal liberation have trouble with the basic natural process of predation. A utilitarian concerned with the lessening of pain in the world would be forced to prevent predation in the wild. The advocate of animal rights would also, it seems, consider the rights of the prey to be violated in the act of predation.[14] But the prevention of predation seems an absurd position to advocate; if the moral consideration of animals implies the implementation of such a moral policy, then animals cannot be morally considerable.

An environmental perspective acknowledges predation as a basic fact of natural existence. Killing other animals for food serves the interests of the individual carnivore by sustaining its life. Predation serves the interests of the carnivore species by preserving its function or niche in the ecological system. In addition, the killing of prey, often the weakest members of the herd, helps preserve and strengthen the species that is preyed upon. In sum, there is no ecological reason to attempt an elimination of pain, killing, and death in the animal kingdom.

Here the advocate of animal moral considerability can offer a serious objection: the use and mistreatment of animals by humans is not normally an act of predation in the wild. Indeed, the few humans who need to hunt for a food supply may be permitted to do so.[15] However, most of the harm inflicted on animals by humanity takes place through factory farming, scientific experimentation, and industrial testing. So, the objection goes, the beneficial instrumental value of pain in the wild is an irrelevant consideration. The pain of animals in slaughterhouses or research laboratories serves no useful natural function.

The answer to this objection lies in a consciously radical environmentalism. From the perspective of ecological holism, the pain of animals in factory farms, slaughterhouses, and research laboratories is not natural pain. The animals suffering the pain are domesticated animals. They are themselves irrelevant to a comprehensive environmental ethic.

This radical environmentalism is based on the fact that most domesticated species of animals are essentially human artifacts. For thousands of years they have been bred for the development of traits important for human life and human use. Recent advances in the technology of agriculture and recombinant DNA research only make this fact clearer. Consider the injection of antibiotics into beef cattle or the genetically altered Harvard mice that are susceptible to forms of cancer.[16] Thus, the animals used by business and industry are human creations designed to fulfill a specific human need. They are artifacts, living artifacts to be sure, but they are no more natural than the wooden table I am using to write this chapter. To consider them the moral equals of wild animals—who, analogously to autonomous humans, pursue their own goals in a natural system—is a serious category mistake.[17]

Nevertheless, there are proper and improper ways to treat human artifacts. Humans may be required to grant direct moral consideration to some artifacts. Works of art seem to be a paradigm example.[18] So the defender of the business use of animals may be led to a kind of moral pluralism in which various kinds of natural and artificial entities, human and nonhuman organisms, natural individuals and collectives, are each determined to have differing amounts of moral value. Adopting a serious environmental ethic may involve remapping the entire landscape of our moral obligations, so that we take into account wild and domestic animals, marginal humans, plants, ecosystems, nonliving natural entities, species, and even future generations. This remapping is clearly a formidable task, but I believe that it will yield more moral truth than the overly easy utilitarian and rights-based arguments proposed by the advocates of animal liberation.[19]

One possible direction for the development of moral pluralism is an emphasis on the context of moral decision making. I criticized the utilitarian consideration of animal pain as being too abstract. The value or disvalue of pain can be understood only in the exact context of an organism's life. This contextual approach to ethical decision making should be generalized to include all practical moral thought. An emphasis on context is inseparable from moral pluralism. This ethical viewpoint implies that there is no one objective overall moral standard. Various criteria—such as sentience, rationality, life, beauty, integrity—are applicable in varying situations. In one situation it may be morally obligatory to treat a dog better than a human; at a different time or situation the human would come first. The point is that no moral decision can be made abstracted from the context of real life. The concrete situation determines the proper moral outcome.

I conclude by returning to the defense of business in its use of animals for food, fur, and research. The argument presented here suggests that business can blunt the criticisms of the animal liberation movement if it adopts an ethic of ecological holism and moral pluralism. Business must stress that the primary value to be promoted in the human interaction with the animal kingdom is the natural fit with ecological processes.[20] Pain and death are not absolute or intrinsic evils. They serve important instrumental functions in the preservation of individuals, species, and systems. They need not be avoided at all costs. As long as animals are used in ways that respect their natural integrity or their natural functions in ecological systems, then they are being treated with the proper moral consideration. Human beings, as natural omnivores, are not acting directly against moral value when they raise and kill animals for food.[21] The human use of domestic animals falls outside the realm of environmental ethics; domestic animals are nothing more than living human artifacts. This conclusion does not deny that there are proper and improper ways of treating animals bred for human purposes; however, these moral constraints are not the absolutes proposed by animal liberationists. Consequently business should argue for a contextual approach to the human treatment of animals. Harms and benefits, value and disvalue, can be determined only in concrete situations. Before making a moral decision, the complex relationship between human and animal, society and nature, individual and species, must be understood.

I have consciously avoided presenting specific proposals. I recommend a general approach to applied ethics that eschews the determination of specific ethical commands abstracted from actual situations. Nevertheless, this defense of the use of animals by business and industry does not imply approbation of current practices. Many of the specific techniques of factory farming, to cite one example, cause pain and suffering that is unnecessary from even a perspective of ecological holism. Although I have argued that pain is not an absolute evil and that it is a mistake to consider it as an evil abstracted from a concrete situation, I am not suggesting that it is never an evil in specific contexts. It can be unnecessary. Humans can reform their practices so that they gain the benefits of using animals without mistreating them. Business and industry ought to modify existing technologies in the raising, harvesting, and slaughtering of animals, even as they defend themselves against the critical attacks of animal liberation.

A final impetus for reform would be the sincere adoption of environmentalist attitudes. An ethic of ecological holism would require major revisions in human activities regarding wildlife and the natural environment. Industry would be compelled to develop alternative technologies with low impact on natural evolutionary processes, such as solar power and organic pesticides. These reforms would affect the animal kingdom in positive ways, for reducing air and water pollution benefits all organic life. However, the reforms required by an attitude of environmentalism are miniscule compared to the reforms demanded by the animal liberation movement. That prudential reason alone should be enough to convince business to adopt an environmental ethic.

NOTES

I thank Michal McMahon for helpful comments on an earlier version of this chapter.

1. One medical researcher gave up fourteen years of research because of protests against animal use. See Sarah Lyall, "Pressed on Animal Rights, Researcher Gives Up Grant," *New York Times,* November 22, 1988, sec. 2, p. 1.

2. The antifur demonstration was reported in Carole Agus, "The Fur and the Fury," *Newsday,* February 21, 1989, pt. 2, pp. 16–18. For more on fur protests see James Hirsch, "Animal-Rights Groups Step Up Attacks on Furriers," *New York Times,* November 27, 1988, sec. 1, p. 50. In the last year, the *New York Times* has printed several articles on the "animal rights" movement—a sure sign of public acceptance of the merits of the debate. See Kirk Johnson, "Arrest Points Up Split in Animal-Rights Movement," *New York Times,* November 13, 1988, sec. 2, p. 40; Robert A. Hamilton, "Advocates of Animal Rights See Influence Grow in State," *New York Times,* November 27, 1988, sec. 23, p. 1; Katherine Bishop, "From Shop to Lab to Farm, Animal Rights Battle Is Felt," *New York Times,* January 14, 1989, sec. 1, p. 1; Barnaby J. Feder, "Research Labs Look Away from Laboratory Animals," *New York Times,* January 29, 1989, sec. 4, p. 24. The Trutt bombing case was originally reported by Robert D. McFadden, "A Bombing Is Thwarted in Norwalk," *New York Times,* November 12, 1988, sec. 1, p. 29, and McFadden, "Norwalk Bomb Inquiry: Did Suspect Have Help?" *New York Times,* November 14, 1989, sec. 2, p. 3.

3. These two lines are represented by Tom Regan, *The Case for Animal Rights* (Berkeley: University of California Press, 1983), and Peter Singer, *Animal Liberation: A New Ethics for Our Treatment of Animals* (New York: Avon Books, 1977).

4. Singer attributes the term *speciesism* to Richard Ryder, author of *Victims of Science* (London: Davis-Poynter, 1975); see *Animal Liberation,* pp. 7, 25.

5. Singer, *Animal Liberation,* p. 8.

6. Hedonistic utilitarianism, the moral doctrine that judges human action by the resulting pleasure and pain, derives from Jeremy Bentham: "Nature has placed mankind under the governance of two sovereign masters, *pain* and *pleasure." An Introduction to the Principles of Morals and Legislation* (1789; rpt. *The Utilitarians,* Garden City, N.Y.: Anchor, 1973), p. 17. Bentham extends the moral significance of pain and pleasure to the animal kingdom; in an oft-quoted passage, he writes: "The French have already discovered that the blackness of the skin is no reason why a human being should be abandoned without redress to the caprice of a tormentor. It may come one day to be recognized, that the number of the legs, the villosity of the skin, or the termination of the *os sacrum,* are reasons equally insufficient for abandoning a sensitive being to the same fate. What else is it that should trace the insuperable line? Is it the faculty of reason, or, perhaps, the faculty of discourse? But a full-grown horse or dog is beyond comparison a more rational, as well as a more conversable animal, than an infant of a day, or a week, or even a month, old. But suppose the case were otherwise, what would it avail? The question is not, Can they *reason?* nor, Can they *talk?* but, Can they *Suffer?" Utilitarians,* p. 381.

7. Jeffrey A. Lockwood, "Not to Harm a Fly: Our Ethical Obligations to Insects," *Between the Species* 4 (3) (1988): 204–11.

8. See John Rodman, "The Liberation of Nature?" *Inquiry* 20 (1977): 83–131, esp. 90–91.

9. One of the most important criticisms of the animal liberationist use of pain can be

found in J. Baird Callicott, "Animal Liberation: A Triangular Affair," *Environmental Ethics* 2 (1980): 311–38, esp. 332–33. Another movement in ethics that emphasizes context is feminist ethics, although many feminists advocate vegetarianism and other nonharmful treatment of animals. I argue that a proper attention to context permits the use and eating of animals. For feminist ethics in general see Carol Gilligan, *In a Different Voice: Psychological Theory and Women's Development* (Cambridge: Harvard University Press, 1982). For a feminist perspective on environmental issues, see Jim Cheney, "Ecofeminism and Deep Ecology," *Environmental Ethics* 9 (1987): 115–45; for a feminist perspective on animals, see Cora Diamond, "Eating Meat and Eating People," *Philosophy* 53 (1978): 464–79.

10. Many animals are treated better than humans. I provide my pet dog, for example, with a better life than millions of humans in the world. His nutritional and medical needs are met to a higher level (I am guessing) than any individual in the entire homeless population of New York City or in the famine regions of the Third World. Since we do not normally condemn this "preferential" treatment of pet animals, we can see that we are not speciesists.

11. The large literature on environmental ethics cannot be cited here. Some of the best book-length treatments of the subject are Mark Sagoff, *The Economy of the Earth* (Cambridge: Cambridge University Press, 1988), Holmes Rolston III, *Environmental Ethics: Duties to and Values in the Natural World* (Philadelphia: Temple University Press, 1988), and Paul Taylor, *Respect for Nature: A Theory of Environmental Ethics* (Princeton: Princeton University Press, 1986). Two excellent anthologies are Donald Scherer and Thomas Attig, eds., *Ethics and the Environment* (Englewood Cliffs, N.J.: Prentice-Hall, 1983), and Donald VanDeVeer and Christine Pierce, eds., *People, Penguins and Plastic Trees: Basic Issues in Environmental Ethics* (Belmont, Calif.: Wadsworth, 1986). Current debates in the field appear in the journal *Environmental Ethics,* edited by Eugene Hargrove, Department of Philosophy, University of Georgia, Athens. I have published an annotated bibliography of recent titles in the field: "Environmental Ethics: A Select Annotated Bibliography, 1983–1987," *Research in Philosophy and Technology* 9 (1989): 251–85.

12. Aldo Leopold, *A Sand County Almanac* (1949; rpt., New York: Ballantine, 1970), p. 262.

13. Rolston, *Environmental Ethics,* pp. 45–125.

14. For more on predation, see Steve F. Sapontzis, "Predation," *Ethics and Animals* 5 (2) (June 1984): 27–38, and J. Baird Callicott's review of Tom Regan's *The Case for Animal Rights* in *Environmental Ethics* 7 (1985): 365–72.

15. So argues Peter Wenz, despite his concern for the moral consideration of animals. See his *Environmental Justice* (Albany: SUNY Press, 1988), pp. 324–31.

16. The creation and patenting of the so-called Harvard mice is reported in "U.S. Plans to Issue First Patent on Animal Today," *New York Times,* April 12, 1988, sec. 1, p. 21, and Keith Schneider, "Harvard Gets a Mouse Patent, a World First," *New York Times,* April 13, 1988, sec. 1, p. 1.

17. See Callicott, "Animal Liberation," pp. 329–36, and Rodman, "Liberation of Nature?" pp. 93–118, for more on domestication and its significance for animal and environmental ethics.

18. For discussion, see Alan Tormey, "Aesthetic Rights," *Journal of Aesthetics and Art Criticism* 32 (1973): 163–70, and a reply by David Goldblatt, "Do Works of Art Have Rights?" *Journal of Aesthetics and Art Criticism* 35 (1976): 69–77.

19. The idea of a morally pluralistic system of ethical value is being discussed seriously in the literature. See Christopher Stone, *Earth and Other Ethics: The Case for Moral Pluralism* (New York: Harper & Row, 1987); Wenz, *Environmental Justice,* esp. pp. 310–43; Callicott, "Animal Liberation and Environmental Ethics: Back Together Again," *Between the Species* 4 (3) (1988): 163–69; and my two articles, "Organism, Community and 'The Substitution Problem,'" *Environmental Ethics* 7 (1985): 241–56, and "Buffalo-killing and the Valuation of Species," in *Values and Moral Standing,* ed. L. W. Sumner (Bowling Green: Bowling Green State University Press, 1986), pp. 114–23.

20. See Rolston, *Environmental Ethics.*

21. But they may be acting indirectly against their interests and the overall health of the biosphere. Meat production is one of the most inefficient means of converting biomass to protein. There would be more food for the human population of the earth if we ceased meat production and shifted to a basic vegetarian diet.

Ethics at Sea: The Dolphin-Tuna Controversy

THOMAS I. WHITE

They live in a dark world miles off the Pacific coast, so even experts understand little about them. We do know that they are highly social, unusually intelligent, friendly, altruistic, and trusting of strangers. Anecdotes over the centuries tell of their helping lost sailors and even saving some people who otherwise would have drowned. Yet they live in the path of an aggressive industry. In fact, since 1959 more than 6 million of them have died in a kind of industrial accident.

This is the plight of dolphins that live in the eastern tropical Pacific. Years ago the tuna industry discovered that dolphins and yellowfin tuna often school together, so by looking for dolphins, the boats could easily find large schools of yellowfin, the very profitable type of fish used in light canned tuna. As long as fishermen used hook and line, there were no casualties among the dolphins. Yet as the industry introduced a new technology, purse seining, dolphins became encircled in the nets and drowned. After Congress enacted protective legislation in 1972, the number of deaths fell dramatically, but the toll is rising again. Every day the dolphins are followed; every day hundreds die. The Marine Mammal Protection Act (MMPA) still permits the U.S. commercial fishing fleet 20,500 dolphin deaths a year. Foreign boats are essentially unregulated and kill even more dolphins than the American fleet.

Organizations like Earth Island Institute, the Marine Mammal Fund, Greenpeace, the Humane Society, and the ASPCA decry the practice. They claim that certain species of dolphin are endangered and contend that it is possible to catch yellowfin without killing dolphin.[1] They further argue that since yellowfin from the eastern tropical Pacific constitutes less than 10 percent of the worldwide tuna catch, not enough benefits come to humans to justify such a large number of dolphin deaths. Accordingly these groups have called for a boycott of all canned tuna.

In response, the tuna industry asserts that dolphin populations are not endangered and that it is not possible to catch enough tuna through other methods. They also claim to be working on bringing dolphin deaths down, particularly the number produced by the foreign fleet.

The dolphin-tuna controversy may at first seem to be no more than one of those clashes that regularly takes place in nature. Tuna is a cheap, healthy source of protein for humans. The dolphins are unfortunate casualties in our search for food. As long as the dolphins are not dying at a rate that threatens their extinction, some would argue, there is no significant ethical problem. In reality, the issue is much more complicated.

The point of this chapter is twofold. First, I briefly survey the wide range of issues this controversy raises. Then I focus on what I take to be the most basic question: whether a dolphin should be granted any special moral standing because of its status as a higher, intelligent mammal. As far as I know, neither of these matters has been fully discussed before.

My aim is to demonstrate the complexity of the ethical problems connected with this case—a complexity representative of the problems that arise whenever we humans take actions that have serious consequences on the lives of other higher animals. As we look more carefully at the ethical dimensions of our dealings, particularly with other primates and the cetaceans, we will find more—not fewer—such issues surfacing. For example, using gorillas or chimpanzees in medical research raises many of the same ethical difficulties. My ultimate hope is that this chapter can serve as a preliminary map for navigating between the Scylla of moral blindness and the Charybdis of raw outrage.

THE RANGE OF ISSUES

Neither the tuna industry nor the opposition recognizes the full dimensions of the controversy. The industry points to the immediate financial harm that would come from further limitations on how they fish. Their opponents combine environmental arguments for preserving certain levels of dolphin populations with humane appeals based on the suffering and wastefulness of the dolphin deaths. In reality, the controversy is much broader, with issues falling into three areas: the dolphins themselves, the federal government's actions, and the tuna industry, the corporations marketing the tuna, their adversaries, and consumers.

The Dolphins

The most basic issues involve special characteristics of the dolphins themselves and stem from dolphins' and humans' sharing several critical traits. In this corner of the controversy, then, the questions are:

Are the dolphins being treated in a way that is morally justifiable?

Do their deaths and injuries count as cruelty or wastefulness of a sort that is morally
    culpable?

Does their ability to experience pain and suffering as we do make us morally obligated to
    accord them special treatment that we do not give the tuna?

Do we have a duty to take into account the dolphins' vital interests? If so, how do we
    balance their interests against the human need for food?

Considering their status as higher mammals, what moral standing do dolphins have?

The Federal Government

A second set of issues involves the actions of the federal government. The
MMPA was passed in 1972 and on balance has been very successful. However,
environmentalists argue that particularly since the beginning of the Reagan administration, the bill has not been vigorously enforced as it pertains to dolphins
dying as a result of tuna fishing. For example, 1984 amendments to the MMPA
call for kill rates by the foreign fleet that are comparable to U.S. rates under
penalty of embargo. More than four years later, the National Marine Fisheries
Service (NMFS) had still not defined "comparability."[2] In this area, then, we
face questions like:

Considering the administration's clear duty to enforce laws enacted by the Congress, is the
    administration morally culpable for its weak enforcement of the MMPA as it relates
    to the tuna-dolphin controversy?

Does this constitute an ethically unjustifiable breach of the explicit agreement the execu-
    tive branch of the government makes to enforce the laws promulgated by the
    Congress?

If an administration thinks that enforcing a law will produce an unacceptable level of
    economic harm, does it have the right to forestall enforcement?

What are we to make of the government's favoring one industry over another when it
    comes to dolphins? That is, what are the ethical implications of the NMFS's letting
    the tuna industry kill dolphins, while the same agency considers suspending the
    tourist industry's dolphin swim programs?

The Business Principals, Their Adversaries, and Consumers

The third set of issues concerns the onshore actions of the fishing and processing industries and their opponents. Since the inception of the MMPA, the fishing
industry has lobbied heavily against the goal to bring dolphin deaths down to
zero. Corporations that buy, process, and market tuna have not themselves lobbied, but they have profited from the lenient enforcement of the MMPA. In
response, opposition groups have called for a boycott. The questions that surface
in this area of the controversy include:

Especially considering the dolphin's status as a higher sentient mammal, have the fishing
    industry's attempts to dilute the legislation been ethically defensible?

Do corporations like Heinz, which owns Star-Kist, have duties to the environment in general or to the dolphins in particular that compete with or surpass their responsibilities to their companies' shareholders and stakeholders?

In the light of the lenient enforcement of the MMPA, what counts as "obeying the law" in this situation? Is abiding by the guidelines of the enforcement agencies sufficient, or should the corporations be bound by the original spirit of the law? Do they have the right to go beyond the letter of the law if it is more expensive to do so?

To be ethically defensible, must the opposition limit its boycott to the products most closely associated with the dolphin deaths (light canned tuna and pet food), or could it include all the products marketed by companies that sell tuna? Considering that an expanded boycott could hurt people not even remotely connected with the fishing industry, is it defensible to call for a boycott of all products marketed by Heinz?

How is management's fiduciary responsibility to the company's stockholders and stakeholders best discharged in the light of the possibility of an expanded boycott and the considerable vulnerability such a company would face?[3]

What about the consumers? Do they have a moral responsibility not to buy a product that brings about so many dolphin deaths?

When we survey the controversy, then, we see a wide variety of issues ranging from animal rights to political and corporate ethics. The first point to appreciate about the controversy, then, is its complexity—a complexity that has not been recognized.

DO DOLPHINS HAVE SPECIAL MORAL STANDING?

Are dolphins entitled to special moral standing because of their unusual characteristics? To anticipate my position I will argue by using the concept of personhood that dolphins are indeed entitled to favored treatment.[4] At the very least, they have the right not to die as they do today in the tuna nets. My argument is based on the fact that dolphins and humans share several critical traits.[5] I contend that there are enough similarities to entitle dolphins to some of the special treatment and protections we claim for ourselves.

Humans, Persons, and Rights

The point to begin with is to ask why we humans think we are entitled to special treatment and protections. The answer, of course, is that we see ourselves as beings with special characteristics, wants, and needs not shared by other living creatures. We assume that we are persons, and they are not. We view a person as "someone"; we see an animal more like "something." We think that we have abilities and the potential for satisfactions beyond "lower" animals. As a result, we claim that as persons we need special conditions in order to live a satisfying human life.

We humans generally refer to these special conditions for human happiness as things we have a right to, for example, rights to life, liberty, justice, fairness, freedom from coercion, protection from cruelty, and the like.[6] Humans argue that without the conditions protected by these rights, our lives as persons would be markedly less satisfying. We consider these rights so critical to our well-being that we say it is morally wrong for them to be violated.

The way humans treat "lower" animals clearly suggests that we consider them to be nonpersons with few, if any, rights. We treat them as nonpersons that do not need what we need in order to enjoy a fundamentally satisfying life. And even if we recognize that their lives could be made more enjoyable through better treatment, we feel absolutely no moral obligation to do so. We seem to assume that they ("something") and we ("someone") are qualitatively different. The bottom line is plain: persons get treated better than nonpersons because we think our needs are so different.

Nonhuman Persons?

The problem with this way of looking at things, however, is that it mistakenly assumes that *human* and *person* are synonyms; however, these concepts are quite different. There is, of course, nothing new about this distinction. "Human" simply means being part of the biological group *homo sapiens*. "Person," however, is an ethical, not a biological, concept. As a rule, virtually all "humans" are also "persons," but the reverse does not have to hold.[7]

There is, then, every reason to accept at least the theoretical possibility of a "nonhuman person." If there are actually alien beings from other planets whom we will one day meet and communicate with, it is unlikely they will be human. Yet we will certainly consider them persons and say that they deserve the special treatment and protections we reserve for ourselves: respect for their rights to life, autonomy, freedom from threats, coercion, manipulation and the like.[8]

But isn't it possible that there already exist "nonhuman persons" on our own planet that we simply have not recognized as such? We have traditionally divided animals into two categories: us (humans, persons) and them (lower animals, nonpersons). Perhaps we should reexamine this assumption. Research over the last couple of decades reveals that the primates and cetaceans show evidence of having many abilities like ours.[9] Dolphins in particular are unquestionably different from most lower animals. But are dolphins high enough on the biological ladder to deserve special treatment? In particular, are dolphins advanced enough to be considered persons?[10]

What Is a Person?

To take up the question of whether dolphins are persons, we need a precise definition of personhood. Although there is some disagreement among thinkers about the essential features of a person, some major characteristics have surfaced in the discussion.[11] A person is a being who is conscious, that is, mentally aware of the world; able to feel pain; capable of emotional states; aware of itself in a special way (self-consciousness); able to control its own behavior; capable of valuing others for their intrinsic worth; and the possessor of high-order intellectual abilities (this includes capacities for analytical, conceptual thought; learning, retaining, and recalling information; solving complicated problems; complex communication; perceiving and ordering reality temporally).[12] The combination of these characteristics result in beings, each unique and special.

IS A DOLPHIN A PERSON?

Dolphins measure up against these characteristics surprisingly well.[13]

Consciousness

It is apparent that dolphins have some kind of mental awareness. That they learn behaviors so easily shows their awareness of the external world. This should come as no surprise, given what Donald Griffin alleges about even lower animals in his landmark work on animal awareness.[14]

Pain

There is no question that dolphins feel physical pain. Their brains, like ours, have pain centers, and their skin is especially sensitive. The ability to feel pain, of course, appears to be present in all animals.

Emotional States

In the opinion of their trainers, dolphins seem to have emotional states. They act in a way that human observers interpret as excitement, depression, surprise, anticipation, anger, and grief. Highly social beings, they appear to feel isolation from other dolphins keenly. Dolphins who have been cut off from their families and schools seem to grieve. They have been known to stop eating and die in such circumstances. Mothers whose calves have died have become listless, apparently mourning their loss. Others cut off from their young have committed suicide by refusing to breathe.[15]

Experts claim that dolphins have distinct personalities—something else that suggests an inner, emotional life. Dolphins can differ in terms of curiosity, timidity, playfulness, aggression, interest in learning, and patience. Some mothers refuse to cut the apron strings, while others encourage their young to become independent. Dolphins also appear to have moods. In captivity, they can be interested in working some days, lackadaisical on others, and flatly refuse at other times.

Self-Consciousness

Mental awareness is one thing, but self-awareness is quite different. The ability to recognize an I in oneself is critical to being a person, and this has often been held up as a unique human achievement. Here, too, dolphins seem to share this feature.[16]

Dolphins have signature whistles that they put at the end of their communications to identify themselves to each other. They can follow commands that contain their own names, the names of other dolphins, and those of their trainers. Most important, their ability to comprehend human language includes pronouns. As Long Marine Laboratories' Kenneth Norris puts it, "They can handle pronouns. They know who they are."

Self-Controlled Behavior

The ability to control one's behavior is another critical criterion of personhood traditionally reserved for humans. We have ascribed only to ourselves the capacity to resist the pull of instinct and to determine fully how we will respond to the stimuli in our environment. Setting aside the question of how much freedom we actually have, it is unlikely that we would consider something to be a person if it could not be the author of its own actions. Especially noteworthy is the following example of cooperative behavior that shows dolphins very much in control of their behavior and able to manipulate their environment to obtain what they want.

Bernd Wursig of the Moss Landing Marine Laboratories reports that when small groups of dolphins in the wild discover a school of anchovies, they herd the fish together and signal nearby dolphins about the catch. Then they wait until the others join them before eating. Even while the feeding is going on, the dolphins take turns at different roles. Some eat while others keep the fish contained, and then they switch. Such feedings can involve as many as 300 dolphins.

Such cooperative behavior suggests that these dolphins have abilities in organization, premeditation about and coordination of different roles, and, above all, patience. This certainly looks like behavior that the dolphins initiate and control internally. Wursig explains,

Herding and holding of prey are not a stereotyped series of actions. At times, the fish school may fragment into smaller balls. When that occurs, a few of the dolphins break off from the group and herd the fish back into the central fish school. It is a dynamic, ever-changing system, which may require organization by these large-brained and communicative social animals. Differential role-playing and premeditation (such as a decision that certain members do particular things in order to meet various contingencies) may be important in this kind of cooperation. The degree of behavioral flexibility to encompass novel situations appears well developed.[17]

Noninstrumental Valuation

Besides wanting a person to control its behavior, we surely expect that a person somehow show in his or her actions recognition of the status of other persons. In essence, this amounts to demonstrating the ability to value something for its intrinsic merit, not just its instrumental worth.[18]

Clearly this is an advanced characteristic. Dolphins probably evidence this in their legendary altruism. Over the centuries there are many stories of dolphins helping humans in distress. The dolphins receive no tangible benefit from such behavior, and there is no reason to think of this as a reflex action. Also dolphins have consistently shown curiosity about and a desire to interact with humans. Yet despite their superior physical strength, this contact has produced few human injuries, despite obvious provocations. It is impossible to know for certain what attitude produces these actions. Nonetheless, it is possible that these behaviors result from the dolphins' ability to recognize humans as beings like themselves and deserving of special consideration.

High-Order Intellectual Abilities

As important as are mental awareness, self-awareness and self-controlled behavior, the degree of intellectual sophistication that a being has is probably the ultimate characteristic we humans respond to. Most of us probably think that if something is enough "like us" to be labeled a "person," it must be "like us" intellectually.

The comparison between dolphin and human brains reveals some interesting facts. Dolphins' brains are usually larger than ours. Human brains range from 900 to 1,800 grams, dolphins' from 1,000 to 6,000 grams. The ratio of brain weight to body weight and brain weight to body length is roughly equivalent between the two species. In addition, if we look at the ratio of the volume of the brain to the surface area of the body (the "encephalization quotient"), we find humans at 7.4, bottle-nose dolphins at 5.6, and chimpanzees at 2.5. Almost all other mammals are lower than 2.0.

The most intriguing comparison between human and dolphin brains lies in the cerebral cortex. Commonly called the brain's gray matter, the cerebral cortex is thought to be the site of higher mental functions in humans. While a dolphin's brain may not be as dense as a human's, it has as many layers to the cerebral cortex, and the cortex is usually more convoluted than the human brain.

Anatomy may not prove higher-order intellectual skills, but dolphin behavior certainly suggests it. Dolphins are not only able to learn complex behaviors, which they then perform on cue, but they have even taught themselves these behaviors.[19] They have shown the capacity to think temporally, to handle abstract concepts like newness, and even to adapt to some extent to the danger presented by the tuna boats.[20]

The most compelling evidence is probably what has been learned about the dolphins' abilities in language and communication.[21] To cite just one example, University of Hawaii psychologist Louis Herman has used hand signals and computer-generated whistles to teach two dolphins a vocabulary of forty words. Herman combines these words into sentences with as many as five words, which instruct the mammals to perform certain tasks. Herman has discovered that the dolphins have little difficulty understanding the commands the first time they are given. In addition, the dolphins are also sensitive to syntax or word order. They know that "hoop pipe fetch" (which tells the dolphin to take a hoop to a nearby pipe) means something different from "pipe hoop fetch." According to Herman, "This is the first convincing evidence that animals can understand syntactical information."[22]

One final example could suggest an impressive level of spontaneous analysis and problem solving. The Dolphin Research Center often takes in sick dolphins from aquariums for rest and recuperation. In one such case the staff decided that in order to ease the transition to a new home, this dolphin would be put in with two others who had lived at the center for a number of years, Mr. Gipper and Little Bit.

This center is situated in a natural habitat on Grassy Key. The dolphins live in a series of pools separated from the ocean only by low fences, which they can easily jump over or make holes in. Mr. Gipper, in particular, often left the center for the ocean and had made a hole in the fence to make it easier. Before putting the new dolphin in with Mr. Gipper and Little Bit, the staff patched the hole so that the sick dolphin would remain at the center for treatment.

Unknown to the staff, however, Mr. Gipper had reopened the hole, and the new dolphin found the hole and headed for the open seas—in her case a serious mistake. Considering how sick she was, if she had gotten lost, she surely would have died; However, Mr. Gipper and Little Bit went after her, turned her around, and brought her back.

When the dolphins returned, the new animal hesitated to go through the hole. Despite the fact that she had gone through it once, she balked about coming back through again. Dolphins instinctively shy away from going through openings like that, so it is surprising that she went through it the first time.[23] While Mr. Gipper stayed with her, Little Bit went back and forth through the hole to show her what to do and that it was not dangerous. Reassured, she went through the fence, and once the three were back inside, the other two kept her away from the hole until it could be blocked again.

Here we have a complicated problem that two dolphins faced: what to do about their sick companion who was endangering herself by leaving the center and then how to get her back inside. While we obviously cannot know for certain what happened, one reasonable possibility is that one or both of the first two dolphins assessed the situation sufficiently to know that the third was in jeopardy, decided on an appropriate course of action, enlisted the other's aid in stopping her and bringing her back, understood why the third would now refuse to reenter the pen, showed her that there was no danger in returning through the fence, and then kept her from leaving again until the hole was patched. If that is actually what happened, it is surely suggestive of a variety of higher-order intellectual skills (analytical thought, implementing an appropriate strategy, and communication).

CONCLUSION

In the light of this admittedly cursory analysis, I think that at least a prima facie case can be made for the claim that a dolphin is a person. Despite our biological differences, dolphins and humans appear to share the combination of features that we have traditionally believed were ours alone: consciousness, the capacity for pain, emotions, self-consciousness, self-controlled behavior, non-instrumental valuation, and a variety of high-order intellectual abilities. I do not claim to have presented an argument impervious to assault; however, I do hope that I have at least called into question two common assumptions: that dolphins are not persons and that humans are the only candidates for personhood on this planet. More important, I believe that I have laid the foundation for a series of positions connected with the three parts of the controversy that I began this chapter with.

First, I hope that I have made a case for the dolphins' characteristics entitling them to special treatment. Even if dolphins are not persons in the same respect that we are, they nonetheless are so close to some form of personhood that I think they should be accorded special consideration. Minimally, they should be recognized as having a right to life. If so, this puts their deaths in the tuna nets in a very different light than has been recognized so far. That is, from an ethical point of view, the dolphins' needless and premeditated deaths would then be something akin to murder.

Second, regarding the actions of the federal government, if dolphins are entitled to special treatment, there is no ethical defense for lenient enforcement of the MMPA. More important, there is no justification for the allowable limit of 20,500 deaths per year.

Third, if dolphins are persons, this means that from an ethical standpoint, the fishing and food processing industries stand under a special obligation about how to treat these animals. As long as tuna fishing is conducted in a way that costs the lives of dolphins, anyone who participates in or benefits from catching yellowfin tuna is morally culpable to a serious degree.

NOTES

1. During the last quarter of 1986 U.S. fishermen were barred from catching tuna "on dolphin" because the yearly mortality quota had already been exceeded; however, the total tuna catch was not materially affected.

2. Congress ultimately defined "comparability" on its own. Even a report by the inspector-general of the Department of Commerce described the National Marine Fisheries Service's enforcement of the MMPA as lenient.

3. Heinz is the only domestic owner of a major tuna label. Heinz markets Star-Kist; Bumble Bee and Chicken of the Sea were sold by Pillsbury and Ralston-Purina, respectively, to Asian concerns. Heinz's vulnerability to a boycott involving all their brand names involves Star-Kist tuna; Heinz ketchup, sauces, pickles, and baby foods; Ore-Ida potato products; Weight Watchers products; Steak-Umm frozen steaks; Nine Lives cat food; and Recipe dog food.

4. Although this analysis is based on the concept of personhood, I do not want to suggest that this is the only way to argue for improving the way we treat nonhuman animals. I am taking this approach because it seems the strongest argument relating to dolphins. For a broader approach, see the work of Peter Singer, *Animal Liberation: A New Ethics for Our Treatment of Animals* (New York: New York Review, 1975). My argument should not be taken to imply that dolphins are the only candidates for nonhuman persons. Some scientists suggest that to varying degrees other animals also evidence traits I have mentioned, for example, chimpanzees, gorillas, orangutans, baboons, pigs, elephants, and the social carnivores.

5. Like humans, dolphins think abstractly, solve difficult problems, and communicate with each other. They can understand human language to some extent. They have a mental life—consciousness and a sense of self. They feel pain and experience a range of emotions. And they have complex social lives. Also noteworthy is that dolphins' brains are larger than ours and that they have a sixth sense (sonar) that we lack. The literature on dolphins is too extensive to cite here. See in particular the work of Louis Herman (University of Hawaii), Kenneth Norris (Long Marine Laboratories, University of California at Santa Cruz), Dianah Reiss (San Francisco State University and Marine World Africa USA), and Bernd Wursig (Moss Landing Laboratories and Texas A&M University at Galveston). This chapter also draws on material from interviews and correspondence with Norris, Reiss, Wursig, Thomas Jefferson (Texas A&M University at Galveston), and Della Schuler and Laura Urian (Dolphin Research Center, Grassy Key, Florida).

6. From this point of view, to claim a right to something is in its most basic feature nothing more than claiming that something is a fundamental condition for happiness.

7. The distinction between "human" and "person" has appeared most often in discussions about the ethical character of abortion. Much of the debate revolves around whether the fetus is a person. There is no doubt that it is alive and human, but there is much disagreement about whether the fetus is simply part of the mother's person, a potential person, or a person in its own right. Advocates of abortion generally argue that the fetus is human but not a person. See, in particular, Mary Anne Warren, "On the Moral and Legal Status of Abortion," *Monist* 57 (1) (January 1973): 43–61, and the writings of Michael Tooley, e.g., "A Defense of Abortion and Infanticide," in *The Problem of Abortion*, ed. Joel Feinberg (Belmont, Calif.: Wadsworth, 1973). Also see the essays in *What Is a Person?* ed. Michael F. Goodman (Clifton, N.J.: Humana Press, 1988). On the possibility of nonhuman persons, see Justin Leiber, *Can Animals and Machines Be Persons?* (Indianapolis: Hackett Publishing Company, 1985). This position is also implicit in Peter Singer, *Practical Ethics* (Cambridge: Cambridge University Press, 1979), esp. chap. 3.

8. Another theoretically possible nonhuman person is a highly advanced computer. If advances in artificial intelligence get us to the point where there is little noticeable difference between dealing with a computer and dealing with a human, we would probably want to call the computer a "person," yet it surely is not "human."

9. Regarding primates, see, for example, Alan and Beatrice Gardner, "Teaching Sign Language to a Young Chimpanzee," *Science* 165 (1969): 664–72, and Francine Patterson and Eugene Linden, *The Education of Koko* (New York: Holt, Rinehart & Winston, 1981). On dolphins, see, for instance, the studies in *Dolphin Cognition and Behavior: A Comparative Approach,* ed. Ronald J. Schusterman, Jeanette A. Thomas, and Forrest G. Wood (Hillsdale, N.J.: Lawrence Erlbaum Associates, 1986).

10. On the theoretical possibility that dolphins may be persons, Michael F. Goodman has written, "Let us consider the dolphin. Studies are proving that this cetaceous mammal is quite intelligent, and it is not inconceivable that the mental capacities of one of these adult creatures are more mature than an adolescent human person. If the dolphin were shown to be rational, self-conscious, able to adopt and reciprocate an attitude of moral concern for another being, in short, if the dolphin were shown to possess all of the relevant conditions of personhood, i.e., all of the qualities we consider relevant for ascribing personhood to ourselves, we would be charged with speciesism and/or self-contradiction if we intentionally failed to recognize them as persons." "Introduction" to *What Is a Person?* p. 7.

11. On the debate about criteria for personhood see, for example, Warren, "On the Moral and Legal Status of Abortion"; Goodman, *What Is a Person?* and Tooley, "A Defense of Abortion and Infanticide."

12. Given the limited aim of this essay, it is beyond its scope to explore such issues as why these are appropriate characteristics, whether they are necessary and/or sufficient, or whether they must be possessed actually or potentially. However, these characteristics do represent a rough consensus among thinkers who have considered the issue.

13. It is impossible here to provide all the documentation that leads me to this assertion. A fuller argument will appear in, "Is a Dolphin a Person?" in my forthcoming *Introduction to Philosophy* (Englewood Cliffs, N.J.: Prentice-Hall).

14. Donald R. Griffin, *The Question of Animal Awareness: Evolutionary Continuity of Mental Experience* (New York: Rockefeller University Press, 1976), and *Animal Thinking* (Cambridge: Harvard University Press, 1984).

15. Unlike humans, dolphins do not breathe automatically. Every breath is a conscious act, so deciding not to breathe is quite possible.

16. Dolphins are probably not the only animal with a concept of the self. See the work of the Gardners, Patterson, and Linden cited in note 9.

17. Bernd Wursig, "The Question of Dolphin Awareness Approached through Studies in Nature," *Cetus* 5 (1) (1985): 6. Another example of self-controlled behavior involves dolphin sexual behavior. One of the critical differences between humans and "lower" animals has traditionally been thought to be sexual activity. Virtually all animals mate because of instinct and forces keyed to their reproductive cycle. Furthermore, they mate only because of this. Humans, on the other hand, choose to have sex for pleasure. That is, we are largely free of the kind of instinctive control of sexual behavior one is accustomed to see in other animals. Dolphins are similar to humans in their sexuality. They, too, appear to have sex for pleasure and not just for reproduction.

18. I owe this point to Karen Bell of California State University at Fresno. Daniel Dennett refers to this criterion as having "the capacity to take a personhood attitude (stance) toward the being in question, [and] the ability to reciprocate such an attitude." Daniel C. Dennett, "Conditions of Personhood," in *What Is a Person?*

19. See Griffin's discussion of reports by University of Hawaii marine biologist Louis Herman in *Animal Thinking,* p. 192.

20. Concerning the dolphin's ability to anticipate future events, see Wursig, "Question of Dolphin Awareness," p. 6. On "newness" and the dolphins' response to the tuna boats, see Griffin's discussion of Karen Pryor's work in *Animal Thinking*, 193–94.

21. The literature on research about dolphins' abilities to communicate is too extensive to summarize. See in particular the work of Louis Herman and Dianah Reiss.

22. Dianah Reiss has discovered that not only can dolphins learn the meaning of computer-generated whistles, but they also integrate them into their own communication and use them in appropriate situations.

23. "Gating," as it is called, is ordinarily difficult to teach dolphins.

Index

About the Editors and Contributors

NANCY W. ANDERSON is director of environmental affairs at the Lincoln Filene Center, Tufts University.

CHARLES BAXTER is an environmental analyst with the Massachusetts Department of Environmental Protection.

NORMAN BOWIE is Elmer L. Andersen Chair in Corporate Responsibility at the Carlson School of Management, University of Minnesota.

DANIEL J. DUDEK is senior economist with the Environmental Defense Fund.

ROBERT E. FREDERICK is assistant professor of philosophy and assistant director of the Center for Business Ethics, Bentley College.

FRANCES GOTCSIK is a doctoral candidate at the College of Business, Rochester Institute of Technology.

LYNN A. GREENWALT is vice-president of the National Wildlife Federation.

DAVID P. HANSON is associate professor of international business in the School of Business and Administration, Duquesne University.

W. MICHAEL HOFFMAN is professor of philosophy and director of the Center for Business Ethics, Bentley College.

JAMES S. HOYTE is a senior member of Choate, Hall and Stewart.

ERIC KATZ is assistant professor in the Department of Humanities, New Jersey Institute of Technology.

ALICE M. LEBLANC is a staff economist with the Environmental Defense Fund.

MICHAEL MCCLOSKEY is chairman of the Sierra Club.

ALAN NEFF is assistant professor of communications and law in the School of Business Administration, Illinois Institute of Technology.

KAREN PAUL is associate professor of management in the College of Business, Rochester Institute of Technology.

EDWARD S. PETRY, JR., is assistant professor of philosophy and research associate of the Center for Business Ethics, Bentley College.

MARK SAGOFF is director of Institute for Philosophy and Public Policy, University of Maryland.

ANDREW W. SAVITZ is general counsel for the Massachusetts Executive Office of Environmental Affairs.

KENNETH SEWALL is an independent economics consultant and adjunct professor at Antioch/New England Graduate School.

THOMAS F. SLAUGHTER, JR., is assistant professor of philosophy at Bentley College.

ROBERT C. SOLOMON is professor of philosophy at the University of Texas.

ROBERT L. SWINTH is professor in the College of Business, Montana State University.

FREDERIC A. WALDSTEIN is director of the Institute for Leadership Education, Wartburg College.

RICHARD A. WEHMHOEFER is John C. Willemssen Distinguished Professor of Ethics at the Graduate School of Business and Public Management, University of Denver.

JACK L. WEIR is professor of philosophy at Morehead State University.

LINDA S. WENNERBERG is an invited fellow at the John McCormack Institute for Public Affairs, University of Massachusetts (Harbor Campus).

THOMAS I. WHITE is associate professor of business ethics in the School of Business Administration, Rider College.

DUANE WINDSOR is associate professor of administrative science and associate dean at Rice University.

Heterick Memorial Library
Ohio Northern University

DUE	RETURNED	DUE	RETURNED
MAR 9 1998 1.	FEB 2 4 1998	13.	
APR 2 0 1999 2.	APR 1 3 1999	14.	
3.		15.	
4.		16.	
5.		17.	
6.		18.	
7.		19.	
8.		20.	
9.		21.	
10.		22.	
11.		23.	
12.		24.	

WITHDRAWN FROM OHIO NORTHERN UNIVERSITY LIBRARY